PENGUIN BOOKS

BY A WOMAN WRITT

To *by a Woman writt* Joan Goulianos brings her experiences as a writer, a critic, and a teacher. She has written for the *Washington Post*, the *Nation*, the *Virginia Quarterly*, and *Modern Fiction Studies*. Her articles on women writers have appeared in the *Village Voice*, the *Massachusetts Review*, and *New Theatre Magazine*. Currently an Associate Professor of Literature at Ramapo College, she has also taught at Columbia University, where she was awarded an M.A. and Ph.D. in English and Comparative Literature and where she received a Woodrow Wilson Fellowship and an American Academy of Poets Prize. As an Assistant Professor of English at New York University, she initiated the extensive research project that was to culminate in *by a Woman writt*. "Working on the book," she writes, "became for me not only an astounding introduction to the many fine women writers I had never learned about before, but also a revelation about myself, my education, my own writing." Born and raised in Detroit, Michigan, Joan Goulianos lives in New York City with her husband.

by a Woman writt

LITERATURE FROM SIX CENTURIES BY AND ABOUT WOMEN

JOAN GOULIANOS

EDITOR

ASSISTANT EDITORS

Sandra Adickes, Bonne August,
Zinta Bibelnieks, Regina Koger Monteith

Penguin Books Inc
Baltimore • Maryland

Penguin Books Inc
7110 Ambassador Road
Baltimore, Maryland 21207, U.S.A.

First published by The Bobbs-Merrill Company, Inc., 1973
Published in Penguin Books, 1974

Did I, my lines intend for publick view,
How many censures, wou'd their faults persue,
Some wou'd, because such words they do affect,
Cry they're insipid, empty, uncorrect.
And many, have attain'd, dull and untaught
The name of Witt, only by finding fault.
True judges, might condemn their want of witt,
And all might say, they're by a Woman writt.
Alas! a woman that attempts the pen,
Such an intruder on the rights of men.

ANNE FINCH, COUNTESS OF WINCHILSEA

(1661–1720)

Staunch Anne! I know your trouble. The same tether
galls us. To be a woman and a writer
is double mischief, for the world will slight her
who slights "the servile house," and who would rather
make odes than beds. Lost lady! Gentle fighter!
Separate in time, we mutiny together.

DILYS LAING

(1906–1960)

Table of Contents

Acknowledgments
ix
Preface
xi
Introduction
xiii

MARGERY KEMPE
3

JANE ANGER
23

ALICE THORNTON
31

MARGARET CAVENDISH, DUCHESS OF NEWCASTLE
55

ANNE FINCH, COUNTESS OF WINCHILSEA
71

APHRA BEHN
87

MARY MANLEY
103

LADY MARY WORTLEY MONTAGU
121

MARY WOLLSTONECRAFT
141

MARY SHELLEY
165

HARRIET MARTINEAU
199

Contents

OLIVE SCHREINER
215

KATE CHOPIN
235

MARY E. WILKINS FREEMAN
255

DOROTHY RICHARDSON
269

ANAÏS NIN
291

DILYS LAING
323

MARGARET WALKER
333

SYLVIA ASHTON-WARNER
343

MURIEL RUKEYSER
363

Acknowledgments

There was sometimes discouragement in the preparation of this work; there was also help and encouragement, often offered when it was most needed.

I especially want to thank Nancy Milford, who helped not only in many practical ways, but in sharing with me her ideas about writing and about the woman writer; Professor Ilse Lind, for her many valuable suggestions and her encouragement; Rosalyn Drexler, Rochelle Owens, and Crystal Field, who discussed with me their experiences as women in the arts; Elaine Showalter and Dorothy B. Simon, for their suggestions about women writers; editor Walter Myers, for his belief and understanding; Helen and George Kotsonis and Ken Milford, for their help; my mother, father, and sister, Anita, for their kindness and support; my husband, Dinos, for his love and care and confidence.

I am grateful for the use of the Princeton University Library, especially its Rare Books Division, and the New York Public Library, where, when I most needed it, I found the Frederick Lewis Allen Memorial Room, a room which, though not "of one's own," is perhaps an even better place in which a woman can write.

Preface

There exists a rich and complex literature by women that goes back to the Middle Ages, a literature that consists of diaries, of autobiographies, of letters, of protests, of novels, of poems, of stories, of plays—a literature in which women wrote about their lives and from which women and men today can draw insight about theirs.

by a Woman writt presents selections from this literature.

When women wrote, they touched upon experiences rarely touched upon by men, they spoke in different ways about these experiences, they often wrote in different forms. Women wrote about childbirth, about housework, about relationships with men, about friendships with other women. They wrote about themselves as girls and as mature women, as wives, mothers, widows, courtesans, workers, thinkers, and rebels. And women writers often wrote about themselves as writers—about the discrimination against them and the pain and courage with which they faced it.

The massive researching, the editing, and the shaping of *by a Woman writt* was done by a group of women. While the book resulted from group work, individual members focused on particular sections. Sandra Adickes contributed eighteenth and nineteenth century selections and researched American material. Bonne August contributed contemporary selections and researched seventeenth and nineteenth century material. Zinta Bibelnieks contributed sixteenth and seventeenth century selections. Joan Goulianos contributed seventeenth century and medieval selections and researched contemporary material. Regina Koger Monteith contributed seventeenth century selections and reseached medieval material. All introductory material was written by Joan Goulianos.

There were two other contributors to this work: Madeline Warren, who worked on the project from the beginning and contributed contemporary selections; and Miriam Kotzin, who contributed nineteenth century American selections.

The selections in *by a Woman writt* represent only a few of hundreds of fine works by women writers, many of which are still

only available in outdated or rare editions. Only works written in
English were chosen, only works which focus on women's experiences, and in the case of nineteenth and twentieth century literature,
only works by writers who had completed substantial bodies of work.
(Medieval material appears in modern translation; sixteenth and
seventeenth century prose material has modernized spelling and punc-
tuation.) Many of the more famous women writers—Virginia Woolf,
Jane Austen, George Eliot—are not included. This is deliberate. For
the aim of *by a Woman writt* is to make available the works of lesser
known writers, writers who deserve more recognition, especially for
the ways in which they wrote about women.

Introduction

What I wish to write about is what it may have meant, what it still may mean, to be a woman writer. I want to tell you how fine these works by women writers are—how they reveal a whole range of women's experiences—how exciting it was to find these works, how maddening to find many of them hidden away in rare books rooms and antiquated editions, how painful to meet the disinterest and ridicule of learned and not so learned professors. But what I really wish to write—what I think I must tell you—is something even more, something about truth and fear.

Months ago, when the selections for this book had been completed, I began to think of ways of introducing these works. These were writings by women from six centuries, many of whom you might not have heard. Good writings. Writings about women's experiences. I could convince you—the works would convince you—that these were moving, important, real experiences, experiences which still occurred. And many of these writings were in unusual forms—autobiographies, diaries, letters, protests. I could convince you too, I thought, that these were valid forms of women's literature. Women had chosen them not only because they were more "acceptable," but because they often suited what was an underlying motive of women's writings—the need to validate one's own experiences. But there was still something that I feared, something that worried me, that stopped me every time I began to write. I had to understand what this was, for when I did, I thought, I would understand something more about these women writers—something that lay at the very heart of their writings.

So I began to reread their works and to read works about women writers. I read scholarly studies about women novelists, playwrights, and poets. I pored over Virginia Woolf's very beautiful, very personal essay, *A Room of One's Own*. I went back to Anaïs Nin's writings about the woman writer. And I studied closely the words of Aphra Behn, the seventeenth century writer, known as the first woman to make money by writing, and those of the seventeenth century poet, Anne Finch, Countess of Winchilsea, and even those of Margery Kempe, a medieval woman, who had described how, when she composed her book, she was sick with fear that her feelings would not be understood. And I talked with women writers, and watched the shapes of their lives. And I tried to understand my own feelings—what was it that made me hesitate, that stopped my words in their tracks?

The subject, of course, was vast. I was talking about writers from many ages. There was a whole new field here. It was not just that works by women writers were being presented, but that, with the contemporary women's movement, these works could be better understood. And the writers themselves were different, individual, each shaped by the circumstances of her own life, her own personality, her own reasons for writing. What was it, I wondered, that Anaïs Nin had in common with Mary Shelley, or Muriel Rukeyser with Aphra Behn, or Dilys Laing with Anne Finch? And as I asked the question, I began to understand that it was not just that these writers had described women's experiences or that many of these writers had written in the same forms, but that, as women, they wrote in a world which was controlled by men, a world in which women's revelations, if they were anything but conventional, might not be welcomed, might not be recognized, and they wrote nevertheless. Their writings were, I thought, not only "literature" but acts of courage. And I wanted to tell you that, and about some of the confusions and perils that courage implied.

It was startling, painful, to read the criticisms of women writers that ran throughout the history of English literature and to realize that these were the criticisms that women faced when they wrote.

Introduction

What was it like for Mary Wollstonecraft, who had written the brilliant *A Vindication of the Rights of Woman,* to be called by Horace Walpole, who refused to read it, "a hyena in petticoats"? As a young woman, Charlotte Brontë had sent some of her work to Robert Southey, Poet Laureate of England. In response, Southey wrote her:

> The day dreams in which you habitually indulge are likely to in-
> duce a distempered state of mind; and in proportion as all the ordi-
> nary uses of the world seem to you flat and unprofitable, you will be
> unfitted for them without becoming fitted for anything else. Litera-
> ture cannot be the business of a woman's life, and it ought not to be.
> The more she is engaged in her proper duties, the less leisure will
> she have for it even as an accomplishment and a recreation.

What was it like for Charlotte Brontë to receive Southey's advice? She wrote back telling him that, at first, she felt "only shame and regret." "I felt a painful heat rise to my face when I thought of the quires of paper I had covered with what once gave me so much delight, but which now was only a source of confusion." But after she had read his letter several times, she came to the conclusion that Southey was not advising her against writing, only against writing for fame. "I trust I shall never more feel ambitious to see my name in print," she wrote. And indeed, later, when she published her works and those of her sisters, Emily and Anne, Charlotte hid the fact that they were women and used the deliberately ambiguous pseudonym of Currer, Ellis and Acton Bell.

I could still remember my own anger and disappointment when I read R. W. Chambers' introduction to the modern version of *The Book of Margery Kempe.* Here was a rare medieval work, a work in which a woman had described pregnancy, post-partum depression, her relations with her husband, her travels, her humiliations, her triumphs, even her times of madness. Yet, here was Chambers, an eminent scholar, praising her work as a medieval document, but warning the reader that "poor Margery is to be classed with those hotels which Baedeker describes as 'variously judged'. You must come to her not expecting too much, and prepared for anything." But it was even more important, I thought, to understand what lay behind these criticisms, what made men characterize women writers as daydreamers, as hyenas, as hotels?

It was here that I came back to the women writers I had read. For, in their own, sometimes guarded, sometimes open, ways, it was they who could provide the answer to my question. It was they who had faced the criticism leveled against them simply because they were women, and who had reached, in their writing, for responses. In Woolf's *A Room of One's Own*, there was a passage that seemed to me full of clues. "Women," wrote Woolf, "have served all these centuries as looking-glasses possessing the magic and delicious power of reflecting the figure of man at twice its natural size." Such mirrors, she went on, "are essential to all violent and heroic action." If woman "begins to tell the truth, the figure in the looking-glass shrinks; his fitness for life is diminished."

But what was even more revealing than Woolf's observation was that she feared to carry it further. Instead, after she had made her observation, she stopped, described herself sitting in a cafe, crumbling her bread, stirring her coffee, paying her bill—grateful for the inheritance an aunt had left her, which allowed her the freedom to write. Woolf had the insight and the independence—she had a room of her own—but she also had the fear, and again and again, in her essay, she would caution women against writing consciously as women—warning them that "anything written with that conscious bias is doomed to death. It ceases to be fertilised." She was wrong, I thought, sadly so, but I could understand what might have made her feel as she did. Finally, it seemed, she was afraid of challenging man, afraid of repercussions, upheavals, changes, loneliness, sterility.

Anaïs Nin had understood these fears better. Creation, she wrote, is "a threat to relation with man." "To create seemed to me such an assertion of the strongest part of me that I would no longer be able to give all those I love the feeling of their being stronger, and they would love me less." Hers was a more direct statement, perhaps because she had come to her understanding with the help of a woman analyst, perhaps because Nin was a different woman. But in her work were keys to our understanding of the woman writer, for again and again, Nin had addressed herself openly to the problems of the woman writer. "Man must fear the effort woman is making to create herself," she wrote, "not to be born of Adam's rib." Why was Henry Miller against Nin writing a diary? She thought it was because he feared "a woman unveiling her own truths." "Woman stuttered about herself," Nin wrote, "out of fear of what she had to say."

For Nin, the response was to adhere to nonfictional forms, in which she could explore these problems—to insist on writing her diary, on writing as a woman, about women—in spite of Miller and others, who were pressuring her to concentrate more on fiction. For Aphra Behn, the response was to preface some of her works with powerful defenses of the woman writer. For Anne Finch, it was to explore, in her poetry, her own situation as a woman poet. What was it like to be a woman poet? Finch would write that it meant that all might say that her poetry was "by a Woman writt," that all would criticize her for neglecting her household duties and for intruding upon the rights of men. And she would write about her fears and her responses: "Be caution'd then my Muse, and still retir'd;/Nor to be dispis'd, aiming to be admir'd." Though her caution was necessary, it was sad as well, for what a poet she could have been, if she did not have to caution her muse to be "still with contracted wing."

When I considered women writers, I thought, I had to consider not only the criticisms they faced—these might be easy enough to counter—but how their lives would affect and be affected by their writing. Women writers were, after all, still women. Most of them depended upon men, not only as their critics but as their sources of support and very often as their sources of identity. There was a passage in the autobiography of Margaret Cavendish, the Duchess of Newcastle, which had haunted me. Here was a seventeenth century woman intellectual, so well known that crowds gathered to see her. Yet, she would justify writing her autobiography by telling her readers that she wrote "for my own sake,"

. . . to tell the truth, lest after ages should mistake, in not knowing I was daughter to one Master Lucas of St. Johns, near Colchester, in Essex, second wife to the Lord Marquis of Newcastle; for My Lord having had two wives, I might easily have been mistaken, especially if I should dye and My Lord marry again.

I thought about her and about Anne Finch. Both mentioned that their husbands approved of their writing—Cavendish even thanking her husband for allowing her to publish, "a favor," she said, "few husbands grant to their wives." But to what extent did this approval limit what Cavendish and Finch wrote? How many women, I wondered, did not publish because their husbands did not approve? And what of the unmarried women writers? Were they not as, or even more, dependent upon men? And how had this shaped what they wrote?

I began to read again about the life of Aphra Behn. Here was a woman who often was credited with being the first woman to earn her living by writing. In a preface to one of her plays, she had described herself as a woman "who is forced to write for Bread and not ashamed to own it," but aside from this statement, there was actually very little known about how she lived. She may have been married and widowed. There were letters that proved she had worked as a spy, letters in which she described herself as desperate for money. There were documents that indicated she had been, for a short time, in debtor's prison. But then there was a gap in what was known about her life. Two years after her imprisonment, she emerged as a playwright, aggressive and risqué. How had this happened, if not, as much that she wrote and much that was written about her clearly suggests, by her becoming the mistress of prominent men?

In one way or another, these women writers all shared this—they were dependent upon men. There were women who were interested in women's writings, and women writers often knew and praised each other's works. But, overall, it was men who were the critics, the publishers, the professors, the sources of support. It was men who had the power to praise women's works, to bring them to public attention, or to ridicule them, to doom them—as was done to many of the works in this book—to obscurity.

by a Woman writt, was, I thought, an attempt to break through this obscurity, an attempt by women to find and to present works that were meaningful to them. I remembered another statement of Woolf's. "There is no reason," she wrote, "to think that the form of the epic or of the poetic play suits a woman any more than the sentence suits her. . . . Yet who shall say that even now 'the novel' . . . who shall say that even this most pliable of all forms is rightly shaped for her use?" It was a radical statement from a woman whose major recognition came from her novels—and a statement important for this book. For what *by a Woman writt* did was not only to present works by women, but to suggest how different women's literature was and could be from men's. Women could define for themselves what their literature was, define it not on the basis of traditional forms and themes, but on the basis of what, in fact, gave shape to their lives.

It was not an idea, I thought, that would be welcomed by the professors with the silver pots and the measuring-rods. I had lived for two years—working on the fascinating materials of this book—hearing, at the same time, that it did not really matter whether or not women writers existed. They were not really very good anyway . . . simply curiosities . . .

When women wrote, I thought, they faced this too, and they wrote, as I would do, about it, in spite of it, in challenge to it. It was no wonder that they often wrote in different forms, that they often wrote about different subjects, that their voices sounded so different—sometimes furious, sometimes full of scorn for their own sex, sometimes fearful, sometimes deadened, yet sometimes compassionate, original, vital, authentic, free. It was no wonder that if there was one phrase that women writers had passed on to each other throughout the centuries—from Margery Kempe to Margaret Cavendish to Virgina Woolf—it was this—that what mattered was to attempt to tell one's truth, to write "what you wish to write."

Joan Goulianos

New York City
February, 1972

by a Woman writt

Drawing by C. Brendel, based on fourteenth century illustration, from *Chaucer's World*, Columbia University Press

Margery Kempe

(ca. 1373–?)

According to her autobiography, Margery Kempe, the proud daughter of the mayor of Lynn, Norfolk, was married at around twenty and soon after pregnant. The birth was a difficult one, and after it, she went mad. She saw devils, she slandered her husband, her friends, and herself, she tore at her own flesh. It was a vision of Christ that brought her back to her senses, and from then on, though she later bore thirteen more children, she devoted herself to becoming a religious mystic, given to visions and to fits of weeping.

Kempe traveled across England, on the continent, and to the Holy Land. She was ridiculed and imprisoned, accused of being a whore as well as a heretic. According to her own account, she was neither. She was simply a woman torn between her obligations to her family and her desire to follow her calling, a woman who explained her fits of weeping as being out of her compassion for the suffering of others, and who struggled to defend and to justify herself.

When she was old, Margery Kempe, who could not write, decided to compose an account of her life and struggled for years with reluctant scribes and with her own fears until she completed it. Her work was lost for nearly five hundred years—an early copy being identified in 1934. Called *The Book of Margery Kempe*, it is the first known extant autobiography in English, and the first known extant work in English, aside from purely religious works, by a woman.

FROM THE BOOK OF MARGERY KEMPE

HER MARRIAGE AND ILLNESS AFTER CHILDBIRTH. SHE RECOVERS.

When this creature was twenty years of age, or some deal more, she was married to a worshipful burgess (of Lynne) and was with child within a short time, as nature would. And after she had conceived, she was belaboured with great accesses till the child was born and then, what with the labour she had in childing, and the sickness going before, she despaired of her life, weening she might not live. And then she sent for her ghostly father, for she had a thing on her conscience which she had never shewn before that time in all her life.

3

For she was ever hindered by her enemy, the devil, evermore saying to her that whilst she was in good health she needed no confession, but to do penance by herself alone and all should be forgiven, for God is merciful enough. And therefore this creature oftentimes did great penance in fasting on bread and water, and other deeds of alms with devout prayers, save she would not shew that in confession.

And when she was at any time sick or dis-eased, the devil said in her mind that she should be damned because she was not shriven of that default. Wherefore after her child was born, she, not trusting to live, sent for her ghostly father, as is said before, in full will to be shriven of all her lifetime, as near as she could. And when she came to the point for to say that thing which she had so long concealed, her confessor was a little too hasty and began sharply to reprove her, before she had fully said her intent, and so she would no more say for aught he might do. Anon, for the dread she had of damnation on the one side, and his sharp reproving of her on the other side, this creature went out of her mind and was wondrously vexed and laboured with spirits for half a year, eight weeks and odd days.

And in this time she saw, as she thought, devils opening their mouths all inflamed with burning waves of fire, as if they would have swallowed her in, sometimes ramping at her, sometimes threatening her, pulling her and hauling her, night and day during the aforesaid time. Also the devils cried upon her with great threatenings, and bade her that she should forsake Christendom, her faith, and deny her God, His Mother and all the Saints in Heaven, her good works and all good virtues, her father, her mother and all her friends. And so she did. She slandered her husband, her friends and her own self. She said many a wicked word, and many a cruel word; she knew no virtue nor goodness; she desired all wickedness; like as the spirits tempted her to say and do, so she said and did. She would have destroyed herself many a time at their stirrings and have been damned with them in Hell, and in witness thereof, she bit her own hand so violently, that the mark was seen all her life after.

And also she rived the skin on her body against her heart with her nails spitefully, for she had no other instruments, and worse she would have done, but that she was bound and kept with strength day and night so that she might not have her will. And when she had long been laboured in these and many other temptations, so that men weened she should never have escaped or lived, then on a time as she lay alone and her keepers were from her, Our Merciful Lord Jesus Christ, ever to be trusted, worshipped be His Name, never forsaking His servant in time of need, appeared to His creature who had forsaken Him, in the likeness of a man, most seemly, most beauteous and most amiable that ever might be seen with man's eye, clad in a mantle of purple silk, sitting upon her bedside, looking upon her with so blessed a face that she was strengthened in all her spirit, and said to her these words:

"Daughter, why hast thou forsaken Me, and I forsook never thee?"

And anon, as He said these words, she saw verily how the air opened as bright as any lightning. And He rose up into the air, not right hastily and quickly, but fair and easily, so that she might well behold Him in the air till it was closed again.

And anon this creature became calmed in her wits and reason, as well as ever she was before, and prayed her husband as soon as he came to her, that she might have the keys of the buttery to take her meat and drink as she had done before. Her maidens and her keepers counselled him that he should deliver her no keys, as they said she would but give away such goods as there were, for she knew not what she said, as they weened.

Nevertheless, her husband ever having tenderness and compassion for her, commanded that they should deliver to her the keys; and she took her meat and drink as her bodily strength would serve her, and knew her friends and her household and all others that came to see how Our Lord Jesus Christ had wrought His grace in her, so blessed may He be, Who ever is near in tribulation. When men think He is far from them, He is full near by His grace. Afterwards, this creature did all other occupations as fell to her to do, wisely and soberly enough, save she knew not verily the call of Our Lord.

HER WORLDLY PRIDE. HER ATTEMPT AT BREWING AND MILL-ING, AND FAILURE AT BOTH. SHE AMENDS HER WAYS.

When this creature had thus graciously come again to her mind, she thought that she was bound to God and that she would be His servant. Nevertheless, she would not leave her pride or her pompous array, which she had used beforetime, either for her husband, or for any other man's counsel. Yet she knew full well that men said of her full much villainy, for she wore gold pipes on her head, and her hoods, with the tippets, were slashed. Her cloaks also were slashed and laid with divers colours between the slashes, so that they should be the more staring to men's sight, and herself the more worshipped.

And when her husband spoke to her to leave her pride, she answered shrewdly and shortly, and said that she was come of worthy kindred—he should never have wedded her—for her father was sometime Mayor of the town of N . . .[1] and afterwards he was alderman of the High Guild of the Trinity in N . . . And therefore she would keep the worship of her kindred whatever any man said.

She had full great envy of her neighbours, that they should be as well arrayed as she. All her desire was to be worshipped by the people. She would not take heed of any chastisement, nor be content with the goods that God had sent her, as her husband was, but ever desired more and more.

Then for pure covetousness, and to maintain her pride, she began to brew, and was one of the greatest brewers in the town of N . . . for three years or four, till she lost much money, for she had never been used thereto. For, though she had ever such good servants, cunning in brewing, yet it would never succeed with them. For when the ale was fair standing under barm as any man might see, suddenly the barm would fall down, so that all the ale was lost, one brewing after another, so that her servants were ashamed and would not dwell with her.

Then this creature thought how God had punished her aforetime— and she could not take heed—and now again, by the loss of her goods. Then she left and brewed no more.

Then she asked her husband's mercy because she would not follow his counsel aforetime, and she said that her pride and sin were the cause of all her punishing, and that she would amend and that she had trespassed with good will.

Yet she left not the world altogether, for she now bethought herself of a new housewifery. She had a horse-mill. She got herself two good

[1] Lynne, now King's Lynn, is evidently referred to. This anonymity is dropped later on.

horses and a man to grind men's corn, and thus she trusted to get her living. This enterprise lasted not long, for in a short time after, on Corpus Christi Eve, befell this marvel. This man, being in good health of body, and his two horses sturdy and gentle, had pulled well in the mill beforetime, and now he took one of these horses and put him in the mill as he had done before, and this horse would draw no draught in the mill for anything the man might do. The man was sorry and essayed with all his wits how he should make this horse pull. Sometimes he led him by the head, sometimes he beat him, sometimes he cherished him and all availed not, for he would rather go backward than forward. Then this man set a sharp pair of spurs on his heels and rode on the horse's back to make him pull, and it was never the better. When the man saw it would work in no way, he set up this horse again in the stable, and gave him corn, and he ate well and freshly. And later he took the other horse and put him in the mill, and like his fellow did, so did he, for he would not draw for anything the man might do. Then the man forsook his service and would no longer remain with the aforesaid creature. Anon, it was noised about the town of N . . . that neither man nor beast would serve the said creature.

Then some said she was accursed; some said God took open vengeance on her; some said one thing and some said another. Some wise men, whose minds were more grounded in the love of Our Lord, said that it was the high mercy of Our Lord Jesus Christ that called her from the pride and vanity of the wretched world.

Then this creature, seeing all these adversities coming on every side, thought they were the scourges of Our Lord that would chastise her for her sin. Then she asked God's mercy, and forsook her pride, her covetousness, and the desire that she had for the worship of the world, and did great bodily penance, and began to enter the way of everlasting life as shall be told hereafter.

HER VISION OF PARADISE. SHE DESIRES TO LIVE APART FROM HER HUSBAND. DOES PENANCE AND WEARS A HAIRCLOTH.

On a night, as this creature lay in her bed with her husband, she heard a sound of melody so sweet and delectable, that she thought she had been in Paradise, and therewith she started out of her bed and said:

"Alas, that ever I did sin! It is full merry in Heaven."

This melody was so sweet that it surpassed all melody that ever might be heard in this world, without any comparison, and caused her, when she heard any mirth or melody afterwards, to have full plenteous and abundant tears of high devotion, with great sobbings and sighings after the bliss of Heaven, not dreading the shames and the spites of this wretched world. Ever after this inspiration, she had in her mind the mirth and the melody that was in Heaven, so much, that she could not well restrain herself from speaking thereof, for wherever she was in any company she would say oftentimes: "It is full merry in Heaven."

And they that knew her behaviour beforetime, and now heard her speaking so much of the bliss of Heaven, said to her:

"Why speak ye so of the mirth that is in Heaven? Ye know it not, and ye have not been there, any more than we." And were wroth with her, for she would not hear nor speak of worldly things as they did, and as she did beforetime.

And after this time she had never desired to commune fleshly with her husband, for the debt of matrimony was so abominable to her that she would rather, she thought, have eaten or drunk the ooze and the muck in the gutter than consent to any fleshly communing, save only for obedience.

So she said to her husband: "I may not deny you my body, but the love of my heart and my affections are withdrawn from all earthly creatures, and set only in God."

He would have his will and she obeyed, with great weeping and sorrowing that she might not live chaste. And oftentimes this creature counselled her husband to live chaste, and said that they often, she knew well, had displeased God by their inordinate love, and the great delectation they each had in using the other, and now it was good that they should, by the common will and consent of them both, punish and chastise themselves wilfully by abstaining from the lust of their bodies. Her husband said it was good to do so, but he might not yet. He would when God willed. And so he used her as he had done before. He would not spare her. And ever she prayed to God that she might live chaste; and three or four years after, when it pleased Our Lord, he made a vow of chastity, as shall be written afterwards, by leave of Jesus.

And also, after this creature heard this heavenly melody, she did great bodily penance. She was shriven sometimes twice or thrice on a day, and specially of that sin she so long had (hid), concealed and covered, as is written in the beginning of the book.

She gave herself up to great fasting and great watching; she rose at two or three of the clock, and went to church, and was there at her prayers unto the time of noon and also all the afternoon. Then she was slandered and reproved by many people, because she kept so strict a life. She got a hair-cloth from a kiln, such as men dry malt on, and laid it in her kirtle as secretly and privily as she might, so that her husband should not espy it. Nor did he, and she lay by him every night in his bed and wore the hair-cloth every day, and bore children in the time.

Then she had three years of great labour with temptations which she bore as meekly as she could, thanking Our Lord for all His gifts, and was as merry when she was reproved, scorned and japed for Our Lord's love, and much more merry than she was beforetime in the worship of the world. For she knew right well she had sinned greatly against God and was worthy of more shame and sorrow than any man could cause her, and despite of the world was the right way Heavenwards, since Christ Himself had chosen that way. All His apostles, martyrs, confessors and virgins, and all that ever came to Heaven, passed by the way of tribulation, and she, desiring nothing so much as Heaven, then was glad in her conscience when she believed that she was entering the way that would lead her to the place she most desired.

And this creature had contrition and great compunction with plenteous tears and many boisterous sobbings for her sins and for her unkindness against her Maker. She repented from her childhood for unkindness, as Our Lord would put it in her mind, full many a time. Then, beholding her own wickedness, she could but sorrow and weep and ever pray for mercy and forgiveness. Her weeping was so plenteous and continuing, that many people thought she could weep and leave off, as she liked. And therefore many men said she was a false hypocrite, and wept before the world for succour and worldly goods. Then full many forsook her that loved her before while she was in the world, and would not know her. And ever, she thanked God for all, desiring nothing but mercy and forgiveness of sin.

HER TEMPTATION TO ADULTERY WITH A MAN, WHO, WHEN SHE CONSENTS, REJECTS HER.

The first two years when this creature was thus drawn to Our Lord, she had great quiet in spirit from any temptations. She could well endure to fast, and it did not trouble her. She hated the joys of the world. She felt no rebellion in her flesh. She was so strong, as she thought, that she dreaded no devil in Hell, as she did such great bodily penance. She thought that she loved God more than He did her. She was smitten with the deadly wound of vainglory, and felt it not, for she many times desired that the crucifix should loosen His hands from the Cross, and embrace her in token of love. Our Merciful Lord Jesus Christ, seeing this creature's presumption, sent her, as is written before, three years of great temptations, one of the hardest of which I purpose to write as an example to those who come after, so that they should not trust in themselves, or have joy in themselves, as she had. For, no dread, our ghostly enemy sleepeth not, but he full busily searcheth our complexions and dispositions and where he findeth us most frail, there, by Our Lord's sufferance, he layeth his snare, which no man may escape by his own power.

So he laid before this woman the snare of lechery, when she believed that all fleshly lust had wholly been quenched in her. And so for a long time she was tempted with the sin of lechery, for aught that she could do. Yet she was often shriven, she wore her hair-cloth, and did great bodily penance and wept many a bitter tear, and prayed full often to Our Lord that He should preserve her and keep her, so that she should not fall into temptation, for she thought she would rather be dead than consent thereto. All this time she had no lust to commune with her husband; but it was very painful and horrible unto her.

In the second year of her temptation, it so fell that a man whom she loved well, said unto her on Saint Margaret's Eve before evensong that, for anything, he would lie by her and have his lust of his body, and she should not withstand him, for if he did not have his will that time, he said he would anyhow have it another time; she should not choose. And he did it to see what she would do, but she thought that he had meant it in full earnest at that time, and said but little thereto. So they parted then and both went to hear evensong, for her church was that of Saint Margaret. This woman was so laboured with the man's words that she could not hear her evensong, nor say her Paternoster, or think any other good thought, but was more troubled than ever she was before.

The devil put into her mind that God had forsaken her, or else she would not be so tempted. She believed the devil's persuasion, and began to consent because she could think no good thought. Therefore thought she that God had forsaken her, and when evensong was done, she went to the man aforesaid, so that he could have his lust, as she thought he had desired, but he made such simulation that she could not know his intent, and so they parted asunder for that night. This creature was so laboured and vexed all that night, that she never knew what she might do. She lay by her husband, and to commune with him was so abominable to her that she could not endure it, and yet it was lawful unto her, in lawful time, if she would. But ever she was laboured with the other man, to sin with him inasmuch as he had spoken to her. At last, through the importunity of temptation, and lack of discretion, she was overcome and consented in her mind, and went to the man to know if he would then consent to her, and he said he never would, for all the gold in this world; he would rather be hewn as small as flesh for the pot.

She went away all shamed and confused in herself at seeing his stability and her own instability. Then thought she of the grace that God had given her before; how she had had two years of great quiet in her soul, repenting of her sin with many bitter tears of compunction, and a perfect will never again to turn to her sin, but rather to die. Now she saw how she had consented in her will to do sin, and then fell she half into despair. She thought she must have been in Hell for the sorrow she felt. She thought she was worthy of no mercy, for her consent was so wilfully done, nor ever worthy to do Him service, because she was so false to Him. Nevertheless she was shriven many times and often, and did whatever penance her confessor would enjoin her to do, and was governed by the rules of the Church. That grace, God gave his creature, blessed may He be, but He withdrew not her temptation, but rather increased it, as she thought.

Therefore she thought He had forsaken her, and dared not trust to His mercy, but was afflicted with horrible temptations to lechery and despair all the next year following. But Our Lord, of His mercy, as she said herself, gave her each day for the most part two hours of sorrow for her sins, with many bitter tears. Afterwards, she was laboured with temptation to despair as she was before, and was as far from feelings of grace, as they that never felt any, and that she could not bear, and so she gave way to despair. But for the time that she felt grace, her labours were so wonderful that she could evil fare with them, but ever mourned and sorrowed as though God had forsaken her.

ON FASTING AND TOKENS.

"Fasting, daughter, is good for young beginners, and discreet penance, especially as their ghostly father giveth them or enjoineth them to do. And to bid many beads is good for those that can do no better, yet it is not perfect. But it is a good way perfection-ward. For I tell thee, daughter, that they who are great fasters, and great doers of penance, they would that it should be held the best life; also they that are given to saying many devotions, they would have that the best life; and they that give much alms, they would that that were held the best life.

"I have oftentimes told thee, daughter, that thinking, weeping, and high contemplation is the best life on earth, and thou shalt have more merit in Heaven for one year of thinking in thy mind than for a hundred years of praying with thy mouth; and yet thou wilt not believe Me, for thou wilt bid many beads whether I will or not. And yet, daughter, I will not be displeased with thee, whether thou think, say, or speak, for I am always well pleased with thee.

"And if I were on earth as bodily as I was before I died on the

Cross, I should not be ashamed of thee, as other men be, for I should take thee by the hand amongst the people, and make thee great cheer, so that they should well know that I loved thee right well.

"For it is fitting for the wife to be homely with her husband. Be he ever so great a lord, and she ever so poor a woman when he weddeth her, yet they must lie together and rest together in joy and peace. Right so must it be between thee and Me, for I take no heed what thou hast been, but what thou wouldst be, and oftentimes have I told thee that I have clean forgiven thee all thy sins. Therefore I must needs be homely with thee, and lie in thy bed with thee.

"Daughter, thou desirest greatly to see Me, and thou mayest boldly, when thou art in thy bed, take Me to thee as thy wedded husband, as thy dearworthy darling, and as thy sweet son, for I will be loved as a son should be loved by the mother, and I will that thou lovest Me, daughter, as a good wife ought to love her husband. Therefore thou mayest boldly take Me in the arms of thy soul and kiss My mouth, My head, and My feet, as sweetly as thou wilt. And as oftentimes as thou thinkest of Me, or wouldst do any good deed to Me, thou shalt have the same reward in Heaven, as if thou didst it to Mine own Precious Body which is in Heaven, for I ask no more of thee but thine heart to love Me, Who loveth thee, for My love is ever ready for thee."

Then she gave thanks and praise to Our Lord Jesus Christ for the high grace and mercy that He shewed unto her, unworthy wretch.

This creature had divers tokens in her bodily hearing. One was a sort of sound as if it were a pair of bellows blowing in her ear. She, being abashed thereby, was warned in her soul no fear to have, for it was the sound of the Holy Ghost. And then Our Lord turned that sound into the voice of a dove, and later on, He turned it into the voice of a little bird which is called a red-breast, that sang full merrily oftentimes in her right ear. And then she would ever have great grace after she heard such a token. She had been used to such tokens for about twenty-five years, at the time of writing this book.

Then said Our Lord Jesus Christ to His creature:

"By these tokens mayest thou well know that I love thee, for thou art to Me a very mother, and to all the world, for that great charity which is in thee; and yet I am the cause of that charity Myself, and thou shalt have great reward therefor in Heaven."

AT LEICESTER SHE IS DISTRESSED BY THE SIGHT OF A CRUCI-
FIX. THE MAYOR ARRESTS HER AND HOLDS HER IN CUSTODY.
THE JAILOR TREATS HER WELL.

Afterwards, set she forth to Leicester, and a good man also—
Thomas Marchale—of whom is written before; and there she came
into a fair church where she beheld a crucifix that was piteously
portrayed and lamentable to behold, through beholding which, the
Passion of Our Lord entered her mind, so that she began all to melt
and to relent by tears of pity and compassion. Then the fire of love
kindled so eagerly in her heart that she could not keep it secret, for,
whether she would or not, it caused her to break out with a loud
voice and cry marvellously, and weep and sob so hideously that many
a man and woman wondered on her therefor.

When it was overcome and she was going out of the church door,
a man took her by the sleeve and said:

"Damsel, why weepest thou so sore?"

"Sir," she said, "it is not you to tell."

So she and the good man, Thomas Marchale went forth, and took
her hostel and there ate their meat. When they had eaten, she prayed
Thomas Marchale to write a letter and send it to her husband, that
he might fetch her home. And while the letter was in writing, the
hosteler came up to her chamber in great haste, and took away her
scrip and bade her come quickly and speak with the Mayor. And so
she did.

Then the Mayor asked her of what country she was, and whose
daughter she was.

"Sir," she said, "I am of Lynne in Norfolk, a good man's daughter
of the same Lynne, who hath been mayor five times of that worshipful borough, and alderman also many years; and I have a good man,
also a burgess of the said town of Lynne, for my husband."

"Ah!" said the Mayor, "Saint Katherine told what kindred she
came of, and yet ye are not like her, for thou art a false strumpet, a
false Lollard, and a false deceiver of the people, and I shall have thee
in prison.

And she answered: "I am as ready, sir, to go to prison for God's
love, as ye are ready to go to church."

When the Mayor had long chidden her and said many evil and horrible words to her, and she, by the grace of Jesus, had reasonably answered to all that he could say, he commanded the jailer's man to lead her to prison.

The jailer's man, having compassion on her with weeping tears, said to the Mayor:

"Sir, I have no house to put her in, unless I put her amongst men."

Then she was moved with compassion for the man who had compassion on her. Praying for grace and mercy to that man, as for her own soul, she said to the Mayor:

"I pray you, sir, put me not among men, that I may keep my chastity, and my bond of wedlock to my husband, as I am bound to do."

Then said the jailer his own self to the Mayor:

"Sir, I will be under bond to keep this woman in safe ward till ye will have her back."

Then was there a man of Boston, who said to the good wife, where she was at hostel:

"Forsooth," he said, "in Boston this woman is held to be a holy woman and a blessed woman."

Then the jailer took her into his ward, and led her home into his own house, and put her in a fair chamber, shutting the door with a key, and commending his wife the key to keep.

Nevertheless, he let her go to church when she would, and let her eat at his own table and made her right good cheer for Our Lord's sake, thanked be Almighty God thereof.

THE STEWARD OF LEICESTER ASSAULTS HER. THE TOWNS-PEOPLE INSIST ON THE RELEASE OF HER FRIENDS.

Then the steward of Leicester, a seemly man, sent for the said creature to the jailer's wife, and she—for her husband was not at home—would not let her go to any man, steward or otherwise. When the jailer knew thereof he came himself, and brought her before the steward. The steward anon, as he saw her, spake Latin unto her, many priests standing about to hear what she would say. She said to the steward:

"Speak English if ye please, for I understand not what ye say."

The steward said to her: "Thou liest falsely, in plain English."

Then she said to him again: "Sir, ask what question ye will in English, and by the grace of My Lord Jesus Christ I will answer you reasonably thereto."

Then asked he many questions, to which she answered so readily and reasonably that he could get no cause against her.

Then the steward took her by the hand, and led her into his chamber and spoke many foul bawdy words unto her, purposing and desiring, as it seemed to her, to oppress her and ravish her. And then she had much dread and much sorrow, crying him for mercy.

She said: "Sir, for the reverence of Almighty God, spare me, for I am a man's wife."

Then said the steward: "Thou shalt tell me whether thou hast this speech of God or the devil, or else thou shalt go to prison."

"Sir," she said, "to go to prison, I am not afraid for My Lord's love, Who suffered much more for my love than I may for His. I pray you do as ye think best."

The steward, seeing her boldness in that she dreaded no prisoning, struggled with her, shewing unclean tokens and ungoodly countenance, wherethrough he scared her so much that she told him how she had her speech and her dalliance of the Holy Ghost and not of her own cunning.

Then he, all astonished at her words, left his business and his lewdness, saying to her, as many a man had done before:

"Either thou art a right good woman, or else a right wicked one," and delivered her again to her jailer, and he led her home again with him. Afterwards they took two of her fellows that went with her on pilgrimage. One was Thomas Marchale, aforesaid, the other, a man of Wisbech, and put them both in prison, for cause of her. Then was she grieved and sorry for their distress, and prayed to God for their deliverance.

Then Our Merciful Lord said to His creature:

"Daughter, I shall, for thy love, so dispose for them, that the people will be right fain to let them go, and not long keep them."

On the next day following, Our Lord sent such weather of lightning, thunder and rain, continuing so that all the people in the town were so afraid that they did not know what to do. They dreaded them it was because they had put the pilgrims in prison.

Then the governors of the town went in great haste and took out both two pilgrims who had lain in prison all the night before, leading them to the Guild Hall, there to be examined before the Mayor and the worshipful men of the town, compelling them to swear if the aforesaid creature were a woman of right faith and right belief, continent and clean of her body, or not.

As far as they knew, they swore, as clearly as God should help them at the Day of Doom, that she was a good woman, of right faith and right belief, clean and chaste in all her behaviour, as far as they could know, in demeanour and bearing, in word and in work.

Then the Mayor let them go whither they would.

And anon, the tempest ceased and it was fair weather, worshipped be Our Lord God.

The pilgrims were glad that they were delivered and durst no longer abide in Leicester, but went ten miles thence, and abode there, that they might have knowledge what should be done with the said creature, for, when they both were put in prison, they had told her themselves that they supposed, if the Mayor might have his will, he would have her burnt.

THE MAN WHOSE WIFE IS INSANE AFTER CHILDBIRTH. MAR-
GERY VISITS HER AND SHE BECOMES NORMAL WITH HER, BUT
STILL INSANE WITH OTHERS. SHE RECOVERS.

As the said creature was in a church of Saint Margaret to say her devotions, there came a man kneeling at her back, wringing his hands and shewing tokens of great grief. She, perceiving his grief, asked him what ailed him. He said it stood right hard with him, for his wife was newly delivered of a child, and she was out of her mind.

"And, dame," he said, "she knoweth not me or any of her neigh-bours. She roareth and crieth so that she maketh folk evil afeared. She will both smite and bite, and therefore is she manacled on her wrists."

Then asked she the man if he would that she went with him and saw her, and he said:

"Yea, dame, for God's love."

So she went forth with him to see the woman; and when she came into the house, as soon as the sick woman, who was alienated from her wits, saw her, she spake to her soberly and kindly and said she was right welcome to her, and she was right glad of her coming, and greatly comforted by her presence, "For ye are," she said, "a right good woman, and I behold many fair angels about you, and therefore, I pray you, go not from me, for I am greatly comforted by you."

And when other folk came to her, she cried and gaped as if she would have eaten them, and said that she saw many devils about them. She would not suffer them to touch her, by her own good will. She roared and cried so, both night and day, for the most part, that men would not suffer her to dwell amongst them, she was so tedious to them.

Then was she taken to the furthest end of the town, into a chamber, so that the people should not hear her crying, and there was she bound, hand and foot, with chains of iron, so that she should smite nobody.

And the said creature went to her each day, once or twice at least; and whilst she was with her, she was meek enough, and heard her speak and chat with good will, without any roaring or crying.

And the said creature prayed for this woman every day, that God should, if it were His will, restore her to her wits again, and Our Lord answered in her soul and said she should fare right well.

Then was she more bold to pray for her curing than she was before, and each day, weeping and sorrowing, prayed for her recovery, till God gave her her wits and her mind again. And then was she brought to church and purified as other women are, blessed may God be.

It was, as they thought that knew it, a right great miracle, for he that wrote this book had never, before that time, seen man or woman, as he thought, so far out of herself as this woman was, nor so evil to rule or to manage.

And later, he saw her sad and sober enough, worship and praise be to Our Lord without end, for His high mercy and His goodness, Who ever helpeth at need.

ON HER FEELINGS. THE END OF THE TREATISE THROUGH THE
DEATH OF THE FIRST WRITER OF IT.

Also, while the aforesaid creature was occupied about the writing
of this treatise, she had many holy tears and weeping, and oftentimes
there came a flame of fire about her breast, full hot and delectable;
and also he that was her writer could not sometimes keep himself
from weeping.

And often in the meantime, when the creature was in church, Our
Lord Jesus Christ with His Glorious Mother and many saints also
came into her soul and thanked her, saying that they were well pleased
with the writing of this book. And also she heard many times a voice
of a sweet bird singing in her ear, and oftentimes she heard sweet
sounds and melodies that passed her wit to tell of. And she was many
times sick while this treatise was in writing, and, as soon as she would
go about the writing of this treatise, she was hale and whole suddenly,
in a manner; and often she was commanded to make herself ready
in all haste.

And, on a time, as she lay in her prayers in the church at the time
of Advent before Christmas, she thought in her heart she would that
God of His goodness would make Master Aleyn to say a sermon as
well as he could; and as quickly as she had thought thus, she heard
Our Sovereign Lord Christ Jesus saying in her soul:

"Daughter, I wot right well what thou thinkest now of Master
Aleyn, and I tell thee truly that he shall say a right holy sermon; and
look that thou believest steadfastly the words that he shall preach, as
though I preached them Myself, for they shall be words of great
solace and comfort to thee, for I shall speak in him."

When she heard this answer, she went and told it to her confessor
and to two other priests that she trusted much on; and when she had
told them her feeling, she was full sorry for dread whether he should
speak as well as she had felt or not, for revelations be hard sometimes
to understand.

And sometimes those that men think were revelations, are deceits
and illusions, and therefore it is not expedient to give readily
credence to every stirring, but soberly abide, and pray if it be sent of
God. Nevertheless, as to this feeling of this creature, it was very truth,

by a Woman writt

shewn in experience, and her dread and her gloom turned into great ghostly comfort and gladness.

Sometimes she was in great gloom for her feelings, when she knew not how they should be understood, for many days together, for dread that she had of deceits and illusions, so that she thought she would that her head had been smitten from her body till God of His goodness declared them to her mind.

For sometimes, what she understood bodily was to be understood ghostly, and the dread that she had of her feelings was the greatest scourge that she had on earth; and especially when she had her first feelings; and that dread made her full meek, for she had no joy in the feeling till she knew by experience whether it was true or not.

But ever blessed may God be, for He made her always more mighty and more strong in His love and in His dread, and gave her increase of virtue with perseverance.

Here endeth this treatise, for God took him to His mercy, that wrote the copy[2] of this book, and, though he wrote it not clearly nor openly to our manner of speaking, he, in his manner of writing and spelling made true sense, which, through the help of God and of herself that had all this treatise in feeling and working, is truly drawn out of the copy into this little book.

[2] By "copy," Margery means the original ill-written book that they have just finished copying here.

IANE ANGER

her Protection

for VVomen.

To defend them againſt the
SCANDALOVS REPORTES OF
a late Surfeiting Louer, and all other like
Venerians that complaine ſo to bee
ouercloyed with womens
kindneſſe.

Written by Ia: A. Gent.

At London

Printed by Richard Ione, and Thomas
Orwin.   1589.

Title page from Jane Anger's PROTECTION FOR WOMEN

Jane Anger

(?)

Jane Anger's *Protection for Women* is one of the earliest examples of an important form of women's writing—the protest. In the *Protection*, Jane Anger attacks an antifeminist work—she calls it *the scandalous reports of a late Surfeiting Lover*—and she attacks the men who produce such works. We do not know who Jane Anger was, nor do we know whether or not she is using a pseudonym. But the emotion behind her militant and bitter work is easily recognizable. As she herself explains, "it was ANGER that did write it."

FROM JANE ANGER HER PROTECTION FOR WOMEN

TO DEFEND THEM AGAINST THE SCANDALOUS REPORTS OF A LATE SURFEITING LOVER, AND ALL OTHER LIKE VENERIANS THAT COMPLAIN SO TO BE OVERCLOYED WITH WOMEN'S KIND-NESS. 1589.

To the Gentlewomen of England, health.

Gentlewomen, though it is to be feared that your settled wits will advisedly condemn that which my choleric vein has rashly set down, and so perchance ANGER shall reap anger for not agreeing with diseased persons. Yet (if with indifference of censure, you consider of the head of the quarrel) I hope you will rather show yourselves defendants of the defender's title, than complainants of the plaintiff's wrong. I doubt judgment before trial, which were injurious to the law, and I confess that my rashness deserves no less, which was a fit of my extremity. I will not urge reasons because your wits are sharp and will soon conceive my meaning, nor will I be tedious least I prove too too troublesome, nor over dark in my writing, for fear of the name of a riddler. But (in a word) for my presumption I crave pardon, because it was ANGER that did write it. Committing your protection and myself to the protection of yourselves, and the judgment of the cause to the censures of your just minds.

Yours ever at commandment,
Ja: A.

To all women in general, and gentle reader whatsoever.

Fie on the falsehood of men, whose minds go oft a madding, and whose tongues can not so soon be wagging, but straight they fall a railing. Was there ever any so abused, so slandered, so railed upon, or so wickedly handled undeservedly as are we women? Will the gods permit it, the goddesses stay their punishing judgments, and we ourselves not pursue their undoings for such devilish practices? Oh Paul's steeple and Charing Cross! A halter hold all such persons! Let the streams of the channels in London streets run so swiftly as they may be able alone to carry them from that sanctuary! Let the stones be as ice, the soles of their shoes as glass, the ways steep like Etna, and every blast a whirlwind puffed out of Boreas his long throat, that these may hasten their passage to the Devil's haven! Shall surfeiters rail on our kindness, you stand still and say nought, and shall not Anger stretch the veins of her brains, the strings of her fingers, and the lists of her modesty to answer their surfeitings? Yes, truly. And herein I conjure all you to aid and assist me in defence of my willingness, which shall make me rest at your commands. Fare you well.

Your friend,
Ja. A.

A Protection for Women. &c.

The desire that every man has to show his true vein in writing is unspeakable, and their minds are so carried away with the manner, as no care at all is had of the matter. They run so into rhetoric as often times they overrun the bounds of their own wits and go they know not whither. If they have stretched their invention so hard on a last as it is at a stand, there remains but one help, which is to write of us women. If they may once encroach so far into our presence as they may but see the lining of our outermost garment, they straight think that Apollo honors them in yielding so good a supply to refresh their sore overburdened heads, through studying for matters to indite of. And, therefore, that the god may see how thankfully they receive his liberality (their wits whetted, and their brains almost broken with botching his bounty), they fall straight to dispraising and slandering our silly[1] sex. But judge what the cause should be of this their so great malice towards simple women. Doubtless the weakness of our wits, and our honest bashfulness, by reason whereof they suppose that there is not one amongst us who can or dare reprove their slanders and false reproaches. Their slanderous tongues are so short, and the time wherein they have lavished out their words freely has been so long, that they know we cannot catch hold of them to pull them out. And they think we will not write to reprove their lying lips, which conceits have already made them cocks, and would (should they not be cravened) make themselves among themselves be thought to be of the game. They have been so daintily fed with our good natures that, like jades, (their stomachs are grown so queasy) they surfeit of our kindness. If we will not suffer them to smell on our smocks, they will snatch at our petticoats. But if our honest natures cannot sway with that uncivil kind of jesting then we are coy, yet if we bear with their rudeness, and be somewhat modestly familiar with them, they will straight make matter of nothing, blaring abroad that they have surfeited with love, and then their wits must be shown in telling the manner how.

Among the innumerable number of books to that purpose of late (unlookedfor), the new surfeit of an old lover (sent abroad to warn those which are of his own kind from catching the like disease) came by chance to my hands, which, because as well women as men are desirous of novelties, I willingly read over. Neither did the ending thereof less please me than the beginning, for I was so carried away with the conceit of the Gent. as that I was quite out of the book, before I thought I had been in the midst thereof: so pithy were his sentences, so pure his words, and so pleasing his style. The chief matters therein contained were of two sorts: the one in the dispraise of man's folly, and the other, invective against our sex, their folly

[1] Helpless.

proceeding of their own flattery joined with fancy, and our faults are through our folly, with which is some faith.

The greatest fault that does remain in us women is that we are too credulous, for could we flatter as they can dissemble, and use our wits well, as they can their tongues ill, then never would any of them complain of surfeiting. But if we women be so so perilous cattle, as they term us, I marvel that the gods made not fidelity as well a man, as they created her a woman, and all the moral virtues of their masculine sex, as of the feminine kind, except their deities knew that there was some sovereignty in us women which could not be in them men. But least some snatching fellow should catch me before I fall to the ground (and say they will adorn my head with a feather, affirming that I roam beyond reason, seeing it is most manifest that the man is the head of the woman, and that therefore we ought to be guided by them), I prevent them with this answer. The gods, knowing that the minds of mankind would be aspiring, and having thoroughly viewed the wonderful virtues wherewith women are enriched, least they should provoke us to pride, and so confound us with Lucifer, they bestowed the supremacy over us to man, that of the coxcomb he might only boast, and therefore, for God's sake, let them keep it. But we return to the surfeit.

Having made a long discourse of the gods' censure concerning love, he leaves them (and I them with him), and comes to the principal object and general foundation of love, which he affirms to be grounded on women. And now beginning to search his scroll, wherein are taunts against us, he begins and says that we allure their hearts to us, wherein he says more truly than he is aware of. For we woo them with our virtues, and they wed us with vanities. And men, being of wit sufficient to consider of the virtues which are in us women, are ravished with the delight of those vanities, which allure and draw the senses of them to serve us, whereby they become ravenous hawks, who do not only seize upon us, but devour us. Our good toward them is the destruction of ourselves; we being well-formed, are by them foully deformed. Of our true meaning they make mocks, rewarding our loving follies with disdainful flouts. We are the grief of man, in that we take all the grief from man: we languish when they laugh, we lie sighing when they sit singing, and sit sobbing when they lie slugging and sleeping. *Mulier est hominis confusio* because her kind heart cannot so sharply reprove their frantic fits as those mad frenzies deserve. *Aut amat, aut odit, non est in tertio:* she loves good things, and hates that which is evil. She loves justice and hates iniquity. She loves truth and true dealing, and hates lies and falsehood. She loves man for his virtues, and hates him for his vices. To be short, there is no *medium* between good and bad, and therefore she can be *in nullo tertio.* Plato his answer to a vicar of fools which asked the question being, that he knew not whether to place women among those creatures which were reasonable or unreasonable, did as much beautify his divine knowledge as all the books he did write. For knowing that women are the greatest help that men have, without whose aide and assistance it is as possible for them to live, as if they wanted meat, drink, clothing, or any other necessity. And knowing also that even then in his age, much more in those ages which should after follow, men were grown to be so unreasonable, as he could not decide whether men or brute beasts were more reasonable. Their eyes are so curious, as be not all women equal with Venus for beauty, they cannot abide the sight of them. Their stomachs so queasy, as do they taste but twice of one dish, they straight surfeit, and needs must a new diet be provided for them. We are contrary to men because they are contrary to that which is good. Because they are purblind, they cannot see into our natures, and we too well (though we had but half an eye) into their conditions, because they are so bad. Our behaviors alter daily because men's virtues decay hourly.

If Hesiod had with equity as well looked into the life of man as he did precisely search out the qualities of us women, he would have said that if a woman trust unto a man, it shall fare as well with her, as if she had a weight of a thousand pounds tied about her neck and then cast into the bottomless seas. For by men are we confounded, though they by us are sometimes crossed. Our tongues are light because earnest in reproving men's filthy vices, and our good counsel is termed nipping injury, in that it accords not with their foolish fancies; our boldness rash, for giving noddies nipping answers, our dispositions naughty, for not agreeing with their vile minds, and our fury dangerous, because it will not bear with their knavish behaviors. If our frowns be so terrible and our anger so deadly, men are too foolish in offering occasions of hatred, which shunned, a terrible death is prevented. There is a continual deadly hatred between the wild boar and tame hounds. I would there were the like between women and men, unless they amend their manners, for so strength should predominate, where now flattery and dissimulation have the upper hand. The lion rages when he is hungry, but man rails when he is glutted. The tiger is robbed of her young ones when she is ranging abroad, but men rob women of their honor undeservedly under their noses. The viper storms when his tail is trodden on, and may not we fret when all our body is a footstool to their vile lust? Their unreasonable minds, which know not what reason is, make them nothing better than brute beasts. But let us grant that Clytemnestra, Ariadne, Delilah and Jezebel were spotted with crimes. Shall not Nero with others innumerable (and therefore unnameable) join hands with them and lead the dance? Yet it grieves me that faithful Deianira should be falsely accused of her husband Heracles's death, seeing she was utterly guiltless (even of thought) concerning any such crime. For had not the Centaur's falsehood exceeded the simplicity of her too too credulous heart, Heracles had not died so cruelly tormented, nor the monster's treason been so unhappily executed. But we must bear with these faults, and with greater than these, especially seeing that he which set it down for a maxim was driven into a mad mood through a surfeit, which made him run quite besides his book, and mistake his case. For where he accused Deianira falsely, he would have had condemned Heracles deservedly.

Marius's daughter, imbued with so many excellent virtues, was too good either for Metellus or any man- living. For though per- adventure she had some small fault, yet doubtless he had detestable crimes. On the same place where *down* is on the hen's head, the *comb* grows on the cock's pate. If women breed woe to men, they bring care, poverty, grief and continual fear to women, which if they be not woes they are worse.

Euthydemus made six kinds of women, and I will approve that there are so many of men, which be poor and rich, bad and good, foul and fair. The great patrimonies that wealthy men leave their children after their death make them rich, but vice and other marthrifts happening into their companies never leave them till they be at the beggar's bush, where I can assure you they become poor. Great eaters being kept at a slender diet never distemper their bodies but remain in good case, but afterwards, once turned forth to liberty's pasture, they graze so greedily as they become surfeiting jades, and always after are good for nothing. There are men which are snout-fair, whose faces look like a cream-pot, and yet those are not the fair men I speak of. But I mean those whose conditions are free from knavery, and I term those foul that have neither civility nor honesty. Of these sorts there are none good, none rich or fair long. But if we do desire to have them good, we must always tie them to the manger and diet their greedy paunches, otherwise they will surfeit. What shall I say? Wealth makes them lavish, wit knavish, beauty effeminate, poverty deceitful, and deformity ugly. Therefore, of me take this counsel:

> Esteem of men as of a broken reed,
> Mistrust them still, and then you well shall speed.

THE

AUTOBIOGRAPHY

OF

MRS. ALICE THORNTON,

OF

EAST NEWTON, CO. YORK.

Alice Thornton;

Published for the Society

BY ANDREWS AND CO., DURHAM;

WHITTAKER AND CO., 13 AVE MARIA LANE;

BERNARD QUARITCH, 15 PICCADILLY;

BLACKWOOD AND SONS, EDINBURGH.

1875.

Title page from THE AUTOBIOGRAPHY OF ALICE THORNTON

Alice Thornton

(1627–1707)

If a life as a wife and mother is "ordinary," Alice Thornton led an ordinary life. She lived in Northern England, married out of duty, bore nine children, six of whom died, and was widowed in middle age. In her old age, she wrote a vividly detailed autobiography, picturing her life as one of almost continual suffering. She wrote of her feelings about marriage, of her sickness from pregnancy and childbirth, of the sicknesses in her family, of the financial difficulties she faced as a widow. Frank and graphic, her work reveals a little known side of the "ordinary" life of a seventeenth century woman.

FROM THE AUTOBIOGRAPHY OF
MRS. ALICE THORNTON

A grateful remembrance of my being preserved from the fury of the wars in the time of the Scots being over the poor country in their madness against us, when I was at Hipswell with my dear mother in 1643–1644.

In this time, after the battle of Hessom Moor, when the blessed King Charles had by treachery lost the field, and his two generals, Prince Rupert and Lord of Newcastle, exposed all the brave white coats' foot that stood the last man till they were murdered and destroyed, and that my poor brother George Wandesford was forced to fly to hide himself at Kirklington, and brought my brother Christopher behind him; after which time we got to Hipswell, and lived as quietly as we could, for the madness of the Scots who quartered all the country over, and insulted over the poor country and English. My dear mother was much grieved to be abused by them in quartering them at her own house, yet could not possibly excuse herself totally from the men and horses, though she paid double pay, and was 1s. 6d. pt. [apiece], when others at ninepence only in a month. She kept of the quartering captains and commanders, and would never yield to have them.

At length there came one Capt. Innis, which was over that troop we had in town, and he coming on a surprise into the house, I could not hide myself from them as I used to do; but coming boldly into my mother's chamber, where I was with her, he began to be much more earnest and violent to have stayed in the house, and said he would stay in his quarters, but we so ordered the matter that we got him out by all the fair means could be to get quit of him, who was so wild a bloody looked man, that I trembled all the time he was in the house; I, calling to mind with dread that he was so infinitely like in person my Lord Macguire, the great rebel in Ireland, was in a great consternation for fear of him. After which time this man impudently told my aunt Norton that he would give all he was worth if she could procure me to be his wife, and offered three or four thousand pounds, and Lord Adair should come and speak for him. She said it was all in vain; he must not presume to look that way, for I was not to be obtained. And she was sure he might not have any encouragement, for I was resolved not to marry, and put him off the best she could; but wrote me private word that my Lord of Adair and he would come to speak to me and my mother about it, and wished me to get out of his way. It was not to further that desire in me, who did perfectly hate him and them all like a todd[1] in such a kind; and immediately acquainted my dear mother, which was surprised and troubled, for she feared they would burn her house and destroy all; wished me to go whither I would to secure myself. And I did so forthwith, ran into the town, and hid myself privately, in great fear and a fright with a good old woman of her tenants, where, I bless God, I continued safely till the visit was over, and at night came home.

We was all joyful to escape so, for my dear mother was forced to give them the best treat she could, and said, indeed, she did not know where I was, and sent out [servants] a little to seek me, but I was safe from them. After which time this villain captain did study to be revenged of my dear mother, and threatened cruelly what he would do to her because she hid me, though that was not true, for I hid myself. And about the time that the Scots was to march into Scotland, being too long here on us, when my mother paid often £25 and £30

---

[1] A fox.

a month to them, this Scot in a boasting manner sent for his pay, and she sent all she ought to him, which he would not take from her, but demanded double money, which she would nor could not do; so on Sunday morning he brought the company, and threatened to break the house and doors, and was most vile and cruel in his oaths and swearing against her and me; and went to drive all her goods in her ground, having this delicate cattle of her own breed. I went up to the leads to see whether he did drive them away, and he looked up and thought it had been my dear mother, cursed me bitterly, and wished the devil blow me blind and into the air, and I had been a thorn in his heel, but he would be a thorn in my side, and drove the cattle away to Richmond, where General Leslie was. So my dear mother was forced to take the pay he was to have, and carried it to the general that laid at my Aunt Norton's, and acquainted him how that captain had abused her and wronged her; which, by mercy of God to her, this General Leslie did take notice of, and took her money, and bid her not trouble herself, for he would make him take it, or punish him for his rudeness. He said more, did Innis, that if ever any of his countrymen came into England, they would burn her and me and all she had; but yet she served that God which did deliver us out of the Irish rebellion and all this bloodshed in England till this time, and did now deliver her and myself and all we had from him.

This was a great deliverance at last, and joined with my own single deliverance from this beast, from being destroyed and deflowered by him, for which I have reason to praise the great and mighty God of mercy to me. There was one of his men that I had cured of his hand, being cut of it and lame; so that fellow did me a signal return of gratitude for it. Thus it was some times a refreshment to me after I had sat up much with my dear weak mother in her illness, or writing of letters for her, that she did bid me walk out to Lowes with her maids to rest myself, so I used this some times. But this captain's man who I cured came to me one day, saying, "Dear mistress, I pray do not think much if I desire you, for God's sake, not to go out with the maids to Lowes." I said, "Why?" He said again, "He was bound to tell me that his captain did curse and swear that he would watch for me, and that very night he had designed with a great many of his comrades to catch me at Lowes, and force me on horseback away with them, and God knows what end he would make of me." I said, "I hoped God would deliver me from all such wickedness;" and so I gave the man many thanks, who was so honest to preserve me from these plots, rewarding him for his pains, and did never go abroad out of the house again, but forced to keep like a prisoner while they was here.

Blessing the great God of heaven, who did not suffer me to fall into the hands of those wicked men, nor into the hand of Sir Jeremy Smithson,[2] who could never prevail by no means to obtain me for his wife, and I was then delivered also from such a force by the discovery of Tom Binkes. Lord make me truly thankful for preservation of me, thy poor handmaid, and make me live to Thy glory. Amen.

The death of my sister Danby, September 30, 1645, at her house at Thorpe.

About this year, my dear and only sister, the Lady Danby, drew near time for delivery of her sixteenth child. Ten whereof had been baptised, the other six were stillborn, when she was above half gone with them, she having miscarried of them all upon frights by fire in her chamber, falls, and such like accidents happening. All her children were sons, saving my two nieces, Katherine and Alice Danby, and most sweet, beautiful, and comely were they all. The troubles and distractions of those sad times did much afflict and grieve her, who was of a tender and sweet disposition, wanting the company of her husband, Sir Thomas, to manage his estate and other concerns. But he, being engaged in his king's service, was not permitted to leave it, nor to come to Thorpe but seldom, till she fell sick. These things, added to the horrid rudeness of the soldiers and Scots quartered then amongst them, which vexing and troubling her much with frights, caused her to fall into travail sooner than she expected, nor could she get her old midwife, being then in Richmond,

---

[2] "A great deliverance from the violence of a rape from Jeremy Smithson, Sir Hugh's son, who had solicited me in marriage by his father and uncle Smithson, who would have settled on him £200 a year if I would have married him; but I would not, but avoided his company, because he was debauched. And he hired some of his own company to have stolen me away from Lowes, but Tom Binks discovered it, I bless God."

which was then shut up, for the plague was exceeding great there, so that all the inhabitants that could get out fled, saving those had the sickness in their houses. At this time did my dear mother and whole family receive grand preservation from the Divine Providence in delivering us from the arrow that flies by day, when as hundreds died so near us, and thousands fell at noonday; nay, all that town was almost depopulated. How did our good and great Lord preserve all us at Hipswell, so that no infection seized upon any one that belonged us, although the malice of the beggars was great to have done harm by rags, notwithstanding all her charitable relief daily with much meat and money. Blessed be the great and ever-merciful Father, Who did not deliver us up to this heavy judgment of the Lord, but did rebuke the destroying angel, and at last stayed this plague in Richmond.

But to return to my poor sister, whose extremities called her friends to her assistance. She had been very ill long time before her delivery, and much altered in the heat of her body, being feverish. After exceeding sore travail she was delivered of a goodly son about August 3d, by one dame Sworre. This boy was named Francis, after another of that name, a sweet child that died that summer of the smallpox. This child came double into the world, with such extremity that she was exceeding tormented with pains, so that she was deprived of the benefit of sleep for fourteen days, except a few frightful slumbers; neither could she eat anything for her nourishment as usual. Yet still did she spend her time in discourse of goodness, excellently pious, godly, and religious, instructing her children and servants, and preparing her soul for her dear Redeemer, as it was her saying she should not be long from Him.

That week when I was left with her, after my lady Armitage and my aunt Norton was gone, though she could not get rest, yet all her discourse was very good and profitable to the hearers, who might learn piety, chastity, holiness, patience, humility and all how to entertain the pleasure of God with contentedness, making so excellent a confession of faith and other Christian virtues and graces that Mr. Siddall exceeding admired her parts and piety, giving her as high a character as could be. She did entreat Sir Thomas, her husband, to send for Mr. Farrer, and to join with her in the receiving of the Holy

Sacrament, but he would not give leave, which was to my knowledge a great grief and trouble to her thoughts. That night she poured out her soul in prayer with such comprehensive and good expressions that could be for her own soul, for pardon and remission of her sins, for grace and sanctification from the Spirit, faith, and assurance; and then for her husband, children, mother, and all her other relations and myself; for the restoration of the king, the church, and the kingdom's peace; with such pathetic and zealous expressions that all did glorify God for [the] things He had done for her. After which, she did in a manner prophesy that God would humble the kingdom by afflictions for their sin and security; but after that, when we were humbled and reformed, whosoever should live to see it (for she should not) should enjoy happy days for church and state. Thus she continued, and with prayers for our enemies, and for they stood in need of our prayers for the forgiveness of all their evils, she called her children, exhorted them abundantly to fear God, serve Him, and love one another, be obedient to their father, with admonishing them and her family. She was kind and dearly affectionate to her husband, to whom, under God, she left the care of her seven young children. Sometimes she did express abundant joy in God, and would sweetly, with a melodious voice, sing aloud His praise and glory in anthems and psalms proper for her condition, with many sweet verses praising Him for all things; nor was she in the least concerned to part with her husband or children, nor any thing in this world, having her hopes and desires fixed upon God, leaving her children freely to the providence of her God, Who had relieved her soul out of all her distress, Who had promised to be a father to the fatherless. All her words were full of sweetness and affection, giving me many hearty thanks for all my pains and care I took with her, and watching a whole week together, if she lived she would requite my love; with an abundance of affectionate expressions to this purpose.

My grief and sorrow was so great for her, that I had brought myself into a very weak condition, insomuch as my mother came to Thorpe with Dafeny Lightfoote, a careful servant, to help with my sister, and sent me home who was almost spent in that time. At which time I took my last leave of my dearest and only sister, never could get to see her for my own illness afterwards. But she, waiting her

Lord's time to be called, was fitting her soul and heart for Him. As the disease increased of the fever, notwithstanding what could be done for her in that condition, it did to her as many others in such extremity, deprive her (for want of sleep and food, which she could not take by reason of a sore throat) of part of the use of understanding for a little while when its fury lasted. But Dafeny was always with her, who she had a great love for, and as she grew weaker after a month's time of her delivery, holding her head on her breast, said to her in a faint, weak voice, "I am going to God, my God, now." Then said Dafeny, "Nay, madame, I hope God will please to spare your life to live amongst your sweet children, and bring them up." "How can that be?" answered my sister, "For I find my heart and vitals all decayed and gone. No; I desire to be dissolved and to be with Christ, which is best of all. I have made my peace with God." And immediately she said with as strong a voice as she could, "Lord Jesus, receive my spirit;" then, giving a little breathing sigh, delivered up her soul into the hands of her Savior, sweetly falling asleep in the Lord.

And thus ended that sweet saint her weary pilgrimage, having her life interwoven with many cares and afflictions. Although she was married to a good estate, yet did she enjoy not much comfort, and I know she received her change with much satisfaction, being, she hoped, to be freed, as she said, from a wicked world, and all the evils therein. Thus departed that good soul, having been young called to walk in the ways of God, and had made His service her continual practice. . . .

The marriage of Alice Wandesford, December 15, 1651.

After many troubles and afflictions under which it pleased God to exercise my mother and self in since the death of my father, she was desirous to see me comfortably settled in the estate of marriage, in which she hoped to receive some satisfaction, finding age and weakness to seize more each year, which added a spur to her desires for the future well-being of her children, according to every one of their capacities. As to myself, I was exceedingly satisfied in that happy and free condition, wherein I enjoyed my time with delight abundantly in the service of my God, and the obedience I owed to such an excellent parent, in whose enjoyment I accounted my days spent with great content and comfort; the only fears which possessed me was lest I should be deprived of that great blessing I had in her life. Nor could I, without much reluctance, draw my thoughts to the change of my single life, knowing too much of the cares of this world sufficiently without the addition of such incident to the married estate. As to the fortune left by my father, it was fair, and more than competent, so that I needed not fear (by God's blessing) to have been troublesome to my friends, but to be rather in a condition to assist them if need had required. Especially more in regard that I was confident of what my dear mother could do for me living and at her death. . . .

Nevertheless, such was my dear mother's affection to the family for its preservation, that she harkened to the proposal made for Mr. Thornton's marriage, albeit therein she disobliged some persons of very good worth and quality which had solicited her earnestly in my behalf, and such as were of large and considerable estates of her neighbor's about her. And, after the first and second view between us, she closed so far with him that she was willing he should proceed in his suit, and that cordially, if I should see cause to accept. For my own particular, I was not hasty to change my free estate without much consideration, both as to my present and future, the first inclining me rather to continue so still, wherein none could be more satisfied. The second would contract much more trouble, twisted inseparably with those comforts God gave in that estate.

Yet might I be hopeful to serve God in those duties incumbent on a wife, a mother, a mistress, and governess in a family. And if it pleased God so to dispose of me in marriage, making me a more public instrument of good to those several relations, I thought it rather duty in me to accept my friends' desires for a joint benefit, than my own single retired content, so that Almighty God might receive the glory of my change, and I more capacitated to serve Him in this generation, in what He thus called me unto. Therefore it highly concerned me to enter into this greatest change of my life with abundance of fear and caution, not lightly, nor unadvisedly, nor, as I may take my God to witness that knows the secrets of hearts, I did it not to fulfill the lusts of the flesh, but in chastity and singleness of heart, as marrying in the Lord.

Alice Thornton

And to that end, that I might have a blessing upon me, in all my undertakings, I poured out my petitions before the God of my life to direct, strengthen, lead, and counsel me what to do in this concern, which so much tended to my future comfort or discomfort. And to order my ways aright, so that if He saw in His wisdom that the married estate was the best for me, that He would please to direct me in it, and incline my heart towards it; but if otherwise it were best for me to be, that I might still continue in the same, but still referring my will to His; and also to order my change so that He would in mercy give me such a one to be my husband as might be an holy, good, and pious Christian, understanding, wise, and affectionate, that we might live in His fear and favor, praying Him to give unto me suitable graces and qualifications which should fit me for that calling, and this for our Savior's sake, I humble begged in Jesus Christ our Lord. Amen.

After which petitions to my God, I was the more inclined to accept of this proposition of my friends' finding; also that the gentleman seemed to be a very godly, sober, and discreet person, free from all manner of vice, and of a good conversation. This was the greatest encouragement to me when I considered the general decay of true religion, in profession and practice, especially the gentry, and with men of quality; too many being given to a sad course of life, through debauchery, made me more cautious in choosing, fearing to meet with such as neither knew God nor cared for their souls, to preserve themselves in a holy course of life and conversation. Nor could I ever have enjoyed comfort in this world to have been matched with the greatest estates or fortunes, had I wanted that first and principal qualification in a husband, which is to be regarded above all the satisfaction this world can afford.

I cannot deny that his estate, which was then favorably given in to my mother, was the least in value which had been offered; yet did my mother hope to find a handsome competency, without much charge, as was represented to her, only the want of a house which he must build; his brothers and sisters being provided for by his mother, that would clear his estate, which was given in to be £600 per annum. This was very well, considering the addition of my father's portion given me by his will and deeds, namely, £500 out of England, at

by a Woman writt

Kirklington, and £1000 to be paid out of his Irish estate of Edough, which would be an addition to increase Mr. Thornton's revenues. Also my dear mother was willing to give me what assistance she could out of her love and affection. The treaty of marriage with Mr. Thornton was very earnestly pursued by himself and friends, and as discreetly managed by my dear mother as she could, for she was in a manner let alone by all our relations. Especially after my brother's death, in regard that self-interest too far prevailed for those to hinder my disposal to any person, by the which they would be deprived of their sinister expectations of my fortune. But, through God's blessing, this treaty was brought to a period to the satisfaction of each party, and with a general consent, and the articles of marriage drawn up by Mr. Thornton for the right settlement of all things concluded upon between my dear mother in my behalf and himself were both justly and honestly done by him. . . .

Alice Wandesford, the daughter of Christopher Wandesford, Esq., late Lord Deputy of Ireland, was married to William Thornton, esquire, of East Newton, at my mother's house in Hipswell, by Mr. Siddall, December the 15th, 1651. Mr. Siddall made a most pious and profitable exhortation to us, showing our duties, and teaching us the fear of the Lord in this our new estate of life, with many zealous prayers for us. . . .

A deliverance from death that day on which I was married, December 15, 1651.

That very day on which I was married, having been in health and strength for many years before, I fell suddenly so ill and sick after two o'clock in the afternoon, that I thought, and all that saw me did believe, it would have been my last night, being surprised with a violent pain in my head and stomach, causing a great vomiting and sickness at my heart, which lasted eight hours before I had any intermissions; but, blessed be the Lord our God, the Father of mercies, Which had compassion on me, and by the means that was used I was strengthened wonderfully beyond expectation, being pretty well about ten o'clock at night. My dear husband, with my mother, was exceeding tender over me, which was a great comfort to my spirits. What the cause of this fit was I could not conjecture, save that I might have brought it upon me by cold taken the night before, when I sat up late in preparing for the next day, and washing my feet at that time of the year, which my mother did believe was the cause of that dangerous fit the next day.[3]

But, however it was, or from what cause it proceeded, I received a great mercy in my preservation from God, and shall ever acknowledge the same in humble gratitude for His infinite loving kindness forever. I looked upon this first business of my new condition to be a little discouragement, although God was able to turn all things for the best, and to my good, that I might not build too much hopes of happiness in things of this world, nor in the comforts of a loving husband, whom God had given me, but set my desires more upon the love of my Lord and God.

Meditations upon the deliverance of my first child, and of the great sickness followed for three quarters of a year; August 6, 1652, lasted till May 12, 1653.

About seven weeks after I married it pleased God to give me the blessing of conception. The first quarter I was exceeding sickly in breeding, till I was with quick child; after which I was very strong and healthy, I bless God, only much hotter than formerly, as is usual in such cases from a natural cause, insomuch that my nose bled much when I was about half gone, by reason of the increase of heat. Mr. Thornton had a desire that I should visit his friends, in which I freely joined, his mother living about fifty miles from Hipswell, and all at Newton and Buttercrambe. In my passage thither I sweat exceedingly, and was much inclining to be feverish, wanting not eight weeks of my time, so that Dr. Wittie said that I should go near to fall into a fever, or some desperate sickness, if I did not cool my blood, by

---

[3] "Which condition was extremely bewailed by my husband and mother and my friends, and looked upon as a sad omen to my future comfort. And I do confess I was very desirous to have then delivered up my miserable life into the hand of my merciful Redeemer, Who I feared I had offended by altering my resolves of a single life . . . Thus was the first entrance of my married life, which began in sickness, and continued in much afflictions, and ended in great sorrows and mournings. So that which was to others accounted the happiest estate was embittered to me at the first entrance, and was a caution of what trouble I might expect in it, as was hinted by St. Paul's Epistle, 'Such shall have trouble in the flesh.' "

by a Woman writt

taking some away, and if I had stayed but two days longer, I had followed his advice. In his return home from Newton, his own estate, I was carried over Hambleton towards Sir William Askough's house, where I passed down on foot a very high wall between Hood Hill and Whitstone cliff, which is above a mile steep down, and indeed so bad that I could not scarce tread the narrow steps, which was exceeding bad for me in that condition, and sore to endure, the way so straight and none to lead me but my maid, which could scarce make shift to get down herself, all our company being gone down before. Each step did very much strain me, being so big with child, nor could I have got down if I had not then been in my full strength and nimble on foot. But, I bless God, I got down safe at last, though much tired, and hot and weary, finding myself not well, but troubled with pains after my walk. Mr. Thornton would not have brought me that way if he had known it so dangerous, and I was a stranger in that place; but he was advised by some to go that way before we came down the hill.

This was the first occasion which brought me a great deal of misery, and killed my sweet infant in my womb. For I continued ill in pain by fits upon this journey, and within a fortnight fell into a desperate fever at Hipswell. Upon which my old doctor, Mr. Mahum, was called, but he could do little towards the cure, because of being with child. I was willing to be ordered by him, but said I found it absolutely necessary to be let blood if they would save my life, but I was freely willing to resign my will to God's, if He saw fit for me, to spare my life, yet to live with my husband; but still with subserviency to my Heavenly Father. Nor was I wanting to supplicate my God for direction what to do, either for life or death. I had very often and frequent impressions to desire the latter before the former, finding no true joy in this life, but I confess also that which moved me to use all means for my recovery, in regard of the great sorrow of my dear and aged mother and my dear husband took for me, far exceeding my deserts, made me more willing to save my life for them, and that I might render praises to my God in the land of the living.

But truly, I found my heart still did cleave to my Maker that I never found myself more desirous of a change to be delivered from this wicked world and body of sin and death, desiring to be dissolved and to be with Christ. Therefore endured I all the rigors and extremity of my sickness with such a share of patience as my God gave me. As for my friends, they were so much concerned for me that, upon the importunity of my husband, although I was brought indeed very weak and desperately ill about eleventh day of my sickness, I did let him send for Dr. Wittie, if it were not too late. The doctor came past the next day, when he found me very weak, and durst not let me blood that night, but gave me cordials, etc., till the next day, and if I got but one hour's rest that night, he would do it the morning following. That night the two doctors had a dispute about the letting me blood. Mr. Mahum was against it, and Dr. Wittie for it; but I soon decided that dispute, and told them, it they would save my life, I must bleed.

So the next day I had six or seven ounces taken which was turned very bad by my sickness, but I found a change immediately in my sight, which was exceeding dim before, and then I see as well as ever clearly, and my strength began a little to return; these things I relate that I may set forth the mercy of my ever gracious God, Who had blessed the means in such manner. Who can sufficiently extoll His Majesty for His boundless mercies to me His weak creature, for from that time I was better, and he had hopes of my life.

The doctor stayed with me seven days during my sickness; my infant within me was greatly forced with violent motions perpetually, till it grew so weak that it had left stirring, and about the 27th of August, I found myself in great pains as it were the colic, after which I began to be in travail, and about the next day at night I was delivered of a goodly daughter, who lived not so long as that we could get a minister to baptize it, though we presently sent for one. This my sweet babe and first child departed this life half an hour after its birth, being received, I hope, into the arms of Him that gave it. She was buried that night, being Friday, the 27th of August, 1652, at Easby church.

The effects of this fever remained by several distempers sucessively, first, after the miscarriage I fell into a most terrible shaking ague, lasting one quarter of a year, by fits each day twice, in much violence, so that the sweat was great with faintings, being thereby weakened till I could not stand or go. The hair on my head came off, my nails of my fingers and toes came off, my teeth did shake, and ready to come out and grew black. After the ague left me, upon a medicine of London treacle, I fell into the jaundice, which vexed me very hardly one full quarter and a half more. I finding Dr. Wittie's judgment true, that it would prove a chronic distemper; but blessed be the Lord, upon great and many means used and all remedies, I was at length cured of all distempers and weaknesses, which, from its beginning, had lasted three quarters of a year full out. Thus had I a sad entertainment and beginning of my change of life, the comforts thereof being turned into much discomforts and weaknesses, but still I was upheld by an Almighty Power, therefore will I praise the Lord my God. Amen.

Upon the birth of my second child and daughter, born at Hipswell on the 3rd of January in the year 1654.

Alice Thornton, my second child, was born at Hipswell near Richmond in Yorkshire the 3rd day of January, 1654, baptized the 5th of the same. Witnesses, my mother the Lady Wandesford, my uncle, Mr. Major Norton, and my cousin Yorke his daughter, at Hipswell, by Mr. Michell Siddall, minister then of Caterick.

It was the pleasure of God to give me but a weak time after my daughter Alice's birth, and she had many preservations from death in the first year, being one night delivered from being overlaid by her nurse, who laid in my dear mother's chamber a good while. One night my mother was writing pretty late, and she heard my dear child make a groaning troublesomely, and stepping immediately to nurse's bedside she saw the nurse fallen asleep, with her breast in the child's mouth, and lying over the child; at which she, being affrighted, pulled the nurse suddenly off from her, and so preserved my dear child from being smothered. . . .

After I was delivered, and in my weary bed and very weak, it fell out that my little daughter Alice, being then newly weaned, and about a year old, being asleep in one cradle and the young infant in another, she fell into a most desperate fit, of the convulsions as supposed to be, her breath stopped, grew black in her face, which sore frightened her maid Jane Flouer. She took her up immediately, and with the help of the midwife, Jane Rimer, to open her teeth and to bring her to life again. But still, afterwards, no sooner that she was out of one fit but fell into another fit, and the remedies could be by my dear mother and Aunt Norton could scarce keep her alive, she having at least twenty fits; all friends expecting when she should have died.

But I lying the next chamber to her and did hear her, when she came out of them, to give great shrieks and suddenly, that it frightened me extremely, and all the time of this poor child's illness I myself was at death's door by the extreme excess of those, upon the fright and terror came upon me, so great floods that I was spent, and my breath lost, my strength departed from me, and I could not speak for faintings, and dispirited so that my dear mother and aunt and friends did not expect my life, but overcome with sorrow for me. Nor durst they tell me in what a condition my dear Naly was in her fits, lest grief for her, added to my own extremity, with loss of blood, might have extinguished my miserable life: but removing her in her cradle into the Blue Parlor, a great way off me, lest I hearing her sad shrieks should renew my sorrows. These extremities did so lessen my milk, that though I began to recruit strength, yet I must be subject to the changes of my condition. After my dear Naly was in most miraculous mercy restored to me the next day, and recruited my strength; within a fortnight I recovered my milk, and was overjoyed to give my sweet Betty suck, which I did, and began to recover to a miracle, blessed be my great and gracious Lord God, Who remembered mercy towards me.

Upon my great fall I had, being with child of my fifth, September 14, 1657, at Hipswell.
Meditations on the deliverance of my first son and fifth child at Hipswell 10th of December.

It pleased God, in much mercy, to restore me to strength to go to my full time, my labor beginning three days; but upon the Wednesday, the ninth of December, I fell into exceeding sharp travail in great extremity, so that the midwife did believe I should be delivered soon. But lo! it fell out contrary, for the child stayed in the birth, and came cross with his feet first, and in this condition continued till Thursday morning between two and three o'clock, at which time I was upon the rack in bearing my child with such exquisite torment, as if each limb were divided from other, for the space of two hours; when at length, being speechless and breathless, I was, by the infinite providence of God, in great mercy delivered. But I having had such sore travail in danger of my life so long, and the child coming into the world with his feet first, caused the child to be almost strangled in the birth, only living about half an hour, so died before we could get a minister to baptize him, although he was sent for.

I was delivered of my first son and fifth child on the 10th of December, 1657. He was buried in Catericke church the same day by Mr. Siddall. This sweet goodly son was turned wrong by the fall I got in September before, nor had the midwife skill to turn him right, which was the cause of the loss of his life, and the hazard of my own. The weakness of my body was exceeding great, of long continuance, that it put me into the beginning of a consumption, none expecting for many days together that I should recover; and when I did recruit a little, then a new trouble seized on me by the loss of blood, in the bleeding of the hemorrhoids every day for a half a year together. Nor did I recover the lameness of my left knee for one whole quarter of a year, in which I could not touch the ground with it. This I got in my labor, for want of the knee to be assisted. But, alas! all these miseries was nothing to what I have deserved from the just hand of God, considering the great failings of my duties is required both as to God and man. And though I am not given over to any sinful enormous crimes which thousands are subject to, yet am I not pure in the sight of God, for there is no man that lives and sins not. . . .

My cure of bleeding at Scarborough, August, 1659.

It was the good pleasure of God to continue me most wonderfully, though in much weakness, after the excessive loss of blood and spirits, in childbed, with the continuance of lameness above twenty weeks after, and the loss of blood and strength by the bleeding of the hemorrhoids, which followed every day by siege, and was caused by my last travail and torment in childbirth, which brought me so low and weak, that I fainted almost every day upon such occasions, when I daily lost about four or five ounces of blood. And it was the opinion of Dr. Wittie that I was deeply gone in a consumption, and

Alice Thornton

if it continued longer I should be barren; all which being considered by my dear husband and mother, they were resolved, from the doctor's opinion, that I should go to Scarborough Spa for the cure of the said distemper, and accordingly I went with Mr. Thornton, staying about a month there; in which time, upon drinking of the waters, I did by the blessing of God recover my strength after the stay of the former infirmity of bleeding, it leaving me within two days totally, and was cleared from those faintings this carried along with it, returning to Oswaldkirk by my sister Denton homewards.

After this great cure which the Spa wrought on me, for which I most humbly return my hearty and faithful acknowledgement of His mercy, we returned home to Hipswell, where we found my dear mother somewhat recovered of a very ill fit of the stone, in which she had been in great danger about two day before, and had sent for me home, her servant meet me at my sister Crathorne's in my way to Hipswell. I was very joyful to find her anything recruited from her extremity, blessed be the Lord Most High, Which had compassion on my dear mother in raising her from death, and easing her from those violent fits of pain and torment, giving her to me, and sparing my life also from that languishing sickness caused by my childbirth, and might have caused my death. About this August, after our return from Scarborough, it pleased God to give me much strength and health, so that I might at length be blessed with a son. For four months together I enjoyed a great deal of comfort and health, being much stronger and lively when I was with my sons than daughters, having great cause to admire the goodness of God, which ever contrary unto hope caused me to recover of that sad distemper wherewith I was afflicted, and giving me hopes to bring forth a son to be a comfort to my dear husband and us all.

The birth of my son Christopher Thornton, my ninth child, November 11, 1667, and of his death December 1, 1667.

. . . The birth of my ninth child was very perilous to me, and I hardly escaped with my life, falling into pangs of labor about the 4th of November, continuing that week; and on Monday, the 11th of November, 1667, I fell in travail, being delivered between the hours of ten and eleven o'clock at night. . . . It pleased the Lord to give another mercy that night, for my daughter Alice, with fear and grief for me, fell so sick in my labor that she was in much danger of death; but blessed be the Lord which preserved her then, and recovered her from that illness the next day, November 12, '67. Christopher Thornton, my ninth child, was born at Newton, on Monday, the 11th November, '67; baptized the 12th at Newton. His godfathers and godmother were my brother Denton, my brother Portington, and Mrs. Anne Danby.

After this comfort of my child I recovered something of my weakness, better recovering my breasts and milk, and giving suck, when he thrived very well and grew strong, being a lovely babe. But, lest I should too much set my heart in the satisfaction of any blessing under heaven, it seemed good to the most infinite wise God to take him from me, giving me some apprehensions thereof, before any did see it as a change in him. And therefore, with a full resignation to His providence, I endeavored to submit patiently and willingly to part with my sweet child to our dear and loving Father, Who see what was better for me than I could, begging that His will might be mine, either in life or death. When he was about fourteen days old, my pretty babe broke into red spots, like the small pox, and through cold, gotten by thinner clothing than either my own experience or practice did accustom to all my children, they following the precept of M.D.; it presently, though then unknown to me, upon this accident, with the extreme cold weather, fell into great looseness, and, notwith-standing all the means I could use, it continued four days, having endured it patiently; then fell into some little struggling, and at length it pleased his Savior and mine, after the fifth sick night and day, to deliver him out of this miserable world. He sweetly fell asleep on Sunday at night, being then the 1st of December, 1667, who was at that time three weeks old on the next day the 2nd, when he was buried at Stonegrave by Mr. Comber, who preached a funeral sermon December 2nd, 1667.

After my dear child's death, I fell into a great and long-continued weakness by the swelling of my milk, he having sucked last, in his pain, of the left breast, had hurt the nipple, causing it to gangrene, and extreme pained with torment of it, made me fall into a fever, which, together with excessive pains in my head and teeth, upon much grief from the unhandsome proud carriage of those I took to be a comfort in my distress, proved the greatest corrosive in my sick and weak condition, I being then the less able to support my spirits under such afflictions; so that such strange, uncharitable dealing kept me from gathering strength, I not being able to stand nor go for four months till February following, witnessed by those servants that attended me then, and was compelled to be carried to and from my bed in a chair. Even at that time did those which had a secret hatred against me (though I neither knew it nor its cause then; for I never in my whole life, by word or act, had the least prejudice or done her any injury to make it, as I must speak to the Lord for truth), yet then she undermined my peace and quiet, and scornfully presenting me real weakness and sad condition to some in secret, saying that I ailed nothing, and I was as well as she, and made myself a talk to my neighbors; all which she carried with much subtlety for the dishonor of my poor despised person, sufficiently afflicted without this addition.

Yet were these but the beginning of sorrows to me upon that account, endeavoring to bear all with abundance of patience, which my God did please to give me in part, hoping with all that, when I met with Tom Danby's wife, I should prevail for her restoration to her children, which she did object daily to me that she had been kept from, because her sister was angry she came, as before, to be with me while I laid in. But I still told her if I had suspected her sister's displeasure for that, I would never have put that to hazard for the world. Nor did she in the least give me notice thereof. But my nephew Kitt's wife did make this an objection, and I believe owed me no good will for it, though she reserved more for an after game (secret) to my ruin. But Thou, O Lord, see and know my integrity for this woman's good, and the love I bore her ever since I knew her; and therefore I desire Thee to pardon what occasion of evil has befallen me from her, and receive my humble and faithful thanks for Thy inexpressible mercy and goodness to me Thy poor creature. . . .

Of the taking Administration of my dear Husband.

After the solemnity of my dear husband's funerals was over, the first and great concern to be done was to have the choice of an administrator, to have a good and honest person got to do justly in that weighty concern. They told me that it by law did fall on myself, as his widow, to take administration of my husband's goods, and to pay debts, etc., by reason there was no will made. As to the making of his will, I had very often put him in mind of it when I saw he did so frequently fall into those palsy fits, desiring he would please to do it for the satisfaction of all the world, and that he would please to order his debts to be paid as he would have them done. All the answer my dear husband was pleased to give me was, "He had settled his estate at Laistrop, as he would have it to pay debts, and for his children; and he desired me to see his debts paid, as he knew I had a good conscience to do." I told him again, "My dear heart, you know there is nothing to maintain my dear son Robert but out of my jointure and estate, and if you leave anything to pay the debts withal, I was not unwilling to do it; but if they were so many and so great, I doubted I could not do it, and to educate my poor child withal." So Mr. Thornton did not make any will, but what he had said of Laistrop for debts. But, after his decease it was necessary that one should take administration to the personal estate, and to order and pay all things according to law, and to have an apprisement of the goods as the law appoints in that case. So my brother Denton told me that it was belonging to me for to do it, and that if I did not take administration myself, I might choose one to take that office upon him. . . . Upon this I told my brother Denton that there was none more fit or proper to undertake so great a trust, and act in that concern, as himself, who was so wise and prudent and knowing a person in all such affairs and the law, to act accordingly; nor no man knew the concerns of Mr. Thornton's estate, and himself and family being so kind and good a friend to my dear husband, and do all things according to equity and justice. If he would please to undertake that trouble, the family would be much obliged to him for it, and I in particular account myself much engaged for his favor. But my brother Denton made his excuse, and said he would serve that family in anything he could, but could not do that; he was a trustee for the children, and could not be both, though he was a trustee for the debts, too, as well in that deed of Laistrop as well as for the children. Then I said, if my brother Portington would do as much as take that trust of administrator on him, I should desire he would please to do it for Mr. Thornton. But

Alice Thornton

Mr. Denton made the same return for him as he had done for himself, so he left me in a great concern how or where to pitch of a right and good man to do it.

At last he said, that if one could be thought upon which had not much estate, but an honest man, and one of an indifferent judgment, that would be advised how to manage the concerns of the estate, it were better to have such an one than have any of a good estate, or were too wise, and would not be advised. So when several was named did not please in one point or other, at last I desired him to nominate one, who, after a little pause, named Mr. Thornton's servant, who he had caused the Warrant house to be built for him to live in, having married Nan Robinson, what so abused me about a great lie she told my brother Thomas of myself and maid, Jane Flouer, and had made my brother ever since my bitter enemy against me. And, to please Mr. Thornton, I had granted that the Warrant house should be built for them to live in, but this people was my great adversaries ever after, and a great loss and destruction to the estate of Mr. Thornton and myself. This man could neither write nor read, and was but of indifferent parts or honesty, not at all, in my thoughts, capable or fit for such a matter of importance of the family, so that I was forced to decline this motion as modestly as I could, and speak my thoughts that, in regard he could neither read nor write, he could not understand the business, nor dispatch anything of that nature. But my brother Denton did incline to none like him, and did pray me to think of it, because, if the debts should come too fast on, he might plead a plea, *"ne administravit."* The unfitness of this man was, indeed, a great trouble to me (being too nimble of his fingers, which I knew, and had proof of in the house, though would not be believed by those [who] proposed him), put me to a great trouble what to do, lest their importunity and fearing to displease might have him cast upon me, so I would not consent, but said I would consider of it.

But behold the gracious goodness and mercy of my God, when, in the midst of my distress, made a way for me to escape the necessity of having such an one to be made a slave to. He caused an unexpected providence to fall out, and as poor Dafeny said, "God had sent me a friend after my own heart." And just as I was in trouble, and pouring out my prayers to Heaven to assist and direct me to one fit for us in this great affair, which concerned, indeed, the right payment of debts, and all things else about the administrator, Dafeny, looking out at the window, heard a horse at the door, cried out, "Oh, mistress, God has heard your prayers, and has sent you a good and honest man, as you desired, to help you, and that is Mr. Anthony Norton, which is come to see you only as a visit since Mr. Thornton's death."

After this good man came to see me, I asked him if he would do me the favor to stand for Mr. Thornton's administrator, to bear the name, and I would take care that the charges should be no way troublesome to him, but should be paid for his journeys and for his expenses, but that he should be saved harmless of anything concerning that business, for I was now extremely weak and sick, and could not be able to travel about it, nor would any of Mr. Thornton's friends do it, nor I could not have any stranger to confide in like him, and hoped that God had in providence sent him hither. When this good man, my cousin Norton, heard me make my request and moan to him, it pleased God to put it into his mind to pity my desolate condition, said, "Dear Madam, I am truly sorry for your loss of good Mr. Thornton, and wish that I could do anything to serve you and your children, but do not understand these things very well, but shall be willing to do you any kindness for your own sake, having a great honor for yourself and family. Indeed, I have done it once for my cousin, Major Norton, but he directed me in all things and proceedings, and by his order I acted and finished that concern for his son Edmund, I hope to his own satisfaction and all creditors; and if you will give me your orders how to act I shall observe it the best I can, or anything else for you lies in my power."

When I heard what this good old man said in a full answer to my desire in this business, I blessed and praised my good God for His mercy to me in granting my humble petitions, hoping this was ordered by His providence for good to me and mine. I acquainted my brother Denton with this opportunity of my cousin, Anthony Norton, being come, and of my gaining his assistance in accepting to be my husband's administrator, which by reason he knew him to be an honest, good man, and his wife's relation and uncle, did approve well of; and so, upon full agreement about this business, proceedings went on. And Mr. Flathers, being rural dean, came to Newton, with orders to take my renunciation of the administration, and my cousin Anthony Norton's name put in, to whom I gave up my power in it. And my cousin Norton took out letters of administration according to law out of the court, and entered bond to the court for right administrating, as in order of law.

After this great matter of the administration was settled, it was requisite I should take the tuition of my poor children, being now by this great change become both father and mother and guardian to them, a duty which I willingly undertook for their own and father's sake, having a threefold tie upon me, as being my own, dearly bought in bringing them forth by exquisite torments and pains in child-bearing, added to many cares and difficulties in their bringing up to their several ages. As to my son Robert, he was solely left to my charge for subsistence, since there was not out of the estate at Laistrop more than what would provide for his two sisters' mainte-nance and portions. . . . For several years together I received not towards my daughter Kate's maintenance, or for her education, the sum of twenty shillings, or of ten, though she should have had equal with her sister, after £40 a year to each of them. But I did borrow for her keeping several years that I wanted out of Laistrop, and never had it made good to me as I ought, out of the land. That is still owing to me the sum of —. Where then could there be anything to bring up my only son Robert but what, by God's providence, I could have out of my jointure and my dear mother's estate at Midlham? all which was so burdened with public charges and debts, which I was forced to contract upon several accounts, fell on me, that I had great straits, which I entered on upon my husband's death, borrowing even from the first to pay funeral charges, and to keep house with, and to main-tain my children. I entered bond to the court for the tuition of my three children. My poor son Robert was but six years old when his dear father was buried, September 19th, 1668; his first tying clothes was mourning for his father. My daughter Alice, her age was, January 3rd, sixteen; my daughter Katherine, her age was, June 2nd, twelve.

Margaret Cavendish, Duchess of Newcastle

Margaret Cavendish,
Duchess of Newcastle

(1623–1673)

Margaret Cavendish was a woman intellectual who believed in the inferiority of women. Though she felt that women ought to be educated, she wrote again and again of their ridiculousness and of their dependency, and of the godlike superiority of men. Cavendish herself was talented, ambitious, and unusual. She was one of the first Englishwomen to publish her work, and she wrote poetry, plays, orations, biography, autobiography, letters, philosophical works, and scientific treatises. She struggled to get her works accepted by the universities, and her greatest hope, which was never realized, was to have them taught there. As if to emphasize the absurdity with which a woman intellectual was viewed in her time, she often appeared in outlandish costumes. Her contemporaries called her "Mad Madge," and if she is remembered at all today, it is, ironically, for the biography she wrote of her husband. Yet, Margaret Cavendish was a brilliant writer. And her work is especially significant because it reveals how deeply a woman could believe in the inferiority of women, and how powerfully she could express this belief.

FROM THE WORLD'S OLIO

THE PREFACE TO THE READER

It cannot be expected I should write so wisely or wittily as men, being of the effeminate sex, whose brains nature has mixed with the coldest and softest elements, and to give my reason why we cannot be so wise as men, I take leave and ask pardon of my own sex, and present my reasons to the judgment of Truth. But I believe all of my own sex will be against me out of partiality to themselves, and all men will seem to be against me, out of compliment to women, or at least for quiet and ease's sake, who know women's tongues are like stings of bees, and what man would endure our effeminate monarchy to swarm about their ears, for certainly he would be stung to death. So I shall be condemned of all sides, but Truth, who helps to defend me.

True it is, our sex make great complaints that men from their first creation usurped a supremacy to themselves, although we were made equal by nature, which tyrannical government they have kept ever since, so that we could never come to be free, but rather more and more enslaved, using us either like children, fools, or subjects, that is, to flatter or threaten us, to allure or force us to obey, and will not let us divide the world equally with them, as to govern and command, to direct and dispose as they do; which slavery has so dejected our spirits, as we are become so stupid that beasts are but a degree below us, and men use us but a degree above beasts. Whereas in nature we have as clear an understanding as men, if we were bred in schools to mature our brains and to manure our understandings, that we might bring forth the fruits of knowledge. But to speak truth, men have great reason not to let us into their governments, for there is great difference between the masculine brain and the feminine, the masculine strength and the feminine. For could we choose out of the world two of the ablest brain and strongest body of each sex, there would be great difference in the understanding and strength. For nature has made man's body more able to endure labor, and man's brain more clear to understand and contrive than woman's, and as great a difference there is between them, as there is between the longest and strongest willow, compared to the strongest and largest oak. Though they are both trees, yet the willow is but a yielding vegetable, not fit nor proper to build houses and ships as the oak, whose strength can grapple with the greatest winds and plow the furrows in the deep. It is true the willows may make fine arbors and bowers, winding and twisting its wreathy stalks about to make a shadow to eclipse the light, or as a light shield to keep off the sharp arrows of the sun which cannot wound deep because they fly far before they touch the earth. Or men and women may be compared to the blackbirds, where the hen can never sing with so strong and loud a voice, nor so clear and perfect notes as the cock: her breast is not made with that strength to strain so high. Even so, women can never have so strong judgment nor clear understanding nor so perfect rhetoric to speak orations with that eloquence as to persuade so forcibly, to command so powerfully, to entice so subtly, and to insinuate so gently and softly into the souls of men.

Or they may be compared to the sun and moon, according to the description in the Holy Writ, which says, "God made two great lights, the one to rule the day, the other the night." So man is made to govern commonwealths, and women their private families. And we find by experience that the sun is more dry, hot, active, and powerful every way than the moon. Besides, the sun is of a more strong and ruddier complexion than the moon, for we find she is pale and wan, cold, moist, and slow in all her operations. And if it be as philosophers hold, that the moon has no light but what it borrows from the sun, so women have no strength nor light of understanding, but what is given them from men. This is the reason why we are not mathematicians, arithmeticians, logicians, geometricians, cosmographers, and the like. This is the reason we are not witty poets, eloquent orators, subtle schoolmen, subtracting chemists, rare musicians, curious limners. This is the reason we are not navigators, architects, exact surveyors, inventive artisans. This is the reason why we are not skillful soldiers, politic statesmen, dispatchful secretaries, or conquering Caesars. But our governments would be weak, had we not masculine spirits and counselors to advise us. And for our strength, we should make but feeble mariners to tug and pull up great ropes and weighty sails in blustering storms. If there were no other pilots than the effeminate sex neither would there be such commerce of nations as there is. Nor would there be so much gold and silver and other minerals fetched out of the bowels of the earth if there were none but effeminate hands to use the pick-axe and spade. Nor so many cities built if there were none but women laborers to cut out great quarries of stone, to hew down great timber trees, and to draw up such materials and engines thereunto belonging. Neither would there be such bars of iron if none but women were to melt and hammer them out, whose weak spirits would suffocate and so faint with the heat, and their small arms would sooner break than lift up such a weight, and beat out a life in striving to beat out a wedge. Neither would there be such steeples and pyramids as there have been in this world, if there were no other than our tender feet to climb, nor could our brains endure the height; we should soon grow dizzy and fall down drunk with too much thin air. Neither have women such hard chests and strong lungs to keep in so much breath to dive to the bottom of the sea to fetch up the treasures that lie in the watery womb. Neither can women bring the furious and wild horse to the bit, quenching his fiery courage and bridling his strong swift speed. This is the reason we are not so active in exercise, nor able to endure hard labor, nor far travels, nor to bear weighty burdens, to run long journeys, and many the like actions which we by nature are not made fit for. It is true education and custom may add something to harden us, yet never make us so strong as the strongest of men, whose sinews are tougher, and bones stronger, and joints closer, and flesh firmer than ours are, as all ages have shown and times have produced.

What woman was ever so strong as Sampson or so swift as Hazael? Neither have women such tempered brains as men, such high imaginations, such subtle conceptions, such fine inventions, such solid reasons, and such sound judgment, such prudent forecast, such constant resolutions, such quick, sharp, and ready-flowing wits. What woman ever made such laws as Moses, Lycurgus, or Solon did? What woman was ever so wise as Solomon or Aristotle, so politic as Achitophel, so eloquent as Tully, so demonstrative as Euclid, so inventive as Seth or Archimedes? It was not a woman that found out the card and needle and the use of the lodestone. It was not a woman that invented perspective glasses to pierce into the moon. It was not a woman that found out the invention of writing letters and the art of printing. It was not a woman that found out the invention of gunpowder and the art of guns. What women were such soldiers as Hannibal, Caesar, Tamburlaine, Alexander, and Scanderbeg? What woman was such a chemist as Paracelsus, such a physician as Hippocrates or Galen, such a poet as Homer, such a painter as Apelles, such a carver as Pygmalion, such an architect as Vitruvius, such a musician as Orpheus? What women ever found out the Antipodes in imagination before they were found out by navigation, as a bishop did. Or whatever did we do but like apes by imitation?

Wherefore women can have no excuse or complaints of being subjects as a hindrance from thinking, for thoughts are free. Those can never be enslaved, for we are not hindered from studying, since we are allowed so much idle time that we know not how to pass it away, but may as well read in our closets, as men in their colleges. And contemplation is as free to us as to men to beget clear speculation. Besides, most scholars marry, and their heads are so full of their school lectures that they preach them over to their wives when they come home, so that they know as well what was spoke as if they had been there. And though most of our sex are bred up to the needle and spindle, yet some are bred in the public theaters of the world, wherefore if nature had made our brains of the same temper as men's, we should have had as clear speculation, and had been as ingenious and inventive as men. But we find she has not, by the effects. And thus we may see by the weakness of our actions, the constitution of our bodies; and by our knowledge, the temper of our brains; by our unsettled resolutions, inconstant to our promises, the perverseness of our wills; by our facile natures, violent in our passions, superstitious in our devotions, you may know our humors: we have more wit than judgment, more active than industrious, we have more courage than conduct, more will than strength, more curiosity than secrecy, more vanity than good housewifery, more complaints than pains, more jealousy than love, more tears than sorrow, more stupidity than patience, more pride than affability, more beauty than constancy, more ill nature than good. Besides, the education and liberty of conversation which men have is both unfit and dangerous to our sex, knowing that we may bear and bring forth branches from a wrong stock, by which every man would come to lose the property of their own children. But nature, out of love to the generation of man, has made women to be governed by men, giving them strength to rule, and power to use their authority.

And though it seem to be natural that generally all women are weaker than men, both in body and understanding, and that the wisest woman is not so wise as the wisest of men, wherefore not so fit to rule, yet some are far wiser than some men. Like earth, for some ground, though it be barren by nature, yet, being well mucked and well manured may bear plentiful crops and sprout forth diverse sorts of flowers, when the fertiler and richer ground shall grow rank and corrupt, bringing nothing but gross and stinking weeds for want of tillage. So women by education may come to be far more knowing and learned than some rustic and rude-bred men. Besides, it is to be observed that nature has degrees in all her mixtures and temperaments, not only to her servile works, but in one and the same matter and form of creatures throughout all her creations. Again, it is to be observed that although nature has not made women so strong of body and so clear of understanding as the ablest of men, yet she has made them fairer, softer, slenderer, and more delicate than they, separating, as it were, the finer parts from the grosser, which seems as if nature had made women as purer white manchet for her own table and palate, where men are like coarse household bread which the servants feed on. And if she has not tempered women's brains to that height of understanding, nor has put in such strong species of imaginations, yet she has mixed them with sugar of sweet conceits. And if she has not planted in their dispositions such firm resolutions, yet she has sowed gentle and willing obedience. And though she has not filled the mind with such heroic gallantry, yet she has laid in tender affections, as love, piety, charity, clemency, patience, humility, and the like, which makes them nearest to resemble angels, which are the most perfect of all her works, where men by their ambitions, extortion, fury, and cruelty resemble the devil. But some women are like devils too when they are possessed with those evils, and the best of men by their heroic, magnanimous minds, by their ingenious and inventive wits, by their strong judgments, by their prudent forecast and wise managements are like to gods.

FROM SOCIABLE LETTERS

XVI

Madam,

I hope I have given the Lady D.A. no cause to believe I am not her friend. For though she has been of P's and I of K's side, yet I know no reason why that should make a difference between us as to make us enemies; no more than cases of conscience in religion, for one may be my very good friend, and yet not of my opinion. Everyone's conscience in religion is between God and themselves, and it belongs to

Margaret Cavendish, Duchess of Newcastle

none other. 'Tis true, I should be glad my friend were of my opinion, or if I thought my friend's opinion were better than mine, I would be of the same. But it should be no breach of friendship if our opinions were different, since God is only to be the judge.

And as for the matter of governments, we women understand them not; yet if we did, we are excluded from intermeddling therewith, and almost from being subject thereto. We are not tied nor bound to state or Crown. We are free, not sworn to allegiance, nor do we take the Oath of Supremacy. We are not made citizens of the commonwealth. We hold no offices, nor bear we any authority therein. We are accounted neither useful in peace, nor serviceable in war. And if we be not citizens in the commonwealth, I know no reason we should be subjects to the commonwealth. And the truth is we are no subjects, unless it be to our husbands, and not always to them, for sometimes we usurp their authority, or else by flattery we get their good wills to govern. But if nature had not befriended us with beauty and other good graces to help us to insinuate ourselves into men's affections, we should have been more enslaved than any other of nature's creatures she has made. But nature be thanked, she has been so bountiful to us as we oftener enslave men than men enslave us. They seem to govern the world, but we really govern the world in that we govern men. For what man is he that is not governed by a woman, more or less? None, unless some dull stoic, or an old miserable usurer, or a cold, old, withered bachelor, or a half-starved hermit, and such like persons, which are but here and there one. And not only wives and mistresses have prevalent power with men, but mothers, daughters, sisters, aunts, cousins, nay, maidservants have many times a persuasive power with their masters, and a landlady with her lodger, or a she-hostess with her he-guest. Yet men will not believe this, and 'tis the better for us, for by that we govern as it were by an insensible power, so as men perceive not how they are led, guided, and ruled by the feminine sex.

But howsoever, Madam, the disturbance in this country has made no breach of friendship between us, for though there has been a civil war in the kingdom, and a general war amongst the men, yet there has been none amongst the women. They have not fought pitched battles, and if they had there has been no particular quarrel between her and me, for her Ladyship is the same in my affection, as if the kingdom had been in a calm peace. In which friendship I shall always remains hers, as also,

Your Ladyship's
Most humble and devoted S.

XLVII

Madam,

The other day the Lady S. M. was to visit me, and I gave her joy. She said she should have joy indeed if it were a son. I said I bid her joy of her marriage, for I had not seen her since she was a wife and had been married, which was some four weeks ago, wherefore I did not know she was with child. But she, rasping wind out of her stomach, as childing women usually do, making sickly faces to express a sickly stomach, and fetching her breath short, and bearing out her body, drawing her neck downward, and standing in a weak and faint posture, as great-bellied wives do bearing a heavy burden in them, told me she had been with child a fortnight, though by her behavior one would not thought she had above a week to go, or to reckon. But she is so pleased with the belief she is with child (for I think she cannot perfectly know herself; at most it is but breeding child), as she makes or believes herself bigger than she appears, and says she longs for every meat that is difficult to be gotten, and eats and drinks from morning till night, with very little intermission, and sometimes in the night. Whereupon I told her if she did so, I believed she would be bigger bellied and greater bodied whether she were with child or not. Besides, eating so much would make her sick if she were not with child. She answered that women with child might eat anything and as much as they would or could, and it would do them no harm.

But I have observed that generally women take more pleasure when they are with child than when they are not with child, not only in eating more and feeding more luxuriously, but taking a pride in their great bellies, although it be a natural effect of a natural cause.

For like as women take a greater pride in their beauty than pleasure or content in their virtue, so they take more pride in being with child than in having a child. For when they are brought to bed and up from their lying-in, they seem nothing so well pleased, nor so proud as when they were great with child. And to prove they are prouder and take more pleasure in being with child and in lying in than in having a child is their care, pains, and cost in getting, making and buying fine and costly childbed linen, swaddling clothes, mantles, and the like, as also fine beds, cradles, baskets, and other furniture for their chambers, as hangings, cabinets, plates, artificial flowers, looking glasses, screens, and many such like things of great cost and charge; besides their banquets of sweetmeats and other junkets, as cakes, wafers, biscuits, jellies, and the like, as also such strong drinks as methinks the very smell should put a childbed wife into a fever, as Hippocras and burnt wine, with hot spices, mulled sack, strong and high-colored ale, well spiced and stuffed with toasts of cake, and the like, all which is more chargeable than to bring up a child when it is born. Nay, they will rather want portions for their children when they are grown to be men or women, or want sufficiency of means to pay for their learning and education than want these extravagances of luxury and vanity at their birth. And their children being christened are like some brides and bridegrooms that are so fine on their wedding day, as they are forced to go in rags all their lives after, which methinks is very strange, that for the vanity and show of one day they will spend so much as to be beggars all their lives after.

But as I said, this proves that women take a greater pride and pleasure in being with child than in having children well-bred and well-bestowed or maintained when grown to years. And that which makes me wonder more is that wise men will suffer their foolish wives to be so foolishly and imprudently expensive. Wherefore such men are worthy to be impoverished that will suffer their wives to be so vain, for it shows them to be better husbands than fathers, kinder to their wives than careful of their children. Also, it shows them fonder husbands than loving children, because they ruin their fore-fathers' posterity by impoverishing their own succession, and that only to please their wives' humors and to expend for their wives' vani-

ties. But leaving the Lady S. M. to her breeding pride or pride
of breeding, to her sick pleasure of pleasurable sickness, to her
luxurious feeding and vain providing, and wishing her a good
gossiping, I rest,

> *Madam,*
> > *Your faithful friend and servant.*

LXII

Madam,

Mrs. C. R. is very much troubled in her mind with doubts and
fears since she has heard that the Lady S. P. did publicly and
privately praise her, for she says she is afraid the Lady S. P. has
observed some error in her behavior, or has heard her speak foolishly,
or has found out some decays of beauty in her face or some de-
formities in her shape, or some of the masculine sex have dispraised her beauty, wit, person, behavior, or the like. Otherwise,
says she, she is confident she would never have praised her, for says
she, it is so unusual for one woman to praise another as it seems
unnatural. Wherefore she does not delight to be praised by her own
sex, and since that time she received your last letter, she will sit in a
silent musing posture, considering and examining herself, as searching to find out what faults she has or what crimes she is guilty of
that the Lady S. P. should praise her. And so peevish and froward
she is for it as I believe she will never be quiet or at rest and peace
in her mind, until she hear that the Lady S. P. has spoken spitefully
of her, or has dispraised her some ways, or other. The truth is, she
does confess as much, for she says she shall never think herself
handsome, conversable, nor virtuous, but ill-favored, foolish, base, or
wicked, unless she be dispraised by her own sex. Wherefore if you
hear, as certainly you cannot choose unless you will stop your ears,
any female discommendations concerning Mrs. C. R., pray send her
word of them, by which you will infinitely oblige her. And in the
meantime I shall endeavor to pacify her thoughts and settle her mind
in peace and quiet, resting,

> *Madam,*
> > *Your faithful friend and servant.*

Margaret Cavendish, Duchess of Newcastle

XCIII

Madam,

You were pleased in your last letter to express to me the reason of the Lady D. S.'s and the Lady E. K.'s melancholy, which was for want of children. I cannot blame the Lady D. S. by reason her husband is the last of his family unless he have children, but the Lady E. K.'s husband being a widower when he married her and having sons to inherit his estate and to keep up his family, I know no reason why she should be troubled for having no children. For though it be the part of every good wife to desire children to keep alive the memory of their husband's name and family by posterity, yet a woman has no such reason to desire children for her own sake. For first her name is lost as to her particular in her marrying, for she quits her own and is named as her husband; also, her family, for neither name nor estate goes to her family according to the laws and customs of this country. Also, she hazards her life by bringing them into the world, and has the greatest share of trouble in bringing them up. Neither can women assure themselves of comfort or happiness by them when they are grown to be men, for their name only lives in sons, who continue the line of succession, whereas daughters are but branches which by marriage are broken off from the root from whence they sprang and engrafted into the stock of another family, so that daughters are to be accounted but as moveable goods or furnitures that wear out. And though sometimes they carry the lands with them for want of heir-males, yet the name is not kept nor the line continued with them, for these are buried in the grave of the males, for the line, name, and life of a family ends with the male issue.

But many times married women desire children, as maids do husbands, more for honor than for comfort or happiness, thinking it a disgrace to live old maids, and so likewise to be barren, for in the Jews' time it was some disgrace to be barren, so that for the most part maids and wives desire husbands and children upon any condition, rather than to live maids or barren. But I am not of their minds, for I think a bad husband is far worse than no husband, and to have unnatural children is more unhappy than to have no children. And where one husband proves good, as loving and prudent, a thousand prove bad, as cross and spendthrifts, and where one child proves good, as dutiful and wise, a thousand prove disobedient and fools, as to do actions both to the dishonor and ruin of their families.

Besides, I have observed that breeding women, especially those that have been married some time and have had no children, are in their behavior like new-married wives, whose actions of behavior and speech are so formal and constrained and so different from their natural way, as it is ridiculous. For new-married wives will so bridle their behavior with constraint or hang down their heads so simply, not so much out of true modesty as a forced shamefacedness. And to their husbands they are so coyly amorous, or so amorously fond and so troublesome kind as it would make the spectators sick, like fulsome meat to the stomach. And if new-married men were not wise men, it might make them ill husbands, at least to dislike a married life, because they cannot leave their fond or amorous wives so readily or easily as a mistress. But, in truth, that humor does not last long, for after a month or two, they are like sufeited bodies that like any meat better than what they were so fond of, so that in time they think their husbands worse company than any other men. Also, women at the breeding of their first children make so many sick faces, although oftentimes the sickness is only in their faces, not but that some are really sick, but not every breeding woman. Likewise, they have such feigned coughs and fetch their breath short, with such feigning laziness and so many unnecessary complaints, as it would weary the most patient husband to hear or see them. Besides, they are so expensive in their longings and perpetual eating of several costly meats as it would undo a man that has but an indifferent estate. But to add to their charge, if they have not what they please for childbed linen, mantles, and a lying-in bed with suitable furniture for their lying chamber, they will be so fretful and discontented, as it will endanger their miscarrying. Again, to redouble the charge, there must be gossiping, not only with costly banquets at the christening and churching, but they have gossiping all the time of their lying-in, for then there is a more set or formal gossiping than at other ordinary times. But I fear that if this letter come to the view of our sex, besides yourself, they will throw more spiteful or angry words out of their mouths against me than the unbelieving Jews did hard stones out of

their hands at Saint Stephen. But the best is they cannot kill me with their reproaches. I speak but the truth of what I have observed amongst many of our sex. Wherefore, pray madam, help to defend me as being my friend and I yours, for I shall continue as long as I live,
Madam,
        Your Ladyship's most faithful and humble Servant.

CLIII

Madam,
    The other day the Lady M. L. was to visit me, and by her sad countenance I perceived she was full of melancholy, ready to be delivered of the burden, as to vent her grief through her mouth. But I, observing she could not readily make her complaints, did as a midwife help them forth by asking her what the cause of her sadness was. With that, tears flowed forth her eyes, as ushers to her complaints. Said she, although I was a joyful bride, yet I am an unhappy wife, for on my wedding day I joyed because I had married such a man as had proved himself to be valiant, generous, and wise, all which I thought was a greater honor, to be the wife of such a worthy man, than if he had been rich, handsome, and dignified with title, although he did neither want those, which was an addition to my joy. Nor did I think myself unhappy that he married me not through his own choice but his friends' persuasions, or that he did seem not to love me. For I thought when time had proved my virtue, duty, and obedience, justice would have persuaded him to have loved me. Neither did I think myself unhappy that he endeavored to make me a servant, nay a slave to his mistress, because I thought he desired by this means to keep me from jealousy and to learn me patience. Neither did I think myself unhappy that he tortured me, nay threatened death to me to force me to serve his concubines, because I took more comfort in that my resolution was so strong as neither pain nor fear of death could alter it, and gloried more in my sufferings than grieved for my pains, as that I would rather die than do a base act, as to be a bawd to my husband's whores. But my unhappiness is that my husband will be divorced from me, which divorcement is far worse than death or bodily pains in life, for in the

grave I shall lie in rest and peace, and if I be not remembered with honor, yet I die not in disgrace. And for the pains in life, it learns me to practice moral philosophy. But to be divorced is to live in disgrace and scorn, which is worse than any pain or death, for he having got the reputation of a worthy man, the world will think I am a very unworthy woman if he forsakes me, and that he knows me to be guilty of some notorious faults, but that he will not divulge them for fear of his own dishonor, or out of respect to the female sex.

Thus, by a divorcement I shall be left to the censure and scandal of the world, whilst he will be thought a wise man for parting from me, as being not honorable for him to live with me. With that she wept as if her eyes had been two perpetual springs and meant to make a deluge of her tears, and with seeing her, my eyes began to drop too. At last I told her I did verily believe her husband did but pretend a divorce only to fright her to what he would have her, and intended not a divorce to grieve her. For though he was a man that did take a liberty of variety of women, knowing that liberty could be no dishonor to the masculine sex, and though he loved a wanton mistress, yet certainly he was not so unjust or unwise as to hate a chaste wife, or to part from a virtuous wife for the sake of a lewd mistress, and therefore I thought she might take comfort, and the best remedy, at least cordial, for grief was patience. For though her husband was an independent to amour, yet he was an orthodox to honor and moral honesty, only he wanted some temperance, at which she smiled. By that I perceived her complaints and my opinion had somewhat removed the heavy oppression of melancholy, and after some time, she took her leave of me, giving me thanks both for hearing her discourse of her own grief and for comforting her. And by this relation you have, as it were, received the same visit, as also a visit from me, so as we have been both with you—only a letter does carry us to you instead of a coach. But now I think it is time to leave you, and rest,

      Madam,
          Your very faithful friend and servant.

MISCELLANY
POEMS,
ON
Several Occasions.

Hamps^h Turkip

Written by a LADY.

The Countess of Winchelsea

T.Inskip

LONDON:

Printed for *J. B.* and Sold by *Benj. Tooke* at
the *Middle-Temple-Gate, William Taylor* in
Pater-Noster-Row, and *James Round* in
Exchange-Alley, Cornhil. 1713.

Title page from MISCELLANY POEMS ON SEVERAL OC-
CASIONS by Anne Finch

Anne Finch, Countess of Winchilsea

(1661–1720)

Beginning a preface to a manuscript of her poems, Anne Finch described the pleasure she took in writing. She went on to describe how, as a young woman at court, she hid her work and nearly stopped writing—knowing that the poetry of a "Versifying Maid of Honour" would meet with "prejudice, if not contempt." It was only years later that Finch published a volume of her poetry, and then the volume was first issued anonymously. Finch wrote love poetry, nature poetry, religious poetry, plays, satires, parodies, fables, translations, and criticism. She often wrote about women—of how it feels for a woman to lose her beauty, of how it feels for a woman to be happily married, of how it feels for a woman writer to be overcome by melancholy. And Finch wrote about the prejudice against the woman writer, of how it can force her—as it had forced Finch—to become essentially a poet in hiding.

THE INTRODUCTION

Did I, my lines intend for publick view,
How many censures, wou'd their faults persue,
Some wou'd, because such words they do affect,
Cry they're insipid, empty, uncorrect.
And many, have attain'd, dull and untaught
The name of Witt, only by finding fault.
True judges, might condemn their want of witt,
And all might say, they're by a Woman writt.
Alas! a woman that attempts the pen,
Such an intruder on the rights of men,
Such a presumptuous Creature, is esteem'd,
The fault, can by no vertue be redeem'd.
They tell us, we mistake our sex and way;
Good breeding, fassion, dancing, dressing, play
Are the accomplishments we shou'd desire;
To write, or read, or think, or to enquire

by a Woman writt

Wou'd cloud our beauty, and exaust our time,
And interrupt the Conquests of our prime;
Whilst the dull mannage, of a servile house
Is held by some, our outmost art, and use.

　　Sure 'twas not ever thus, nor are we told
Fables, of Women that excell'd of old;
To whom, by the diffusive hand of Heaven
Some share of witt, and poetry was given.
On that glad day, on which the Ark return'd,
The holy pledge, for which the Land had mourn'd,
The joyfull Tribes, attend itt on the way,
The Levites do the sacred Charge convey,
Whilst various Instruments, before itt play;
Here, holy Virgins in the Concert joyn,
The louder notes, to soften, and refine,
And with alternate verse, compleat the Hymn Devine.
Loe! the yong Poet, after Gods own heart,
By Him inspired, and taught the Muses Art,
Return'd from Conquest, a bright Chorus meets,
That sing his slayn ten thousand in the streets.
In such loud numbers they his acts declare,
Proclaim the wonders, of his early war,
That Saul upon the vast applause does frown,
And feels, itts mighty thunder shake the Crown.
What, can the threat'n'd Judgment now prolong?
Half of the Kingdom is already gone;
The fairest half, whose influence guides the rest,
Have David's Empire, o're their hearts confess't.

　　A Woman here, leads fainting Israel on,
She fights, she wins, she tryumphs with a song,
Devout, Majestick, for the subject fitt,
And far above her arms, exalts her witt,
Then, to the peacefull, shady Palm withdraws,
And rules the rescu'd Nation, with her Laws.
How are we fal'n, fal'n by mistaken rules?
And Education's, more then Nature's fools,

Anne Finch, Countess of Winchilsea

Debarr'd from all improve-ments of the mind,
And to be dull, expected and dessigned;
And if some one, wou'd Soar above the rest,
With warmer fancy, and ambition press't,
So strong, th' opposing faction still appears,
The hopes to thrive, can ne're outweigh the fears,
Be caution'd then my Muse, and still retir'd;
Nor be dispis'd, aiming to be admir'd;
Conscious of wants, still with contracted wing,
To some few freinds, and to thy sorrows sing;
For groves of Lawrell, thou wert never meant;
Be dark enough thy shades, and be thou there content.

THE APOLOGY

'Tis true I write and tell me by what Rule
I am alone forbid to play the fool
To follow through the Groves a wand'ring Muse
And fain'd Idea's for my pleasures chuse
Why shou'd it in my Pen be held a fault
Whilst Mira paints her face, to paint a thought
Whilst Lamia to the manly Bumper flys
And borrow'd Spiritts sparkle in her Eyes
Why shou'd itt be in me a thing so vain
To heat with Poetry my colder Brain
But I write ill and there-fore shou'd forbear
Does Flavia cease now at her fortieth year
In ev'ry Place to lett that face be seen
Which all the Town rejected at fifteen
Each Woman has her weaknesse; mind [*sic*] indeed
Is still to write tho' hoplesse to succeed
Nor to the Men is this so easy found
Ev'n in most Works with which the Witts abound
(So weak are all since our first breach with Heav'n)
Ther's lesse to be Applauded then forgiven.

ARDELIA[1] TO MELANCHOLY

At last, my old inveterate foe,
No opposition shalt thou know.
Since I by struggling, can obtain
Nothing, but encrease of pain,
I will att last, no more do soe,
Tho' I confesse, I have apply'd
Sweet mirth, and musick, and have try'd
A thousand other arts beside,
To drive thee from my darken'd breast,
Thou, who hast banish'd all my rest.
But, though sometimes, a short repreive they gave,
Unable they, and far too weak, to save;
All arts to quell, did but augment thy force,
As rivers check'd, break with a wilder course.

Freindship, I to my heart have laid,
Freindship, th' applauded sov'rain aid,
And thought that charm so strong wou'd prove,
As to compell thee, to remove;
And to myself, I boasting said,
Now I a conqu'rer sure shall be,
The end of all my conflicts, see,
And noble tryumph, wait on me;
My dusky, sullen foe, will sure
N'er this united charge endure.
But leaning on this reed, ev'n whilst I spoke
It peirc'd my hand, and into peices broke.
Still, some new object, or new int'rest came
And loos'd the bonds, and quite disolv'd the claim.

These failing, I invok'd a Muse,
And Poetry wou'd often use,

---

[1] In her poetry, Anne Finch often referred to herself as "Ardelia" and to her husband as "Daphnis" or "Flavio."

Anne Finch, Countess of Winchilsea

To guard me from thy Tyrant pow'r;
And to oppose thee ev'ry hour
New troops of fancy's, did I chuse.
Alas! in vain, for all agree
To yeild me Captive up to thee,
And heav'n, alone, can sett me free.
Thou, through my life, wilt with me goe,
And make ye passage, sad, and slow.
All, that cou'd ere thy ill gott rule, invade,
Their uselesse arms, before thy feet have laid;
The Fort is thine, now ruin'd, all within,
Whilst by decays without, thy Conquests too, is seen.

THE CONSOLATION

See, Phœbus breaking from willing skies,
See, how the soaring Lark, does with him rise,
And through the air, is such a journy borne
As if she never thought of a return.
Now, to his noon, behold him proudly goe,
And look with scorn, on all that's great below.
A Monark he, and ruler of the day,
A fav'rite She, that in his beams does play.
Glorious, and high, but shall they ever bee,
Glorious, and high, and fixt where now we see?
No, both must fall, nor can their stations keep,
She to the Earth, and he below the Deep,
At night both fall, but the swift hand of time
Renews the morning, and again they climb,
Then lett no cloudy change, create my sorrow,
I'll think 'tis night, and I may rise to-morrow.

ON MYSELFE

Good Heav'n, I thank thee, since it was design'd
I shou'd be fram'd, but of the weaker kinde,
That yet, my Soul, is rescu'd from the Love

by a Woman writt

Of all those Trifles, which their Passions move.
Pleasures, and Praise, and Plenty haue with me
But their just value. If allow'd they be,
Freely, and thankfully as much I tast,
As will not reason, or Religion wast.
If they're deny'd, I on my selfe can Liue,
And slight those aids, unequal chance does give.
When in the Sun, my wings can be display'd,
And in retirement, I can bless the shade.

A LETTER TO DAFNIS APRIL: 2D 1685

This to the Crown, and blessing of my life,
The much lov'd husband, of a happy wife.
To him, whose constant passion found the art
To win a stubborn, and ungratefull heart;
And to the World, by tend'rest proof discovers
They err, who say that husbands can't be lovers.
With such return of passion, as is due,
Daphnis I love, Daphnis my thoughts persue,
Daphnis, my hopes, my joys, are bounded all in you:
Ev'n I, for Daphnis, and my promise sake,
What I in women censure, undertake.
But this from love, not vanity, proceeds;
You know who writes; and I who 'tis that reads.
Judge not my passion, by my want of skill,
Many love well, though they express itt ill;
And I your censure cou'd with pleasure bear,
Wou'd you but soon return, and speak itt here.

TO MR. F. NOW EARL OF W.

Who going abroad, had desired ARDELIA *to write some Verses
upon whatever Subject she thought fit,
against his Return in the Evening.*

Written in the Year 1689.

No sooner, FLAVIO, was you gone,
But, your Injunction thought upon,

Anne Finch, Countess of Winchilsea

ARDELIA took the Pen;
Designing to perform the Task,
Her FLAVIO did so kindly ask,
    Ere he returned agen.

Unto *Parnassus* strait she sent,
And bid the Messenger, that went
    Unto the *Muses* Court,
Assure them, she their Aid did need,
And begg'd they'd use their utmost Speed,
    Because the Time was short.

The hasty Summons was allow'd;
And being well-bred, they rose and bow'd,
    And said, they'd poste away;
That well they did ARDELIA know,
And that no Female's Voice below
    They sooner wou'd obey:

That many of that rhiming Train,
On like Occasions, sought in vain
    Their Industry t'excite;
But for ARDELIA all they'd leave:
Thus flatt'ring can the Muse deceive,
    And wheedle us to write.

Yet, since there was such haste requir'd;
To know the Subject 'twas desir'd,
    On which they must infuse;
That they might temper Words and Rules,
And with their Counsel carry Tools,
    As Country-*Doctors* use.

Wherefore to cut off all Delays,
'Twas soon reply'd, a *Husband's* Praise
    (Tho' in these looser Times)
ARDELIA gladly wou'd rehearse
A *Husband's*, who indulg'd her Verse,
    And now requir'd her Rimes.

by a Woman writt

A *Husband!* eccho'd all around:
And to *Parnassus* sure that Sound
   Had never yet been sent;
Amazement in each Face was read,
In haste th' affrighted Sisters fled,
   And unto Council went.

Erato cry'd, since *Grizel's* Days,
Since *Troy*-Town pleas'd, and *Chivey-chace*,
   No such Design was known;
And 'twas their Bus'ness to take care,
It reach'd not to the publick Ear,
   Or got about the Town:

Nor came where Evening *Beaux* were met
O'er *Billet-doux* and *Chocolate*,
   Lest it destroy'd the House;
For in that Place, who cou'd dispence
(That wore his Cloaths with common Sense)
   With mention of a *Spouse?*

'Twas put unto the Vote at last,
And in the Negative it past,
   None to her Aid shou'd move;
Yet since ARDELIA was a Friend,
Excuses 'twas agreed to send,
   Which plausible might prove:

That *Pegasus* of late had been
So often rid thro' thick and thin,
   With neither Fear nor Wit;
In *Panegyrick* been so spurr'd,
He cou'd not from the Stall be stirr'd,
   Nor wou'd endure the Bit.

Melpomene had given a Bond,
By the new House alone to stand,
   And write of War and Strife;

Anne Finch, Countess of Winchilsea

Thalia, she had taken Fees,
And Stipends from the Patentees,
   And durst not for her Life.

Urania only lik'd the Choice;
Yet not to thwart the publick Voice,
   She whisp'ring did impart:
They need no Foreign Aid invoke,
No help to draw a moving Stroke,
   Who dictate from the Heart.

Enough! the pleas'd ARDELIA cry'd;
And slighting ev'ry Muse beside,
   Consulting now her Breast,
Perceiv'd that ev'ry tender Thought,
Which from abroad she'd vainly sought,
   Did there in Silence rest:

And shou'd unmov'd that Post maintain,
Till in his quick Return again,
   Met in some neighb'ring Grove,
(Where Vice nor Vanity appear)
Her FLAVIO them alone might hear,
   In all the Sounds of Love.

For since the World do's so despise
Hymen's Endearments and its Ties,
   They shou'd mysterious be;
Till We that Pleasure too possess
(Which makes their fancy'd Happiness)
   Of stollen Secrecy.

CLARINDA'S INDIFFERENCE AT PARTING WITH HER BEAUTY

Now, age came on, and all the dismal traine
That fright the vitious, and afflicte the vaine.
Departing beauty, now Clarinda spies

Pale in her cheeks, and dying in her eyes;
That youthfull air, that wanders ore the face,
That undescrib'd, that unresisted grace,
Those morning beams, that strongly warm, and shine,
Which men that feel and see, can ne're define,
Now, on the wings of restlesse time, were fled,
And ev'ning shades, began to rise, and spread,
When thus resolv'd, and ready soon to part,
Slighting the short repreives of proffer'd art
She spake—
And what, vain beauty, didst thou 'ere atcheive,
When at thy height, that I thy fall shou'd greive,
When, did'st thou e're succesfully persue?
When, did'st thou e're th' appointed foe subdue?
'Tis vain of numbers, or of strength to boast,
In an undisciplin'd, unguided Host,
And love, that did thy mighty hopes deride,
Wou'd pay no sacrafice, but to thy pride.
When, did'st thou e're a pleasing rule obtain,
A glorious Empire's but a glorious pain,
Thou, art indeed, but vanity's cheife sourse,
But foyle to witt, to want of witt a curse,
For often, by thy gaudy sign's descry'd
A fool, which unobserv'd, had been untry'd,
And when thou doest such empty things adorn,
'Tis but to make them more the publick scorn.
I know thee well, but weak thy reign wou'd be
Did n'one adore, or prize thee more then me.
I see indeed, thy certain ruine neer,
But can't affoard one parting sigh, or tear,
Nor rail at Time, nor quarrell with my glasse,
But unconcern'd, can lett thy glories passe.

THE UNEQUAL FETTERS

Cou'd we stop the time that's flying
Or recall itt when 'tis past

Anne Finch, Countess of Winchilsea

Put far off the day of Dying
    Or make Youth for ever last
To Love wou'd then be worth our cost.

But since we must loose those Graces
    Which at first your hearts have wonne
And you seek for in new Faces
    When our Spring of Life is done
It wou'd but urdge our ruine on

Free as Nature's first intention
    Was to make us, I'll be found
Nor by subtle Man's invention
    Yeild to be in Fetters bound
By one that walks a freer round.

Mariage does but slightly tye Men
    Whil'st close Pris'ners we remain
They the larger Slaves of Hymen
    Still are begging Love again
At the full length of all their chain.

A SONG

'Tis strange, this Heart within my breast,
    Reason opposing, and her Pow'rs,
Cannot one gentle Moment rest,
    Unless it knows what's done in Yours.

In vain I ask it of your Eyes,
    Which subt'ly wou'd my Fears controul;
For Art has taught them to disguise,
    Which Nature made t' explain the Soul.

In vain that Sound, your Voice affords,
    Flatters sometimes my easy Mind;

by a Woman writt

But of too vast Extent are Words
  In them the Jewel Truth to find.

Then let my fond Enquiries cease,
  And so let all my Troubles end:
For, sure, that Heart shall ne'er know Peace,
  Which on Anothers do's depend.

JEALOUSIE IS THE RAGE OF A MAN

Whilst with his falling wings, the courtly Dove
Sweeps the low earth, and singles out his Love,
Now murmurs soft, then with a rowling note
Extends his crop, and fills his am'rous throate,
On ev'ry side accosts the charming Fair,
Turns round, and bows with an inticing ayre,
She, carelessly neglecting all his pain,
Or shifts her ground, or pecks the scatter'd grain.
But if he cease, and through the flight wou'd range,
(For though renown'd for truth, e'vn Doves will change)
The mildnesse of her nature laid aside,
The seeming coldnesse, and the carelesse pride,
On the next Rival, in a rage she flies;
Smooth, ev'ry clinging plume, with anger lies,
Employs in feeble fight her tender beck,
And shakes the Favrites, parti-colour'd neck.
Thus, jealousy, through ev'ry species moves;
And if so furious, in the gallesse Doves,
No wonder, that th' experienc'd Hebrew sage,
Of Man, pronounc'd itt the extremest Rage.

TO THE NIGHTINGALE

Exert thy Voice, sweet Harbinger of Spring!
  This Moment is thy Time to sing,
  This Moment I attend to Praise,
And set my Numbers to thy Layes.

Anne Finch, Countess of Winchilsea

Free as thine shall be my Song;
 As thy Musick, short, or long.
Poets, wild as thee, were born,
 Pleasing best when unconfin'd,
 When to Please is least design'd,
Soothing but their Cares to rest;
 Cares do still their Thoughts molest,
 And still th' unhappy Poet's Breast,
Like thine, when best he sings, is plac'd against a Thorn.
She begins, Let all be still!
 Muse, thy Promise now fulfill!
Sweet, oh! sweet, still sweeter yet
Can thy Words such Accents fit,
Canst thou Syllables refine,
Melt a Sense that shall retain
Still some Spirit of the Brain,
Till with Sounds like these it join.
 'Twill not be! then change thy Note;
 Let division shake thy Throat.
Hark! Division now she tries;
Yet as far the Muse outflies.
 Cease then, prithee, cease thy Tune;
 Trifler, wilt thou sing till *June?*
Till thy Bus'ness all lies waste,
And the Time of Building's past!
 Thus we Poets that have Speech,
Unlike what thy Forests teach,
 If a fluent Vein be shown
 That's transcendent to our own,
Criticize, reform, or preach,
Or censure what we cannot reach.

A NOCTURNAL REVERIE

In such a *Night*, when every louder Wind
Is to its distant Cavern safe confin'd;
And only gentle *Zephyr* fans his Wings,

And lonely *Philomel*, still waking, sings;
Or from some Tree, fam'd for the *Owl's* delight,
She, hollowing clear, directs the Wand'rer right:
In such a *Night*, when passing Clouds give place,
Or thinly vail the Heav'ns mysterious Face;
When in some River, overhung with Green,
The waving Moon and trembling Leaves are seen;
When freshen'd Grass now bears it self upright,
And makes cool Banks to pleasing Rest invite,
Whence springs the *Woodbind*, and the *Bramble*-Rose,
And where the sleepy *Cowslip* shelter'd grows;
Whilst now a paler Hue the *Foxglove* takes,
Yet checquers still with Red the dusky brakes
When scatter'd *Glow-worms*, but in Twilight fine,
Shew trivial Beauties watch their Hour to shine;
Whilst *Salisb'ry* stands the Test of every Light,
In perfect Charms, and perfect Virtue bright:
When Odours, which declin'd repelling Day,
Thro' temp'rate Air uninterrupted stray;
When darken'd Groves their softest Shadows wear,
And falling Waters we distinctly hear;
When thro' the Gloom more venerable shows
Some ancient Fabrick, awful in Repose,
While Sunburnt Hills their swarthy Looks conceal,
And swelling Haycocks thicken up the Vale:
When the loos'd *Horse* now, as his Pasture leads,
Comes slowly grazing thro' th' adjoining Meads,
Whose stealing Pace, and lengthen'd Shade we fear,
Till torn up Forage in his Teeth we hear:
When nibbling *Sheep* at large pursue their Food,
And unmolested Kine rechew the Cud;
When *Curlews* cry beneath the Village-walls,
And to her straggling Brood the *Partridge* calls;
Their shortliv'd Jubilee the Creatures keep,
Which but endures, whilst Tyrant-*Man* do's sleep;
When a sedate Content the Spirit feels,
And no fierce Light disturbs, whilst it reveals;

But silent Musings urge the Mind to seek
Something, too high for Syllables to speak;
Till the free Soul to a compos'dness charm'd,
Finding the Elements of Rage disarm'd,
O'er all below a solemn Quiet grown,
Joys in th' inferiour World, and thinks it like her Own:
In such a *Night* let Me abroad remain,
Till Morning breaks, and All's confus'd again;
Our Cares, our Toils, our Clamours are renew'd,
Or Pleasures, seldom reach'd, again pursu'd.

Aphra Behn

Aphra Behn

(ca. 1640–1689)

With the production of her play, *The Forc'd Marriage*, Aphra Behn—the first known Englishwoman to write for money—became a celebrity and a curiosity. At a time when few women became writers, Behn had become a professional playwright. The prologue to her play touted the novelty of a woman as author. And Behn became the subject of praise and ridicule—both focusing as much on her sex as on her talent. She was hailed for having the body of a Venus and the mind of a Minerva, for being "the English Sappho"; she was satirized as "that lewd harlot" and as "Sappho, famous for her Gout, and Guilt."

Behn wrote plays, novels, short stories, poetry, letters, and translations. She was innovative—experimenting with realism, writing one of the first novels to expose the horrors of slavery, and creating portraits of aggressive women. And she was courageous—vigorously defending her own work and the rights of women writers. The following selection from Behn's poetry reveals how candidly she could write about passion; the selection from "An Epistle to the Reader," a defense of the woman playwright, suggests how directly Behn confronted her opponents, and how clearly she understood them.

SONG.

Love Arm'd.

LOVE in Fantastique Triumph satt,
Whilst Bleeding Hearts a round him flow'd,
For whom Fresh paines he did Create,
And strange Tryanick power he show'd;
From thy Bright Eyes he took his fire,
Which round about, in sport he hurl'd;
But 'twas from mine he took desire,
Enough to undo the Amorous World.

From me he took his sighs and tears,
From thee his Pride and Crueltie;
From me his Languishments and Feares,

by a Woman writt

And every Killing Dart from thee;
Thus thou and I, the God have arm'd,
And sett him up a Deity;
But my poor Heart alone is harm'd,
Whilst thine the Victor is, and free.

SONG.

Pan, grant that I may never prove
So great a *Slave* to fall in love,
And to an Unknown *Deity*
Resign my happy Liberty:
I love to see the Amorous *Swains*
   Unto my Scorn their Hearts resign:
With Pride I see the Meads and Plains
   Throng'd all with *Slaves*, and they all mine:
Whilst I the whining Fools despise,
That pay their Homage to my Eyes.

SONG.

The Willing Mistriss.

Amyntas led me to a Grove,
   Where all the Trees did shade us;
The Sun it self, though it had Strove,
   It could not have betray'd us:
The place secur'd from humane Eyes,
   No other fear allows,
   But when the Winds that gently rise,
Doe Kiss the yeilding Boughs.

Down there we satt upon the Moss,
   And did begin to play
A Thousand Amorous Tricks, to pass
   The heat of all the day.
A many Kisses he did give:

Aphra Behn

And I return'd the same
Which made me willing to receive
    That which I dare not name.

His Charming Eyes no Aid requir'd
    To tell their softning Tale;
On her that was already fir'd,
    'Twas Easy to prevaile.
He did but Kiss and Clasp me round,
    Whilst those his thoughts Exprest:
And lay'd me gently on the Ground;
    Ah who can guess the rest?

THE DISAPPOINTMENT.

I.

ONE day the Amorous *Lysander*,
By an impatient Passion sway'd,
Surpriz'd fair *Cloris*, that lov'd Maid,
Who could defend her self no longer.
All things did with his Love conspire;
The gilded Planet of the Day,
In his gay Chariot drawn by Fire,
Was now descending to the Sea,
And left no Light to guide the World,
But what from *Cloris* Brighter Eyes was hurld.

II.

In a lone Thicket made for Love,
Silent as yielding Maids Consent,
She with a Charming Languishment,
Permits his Force, yet gently strove;
Her Hands his Bosom softly meet,
But not to put him back design'd,
Rather to draw 'em on inclin'd:

by a Woman writt

Whilst he lay trembling at her Feet,
Resistance 'tis in vain to show;
She want the pow'r to say—*Ah! What d'ye do?*

III.

Her Bright Eyes sweet, and yet severe,
Where Love and Shame confus'dly strive.
Fresh Vigor to *Lysander* give;
And breathing faintly in his Ear,
She cry'd—*Cease, Cease—your vain Desire,*
Or I'll call out—What would you do?
My Dearer Honour ev'n to You
I cannot, must not give—Retire,
Or take this Life, whose chiefest part
I gave you with the Conquest of my Heart.

IV.

But he as much unus'd to Fear,
As he was capable of Love,
The blessed minutes to improve,
Kisses her Mouth, her Neck, her Hair;
Each Touch her new Desire Alarms,
His burning trembling Hand he prest
Upon her swelling Snowy Brest,
While she lay panting in his Arms.
All her Unguarded Beauties lie
The Spoils and Trophies of the Enemy.

V.

And now without Respect or Fear,
He seeks the Object of his Vows,
(His Love no Modesty allows)
By swift degrees advancing—where
His daring Hand that Altar seiz'd,
Where Gods of Love do sacrifice:
That Awful Throne, that Paradice

Aphra Behn

Where Rage is calm'd, and Anger pleas'd;
That Fountain where Delight still flows,
And gives the Universal World Repose.

VI.

Her Balmy Lips incountring his,
Their Bodies, as their Souls, are joyn'd;
Where both in Transports Unconfin'd
Extend themselves upon the Moss.
Cloris half dead and breathless lay;
Her soft Eyes cast a Humid Light,
Such as divides the Day and Night;
Or falling Stars, whose Fires decay:
And now no signs of Life she shows,
But what in short-breath'd Sighs returns and goes.

VII.

He saw how at her Length she lay;
He saw her rising Bosom bare;
Her loose thin *Robes,* through which appear
A Shape design'd for Love and Play;
Abandon'd by her Pride and Shame.
She does her softest Joys dispence,
Off'ring her Virgin-Innocence
A Victim to Loves Sacred Flame;
While the o'er-Ravish'd Shepherd lies
Unable to perform the Sacrifice.

VIII.

Ready to taste a thousand Joys,
The too transported hapless Swain
Found the vast Pleasure turn'd to Pain;
Pleasure which too much Love destroys:
The willing Garments by he laid,
And Heaven all open'd to his view,
Mad to possess, himself he threw

by a Woman writt

On the Defenceless Lovely Maid.
But Oh what envying God conspires
To snatch his Power, yet leave him the Desire!

IX.

Nature's Support, (without whose Aid
She can no Humane Being give)
It self now wants the Art to live;
Faintness its slack'ned Nerves invade:
In vain th' inraged Youth essay'd
To call its fleeting Vigor back.
No motion 'twill from Motion take;
Excess of Love his Love betray'd:
In vain he Toils, in vain Commands;
The Insensible fell weeping in his Hand.

X.

In this so Amorous Cruel Strife,
Where Love and Fate were too severe,
The poor *Lysander* in despair
Renounc'd his Reason with his Life:
Now all the brisk and active Fire
That should the Nobler Part inflame,
Serv'd to increase his Rage and Shame,
And left no Spark for New Desire:
Not all her Naked Charms cou'd move
Or calm that Rage that had debauch'd his Love.

XI.

Cloris returning from the Trance
Which Love and soft Desire had bred,
Her timerous Hand she gently laid
(Or guided by Design or Chance)
Upon that Fabulous *Priapus*,
That Potent God, as Poets feign;
But never did young *Shepherdess*,

Aphra Behn

Gath'ring of Fern upon the Plain,
More nimbly draw her Fingers back,
Finding beneath the verdant Leaves a Snake:

XII.

Than *Cloris* her fair Hand withdrew,
Finding that God of her Desires
Disarm'd of all his Awful Fires,
And Cold as Flow'rs bath'd in the Morning Dew.
Who can the *Nymph's* Confusion guess?
The Blood forsook the hinder Place,
And strew'd with Blushes all her Face,
Which both Disdain and Shame exprest:
And from *Lysander's* Arms she fled,
Leaving him fainting on the Gloomy Bed.

XIII.

Like Lightning through the Grove she hies,
Or *Daphne* from the *Delphick God*,
No Print upon the grassey Road
She leaves, t' instruct Pursuing Eyes.
The Wind that wanton'd in her Hair,
And with her Ruffled Garments plaid,
Discover'd in the Flying Maid
All that the Gods e'er made, if Fair.
So *Venus*, when her *Love* was slain,
With Fear and Haste flew o'er the Fatal Plain.

XIV.

The *Nymph's* Resentments none but I
Can well Imagine or Condole:
But none can guess *Lysander's* Soul,
But those who sway'd his Destiny.
His silent Griefs swell up to Storms,
And not one God his Fury spares;
He curs'd his Birth, his Fate, his Stars;

by a Woman writt

But more the *Shepherdess's* Charms,
Whose soft bewitching Influence
Had Damn'd him to the *Hell* of Impotence.

TO LYSANDER, ON SOME VERSES
HE WRIT, AND ASKING MORE FOR
HIS HEART THEN 'TWAS WORTH.

I.

TAKE back that Heart, you with such Caution give,
    Take the fond valu'd Trifle back;
I hate Love-Merchants that a Trade wou'd drive;
    And meanly cunning Bargains make.

II.

I care not how the busy Market goes,
    And scorn to Chaffer for a price:
Love does one Staple Rate on all impose,
    Nor leaves it to the Traders Choice.

III.

A heart requires a Heart Unfeign'd and True,
    Though Subt'ly you advance the Price,
And ask a Rate that Simple Love ne'er knew:
    And the free Trade Monopolize.

IV.

An Humble *Slave* the Buyer must become,
    She must not bate a Look or Glance,
You will have all, or you'll have none;
    See how Loves Market you inhaunce.

V.

Is't not enough, I gave you Heart for Heart,
    But I must add my Lips and Eies;

Aphra Behn

I must no friendly Smile or Kiss impart;
    But you must *Dun* me with Advice.

VI.

And every Hour still more unjust you grow,
    Those Freedoms you my life deny,
You to *Adraste* are oblig'd to show,
    And give her all my Rifled Joy.

VII.

Without Controul she gazes on that Face,
    And all the happy Envyed Night,
In the pleas'd Circle of your fond imbrace:
    She takes away the Lovers Right.

VIII.

From me she Ravishes those silent hours,
    That are by Sacred Love my due;
Whilst *I* in vain accuse the angry Powers,
    That make me hopeless Love pursue.

IX.

Adrastes Ears with that dear Voice are blest,
    That Charms my Soul at every Sound,
And with those *Love-Inchanting* Touches prest:
    Which *I* ne'er felt without a Wound.

X.

She has thee all: whilst *I* with silent Greif,
    The Fragments of thy Softness feel,
Yet dare not blame the happy licenc'd Thief:
    That does my Dear-bought Pleasures steal.

XI.

Whilst like a Glimering Taper still *I* burn,
    And waste my self in my own flame,
Adraste takes the welcome rich Return:
    And leaves me all the hopeless Pain.

XII.

Be just, my lovely *Swain*, and do not take
    Freedoms you'll not to me allow;
Or give *Amynta* so much Freedom back:
    That she may Rove as well as you.

XIII.

Let us then love upon the honest Square,
    Since Interest neither have design'd,
For the sly Gamester, who ne'er plays me fair,
    Must Trick for Trick expect to find.

TO THE FAIR CLARINDA,
WHO MADE LOVE TO ME,
IMAGIN'D MORE THAN WOMAN.

FAIR lovely Maid, or if that Title be
Too weak, too Feminine for Nobler thee,
Permit a Name that more Approaches Truth:
And let me call thee, Lovely Charming Youth.
This last will justifie my soft complaint,
While that may serve to lessen my constraint;
And without Blushes I the Youth persue,
When so much beauteous Woman is in view.
Against thy Charms we struggle but in vain
With thy deluding Form thou giv'st us pain,
While the bright Nymph betrays us to the **Swain**.
In pity to our Sex sure thou wer't sent,
That we might Love, and yet be Innocent:
For sure no Crime with thee we can commit;

Aphra Behn

Or if we shou'd—thy Form excuses it.
For who, that gathers fairest Flowers believes
A Snake lies hid beneath the Fragrant Leaves.

Thou beauteous Wonder of a different kind,
Soft *Cloris* with the dear *Alexis* join'd;
When e'r the Manly part of thee, wou'd plead
Thou tempts us with the Image of the Maid,
While we the noblest Passions do extend
The Love to *Hermes*, *Aphrodite* the Friend.

TO ALEXIS IN ANSWER TO
HIS POEM AGAINST FRUITION.

AH hapless sex! who bears no charms,
But what like lightning flash and are no more,
    False fires sent down for baneful harms,
Fires which the fleeting Lover feebly warms
    And given like past Beboches o're,
        Like Songs that please (tho bad,) when new,
        But learn'd by heart neglected grew.

In vain did Heav'n adorn the shape and face
With Beautyes which by Angels forms it drew:
In vain the mind with brighter Glories Grace,
While all our joys are stinted to the space
        Of one betraying enterview,
With one surrender to the eager will
We're short-liv'd nothing, or a real ill.

Since Man with that inconstancy was born,
To love the absent, and the present scorn,
    Why do we deck, why do we dress
    For such a short-liv'd happiness?
    Why do we put Attraction on,
Since either way tis we must be undon?

They fly if Honour take our part,
Our Virtue drives 'em o're the field.
We lose 'em by too much desert,
And Oh! they fly us if we yeild.
Ye Gods! is there no charm in all the fair
To fix this wild, this faithless, wanderer?

Man! our great business and our aim,
For whom we spread our fruitless snares,
No sooner kindles the designing flame,
But to the next bright object bears
The Trophies of his conquest and our shame:
Inconstancy's the good supream
The rest is airy Notion, empty Dream!

Then, heedless Nymph, be rul'd by me
If e're your Swain the bliss desire;
Think like *Alexis* he may be
Whose wisht Possession damps his fire;
The roving youth in every shade
Has left some sighing and abandon'd Maid,
For tis a fatal lesson he has learn'd,
After fruition ne're to be concern'd.

FROM "AN EPISTLE TO THE READER," THE PREFACE TO BEHN'S PLAY THE DUTCH LOVER

Indeed that day 'twas acted first, there comes me into the pit a long, lithe, phlegmatic, white, ill-favored, wretched fop, an officer in masquerade newly transported with a scarf and feather out of France, a sorry animal that has nought else to shield it from the uttermost contempt of all mankind, but that respect which we afford to rats and toads, which though we do not well allow to live, yet when considered as a part of God's creation, we make honorable mention of them. A thing, reader—but no more of such a smelt: this thing, I tell you, opening that which serves it for a mouth, out issued such a noise as this to those that sat about it, that they were to expect a woeful play, God damn him, for it was a woman's. Now how this came about I am not sure, but I suppose he brought it piping hot from some who had with him the reputation of a villainous wit: for creatures of his size of sense talk without all imagination, such scraps as they pick up from other folks. I would not for a world be taken arguing with such a property as this; but if I thought there were a man of any tolerable parts, who could upon mature deliberation distinguish well his right hand from his left, and justly state the difference between the number of sixteen and two, yet had this prejudice upon him; I would take a little pains to make him know how much he errs. For waiving the examination why women having equal education with men, were not as capable of knowledge, of whatsoever sort as well as they: I'll only say as I have touched before, that plays have no great room for that which is men's great advantage over women, that is learning; we all well know that the immortal Shakespeare's plays (who was not guilty of much more of this than often falls to women's share) have better pleased the world than Jonson's works, though by the way 'tis said that Benjamin was no such rabbi neither, for I am informed that his learning was but grammar high; (sufficient indeed to rob poor Salust of his best orations) and it has been observed that they are apt to admire him most confoundedly, who have just such a scantling of it as he had; and I have seen a man the most severe of Jonson's sect, sit with his hat removed less than a hair's breadth from one sullen posture for almost three hours at the *The Alchymist*; who at that excellent play of *Harry the Fourth* (which yet I hope is far enough from farce) has very hardly kept his doublet whole; but affectation has always had a greater share both in the action and discourse of men than truth and judgment have; and for our modern ones, except our most inimitable laureate, I dare to say I know of none that write at such a formidable rate, but that a woman may well hope to reach their greatest heights. Then for their musty rules of unity, and God knows what besides, if they meant anything, they are enough intelligible and as practicable by a woman; but really methinks they that disturb their heads with any other rule of plays besides the making them pleasant, and avoiding of scurrility, might much better be employed in studying how to improve men's too imperfect knowledge of that ancient English game which hight long Laurence: and if comedy should be the picture of ridiculous mankind I wonder anyone should think it such a sturdy task, whilst we are furnished with such precious originals as him I lately told you of; if at least that character do not dwindle into farce, and so become too mean an entertainment for those persons who are used to think. Reader, I have a complaint or two to make to you and I have done.

O Sacred Truth inspire and rule my Page —
So may reforming Satyr mend a vicious Age —
Whilst thy Enlightning Rays adorn & guard ye Place,
Astrea's glorious Form Surveys the Peace —
And Virtue wears the bright Ormonda's Face.

Frontispiece from Mary Manley's SECRET MEMOIRS

Mary Manley

(ca. 1663–1724)

Mary Manley described herself as "a ruined woman." Her father had been a high ranking officer and a writer. According to a semiautobiographical account, she was tricked into a false marriage to her cousin, who took her inheritance and deserted her. She went on to become a successful and prolific writer, and the mistress of several prominent men.

Perhaps due to her own experiences, Manley wrote with compassion about "ruined women." She attacked the double standard, by which women are condemned for acts which men are free to commit, and she spoke out for women and for women writers. Her own life seems to have been marked by the qualities she often gave her female characters—strength, insight born of hard experience, passion, and desperate courage.

Manley wrote plays, long satiric prose works, stories, letters, and political articles. She succeeded Jonathan Swift as the editor of the Tory publication, the *Examiner*, and she is credited with being the first Englishwoman to be a political journalist, the first to be the author of a best seller, and the first to be arrested for her writing. Her *Secret Memoirs and Manners of Several Persons of Quality of Both Sexes From the New Atalantis, an Island in the Mediterranean* was a best selling satiric work, intended to expose the personal scandals of the opposing Whig party. The work apparently had an impact, for Manley and her publishers were arrested because of it. To Manley's contemporaries, the stories in the *Secret Memoirs* must have been intriguing, for they supposedly were about real people. To readers today, the stories should hold special interest, for many of them, like "Corinna"—about a girl who refuses to marry—and "The Cabal"—about a lesbian group—are revealing accounts of women's lives.

FROM SECRET MEMOIRS
AND MANNERS OF SEVERAL PERSONS OF
QUALITY OF BOTH SEXES.
FROM THE NEW ATALANTIS,
AN ISLAND IN THE MEDITERRANEAN.

In the *Secret Memoirs*, Manley links together a collection of stories by using a frame story, in which Astrea, a goddess, comes back to earth and visits a mythical

by a Woman writt

island in the Mediterranean, called Atalantis. Here she meets Virtue and her mother, Intelligence, and the three travel together and tell the stories of what they see.

CORINNA

Astrea. The next house furnishes with a scene no less an object of satire: you will see there a young lady, who has long suffered under the barbarous persecution of her mother; she would persuade her she was a lunatic, and used her accordingly, till at length she has in reality made her not very far from one. As a proof of it, she is gone to live with her again; notwithstanding all her ill usage. We find the lady born with an elevated genius in a family of considerable circumstances, her father a chevalier. Corinna had a genteel, agreeable person, with an abundance of roving wit, superficial sparklings, without much conduct or any judgment. Her mother, a severe parsimonious lady, allowed her no advantages from education at home, or conversation abroad, so that Corinna bred herself, and took a bent not easily to be straightened. She had so much of my lady in her temper, as to be covetous; to which she has owed her misfortunes. The original of her mother's aversion for her, had its rise from an intercepted letter that Corinna wrote to a confidant; where complaining of the little diversions she met with at home, she summed up the family in these two lines.

> A hen-pecked father, an imperious mother,
> A deaf sister, and a lame brother.

From which she desired her to make a judgment of the agreeableness of her entertainment, and whether such company could have any part in her fondness. My lady was resolved to make good the character her daughter gave her, and used her with such tyranny and ill-nature, that Corinna could not support it. The chevalier her father was concerned at it; but according to what his daughter had said, durst not complain. The young lady made him a request, that she could not very easily expect to have had granted. My dear Papa, says the caressing Corinna, I know you do; as if you loved my mother, never contradicting her anything; but I am sure you love your girl, because you are uneasy at her contradicting me in every thing: you know, my dear Papa, that I'm an excellent housewife, my lady herself can't say against it; all she will allow me to be her daughter in, is, because I have a great deal of her preserving temper. I have no inclination to marry, rather an aversion that way; you have said my fortune shall be forty thousand crowns, this you would not scruple to pay down upon the nail, to any old curmudgeonly deformed abject monster, that shall hit my mother's foible. For if she says it must be done, there's no remedy; we must both consent, tho' my eternal quiet is sacrificed to her caprice. Such a one I'm informed she is in treaty with; old Adorno, you know him, my dear Papa; but what are his large possessions to me? I shall ever hate him; can your girl be happy with such unequal merit? When my lady has brought things to a conclusion, if you refuse your consent, it will make a perpetual quarrel; if you grant, then Corinna's mortified and undone. Therefore, my dear Papa, trust your poor girl for once; give me the possession of those crowns, I'll take a little house, two maidservants, a woman, one footman, and a coachman, and you shall see how distinguishingly I shall live. Resolving never to marry, you will have my house to be easy in, when my mother makes you otherwise at home. If you can be so obliging, you will render me eternally happy, and if I prophesy right, you'll have no occasion to repent of it. I will at least answer on my part, unless some unfortunate whirl of fate thrust between me and happiness, to poison that quiet I promise to my self; but however, this I may almost venture to be a sybil in, my disappointment shall never arise from love; and what young woman was ever yet known entirely miserable without it?

To be short, she gained her point, the chevalier made her absolute mistress of forty thousand crowns, and of her own conduct, settled her in a very pretty house, for which he paid the highest price, I mean his own life. My lady grew so outrageous to see her daughter entirely out of her dominion, that she never ceased a moment from teasing her husband; who so well knew her temper, and the ascendancy she had over him, by his love of ease, and refusing to exert himself, that he had put it out of his power to recall Corinna's fortune, as he certainly must have done, if possible. My lady would, however, take out her revenge upon his quiet, and so successfully pursued her point, that he fell a martyr to her tongue. A landmark for husbands, how they suffer the growth of authority in that tyrannical unruly member!

The gentleman who owned the house Corinna lived in, was a cadet of justice, with no large estate, but that was then the worst part of him, for his person was agreeable enough, his temper soft and amorous, exact in his dress, not wholly free from foppery in his manner; he could not see his fair tenant without a tenderness for her. She had many pretenders, and some admirers; but Don Alonzo, so was he called, proved to be the man. She had some relish of his conversation, had read a great deal, and much of love, but was never touched with anything that interfered with interest; she liked with her eyes, but her heart had still a true regard to the world, more than merit. However, finding her self mistress of an easy fortune, resolved against the marriage chain, and entirely at her own dispose, she waived too scrupulous an inquiry into what she owed her virtue, and determined not to deny her satisfaction for a circumstance. She had an idea of the joys of love from others; all who have ever felt it, speak with rapture of its delights. Those who can write but indifferently on other subjects, if once they have been truly agitated by it, write well of that. Her curiosity taught her to prove whether there was in it that pang of pleasure, as she had been made to believe; but the affair was a little nice, Don Alonzo had an honorable opinion of her virtue, and visited her accordingly. 'Twas true she was a virgin, but weary of being such, and yet she did not know how to exchange her condition, without making her self that slave a wife, as she called it. However, a lady, or her lover, must be very dull indeed, in the freedom of conversation, if one cannot give, and the other explain, their desires without speaking. Don Alonzo was perhaps as long again in guessing at her design, as another less prepossessed would have been; because he desired to marry her, and was very unwilling to believe but indifferently of a lady he had such an intention towards: he pressed hard upon the point, but she was deaf as storms on that side; but when he would urge the excess of his passion, the height of his respective flames, the ardor of his pains, his impatiency for happiness; she would smile him a gracious look of approbation, suffered him to kneel at her feet, to grasp her knees, to meet the softness of her eyes, with greater of his own; would lean her face to his, where (all coward, as love had made him) the kindling youth could not be so lost to native hope and instinct, as not to attempt the hanging cherry of her lip, that seemed to stoop for pressure. But oh! which was greater, his astonishment or delight? when he found that an action which he feared had merited death, was feelingly received, and repayed with blushing usury; his heart throbbed as if 'twould leave his breast; he felt inestimable pleasures, between his fears and his desires. Her sparkling eyes cast a day of hope around him, to animate his doubting love. The virgin-guard of awful modesty was willingly thrown by, she left the dazzled youth no time to pause or recollect, but answering all his eager sighs, his kisses and desires, she leaned upon a bed was near her, whither the amorous youth in heat of ecstasy pursued her. Then was his time (he thought) to gain the warmed, the yielding maid's consent; he pressed for happiness, he pressed to marry her—to lengthen out his part of bliss, and make it durable as great—Corinna paused—and yawned upon the importunity.—Have you ever seen water thrown upon aspiring flames, that rise to cover all they meet with ruin? such, and so damped, seemed the burnings of the defeated maid. At length obliged to answer his repeated proposition, emboldened as he grew by that degree of favor she had lately shown him;—Why, ay, Alonzo—answered she—'tis true—marriage is indeed for life,—but who can tell what sort of a life?—Do you think we can't love without marrying? at least it seems rational to us that have our understanding about us, to try those nearer intimacies, which are said, either to ravish or disgust! to make us fonder or more indifferent. Whatever false notion the world or you may have of virtue, I must confess I should be very loathe to bind my self to a man for ever, before I was sure I should like him for a night; I don't take you to be so dull, that I need explain my self any further. I have hinted to you my inclinations, I think it is now your business to convince me of the extent of yours.

Don Alonzo, who had an early taint in his composition of self-conceit, did not fear that possession could abate of her inclination towards his fine person; he rather believed it would heighten it, a received maxim, that women become fonder of whomsoever they admit to those intimacies. He did not doubt his charms, nor his good fortune, by a mistaken notion, concluding it would give him a right over the dishonored fair, and that then she would be glad to marry him with the soonest, at least if she should happen to be pregnant.

But he had to deal with a lady infinitely more politic; she had gratified her curiosity, and became dotingly fond of his conversation, perpetually teasing and sending after him when he was never so little a time absent from her; but still she would not, she was too wise, or too covetous, to marry him. A neighboring lady, whom he had introduced to her intimacy, pressed her hard on Don Alonzo's part, to make his happiness lawful, representing a thousand things to engage; among the rest, his vast respect, nay, adoration for her person. Corinna said, she was indeed obliged to him; but, Madam, she pursued, what should I marry him for, to make him the master of my self and fortune, only for a name? I love his company, whilst he is thus obliging, insinuating, careful of displeasing, tender, complaisant, amorous and ardent; but these qualities, so conspicuous and valuable in a lover, will be lost, or vanish in the husband: neglectful, sullen, perhaps morose; all his attributes will be inverted; he will then expect to be pleased, 'twill be my turn to oblige and obey, at least I must endeavor it, and perhaps without succeeding, I shall find him positive, arbitrary, cold, as if he never had had any fire, or that I had lost the art of kindling it; tho' I must confess to you, the defect of my own constitution, I should not stick with him for that trifle, because whatever lovers may talk of joys, I find there's nothing in't. If I were to judge of all ladies by my self, I should think it lay chiefly in the head; therefore must be mad to give up my possessions for nothing, to lose all that is endearing in Don Alonzo's conversation, and not be able to find my account any other way: no, no, madam, I'm wiser than that comes to. I am mistress of my own liberty and fortune, I shall put on none of his fetters, since all I shall be entitled to by 'em is, clearing his mortgaged estate, and paying his other debts.

Mean time, her mother (thro' some extravagant sparklings in the daughter's unheeded conversation, with her intimates, who ridiculed

Mary Manley

a wit they did not understand) failed not to represent her in all companies as lunatic; she thought if she could but succeed, her forty thousand crowns would fall to her share: the truly covetous have never enough! The charge of keeping her under those circumstances woud be insignificant; at length she proceeded so far, as to have her seized in her own house, by doctors and nurses, and put under the operation. Don Alonzo rescued her, they had a trial at law, where Corinna's woman deposed, that for a length of time together, she had given her a powder every morning in her chocolate, that my lady had furnished her with, pernicious to health, and capable, by slow degrees, of ruining the strongest constitution. Don Alonzo pleaded merit from the service he had done her, and urged her to marry him, which perhaps she might have been brought to, since the name and quality of a husband, was all that was left to screen her from her mother's malicious designing pretenses, if an unlucky story had not reached her ear. It seems, during the time of her persecution, Don Alonzo had the reputation of courting a lady only for his pleasure, who made no scruple to receive his visits and his presents; but yet at the long run refused him her favors: he was out of patience with the jilting fair one, and as the scandalous chronicle recites, having one day found a lone opportunity, he very robustly gave her two or three sound blows that stunned her and threw her on the ground; where, as 'tis reported, he took the opportunity of accomplishing his desire. The cadet so used to do justice to others, would not refuse it to himself; for, as he said, his presents had bought the lady; the favors she had to bestow were his, and he would take 'em where-ever he had an opportunity.

This ruined him with Corinna, who tho' she had found nothing in't, was not very willing another should. Her mother got her again, and kept her a prisoner at a house in the country, whence to free her self, she did the thing in the world she had least inclination for, and that was to marry the son of the family she was in, a pert young man, without the ballast of understanding. He might have made himself and Corinna happy; but with weak heads, good fortune has fumes that very often turns the brain. They were forced to submit to another trial at law, to acquit her from being a lunatic; one (no undiverting) circumstance, inclined the judge to give sentence in her favor. A gentleman of the long robe, named Vagellius, was eminently against her.

> ————One reputed long,
> For strength of lungs and pliancy of tongue:
> Which way he pleases, he can mold a cause,
> The worst has merits, and the best has flaws.
> Five pieces makes a criminal to day,
> And ten to morrow takes the stain away:
> Whatever he affirms is undenied, &c.

To be short, nothing can be added to the satirist's excellent description of him, but a word or two of his person: where we find a studied elegance of dress, and stiffness of behavior, that distinguishes him as much as his tongue. This spruce, affected, not unhandsome lawyer, had made the overture of his fair person to Corinna. You have heard that only necessity could determine her resolutions (against her inclinations) to marry at all, and therefore when she was not under that necessity, she refused Vagellius, who as little in his revenge, as he was great in rhetoric, engaged himself of her mother's side, and said all that could be said, to convince the judge she was a lunatic. Corinna begged his lordship to hear her but one word upon that head, related the circumstances of Vagellius's courtship, and then appealed to his lordship's judgment, if they could rationally condemn her for a lunatic, who had been so wise as to refuse to marry him, with his little share of real estate, and his large portion of children, for he had six. This determined the court of her side; she was discharged, and left to her own and her husband's management, who in a little time behaved himself unworthily to her, kept two women for his pleasure, in her very eye, and rioted out the income of her fortune in such blamable diversions, till he had quite wearied her out, and forced her to take up with her mother's house, to revenge herself upon her husband. He quickly, upon her desertion, fell into a want of money, and failing to carry her off, when he came to my lady's to demand her, he fell into a lunacy; the first effects of it was fatal to his friend, whom he had brought to assist him; for, without any provocation, as they were walking, he let him go a little before, and then discharging a pistol behind, shot him into the body, of which he died. He also let fly another at the first person that he saw in the road. He was seized, and brought to justice; but his madness saved his life. He is now under cure, and Corinna buried and forgotten in her mother's persecutions; a lady, who bating some circumstances, deserved better fortune, all her misery and wrongs being derived from her that should, by nature and duty, have done her utmost to shelter her from being wronged by others.

THE CABAL

Astrea. Does your ladyship's Intelligence extend to the knowledge of those ladies (we know 'em to be such by their voices) who fill those three coaches, that run along the gravel road on the right hand of us? they laugh loud and incessantly. 'Tis certain they have neither the spleen nor vapors! or for the present seem to have forgot 'em. Can any persons be more at their ease? Sure these seem to unknow that there is a certain portion of misery and disappointments allotted to all men, which one time or other will assuredly overtake 'em. The very consideration is sufficient, in my opinion, to put a damp upon the serenest, much more a tumultuous joy.

Intell. That is afflicting themselves unprofitably; nothing ought to hinder a man from enjoying the present, no reflection of the future carry away his relish of the instant, provided it be innocently employed. To one of right understanding it will certainly happen thus; provided he be free from bodily pains, which, notwithstanding the vain celebrated apathy of the Stoics, none was ever found to be insensible of, and whoever has pretended to the contrary, must be as ridiculous as affected.

But to satisfy your excellency, these ladies are of the new Cabal; a sect (however innocent in itself) that does not fail from meeting its share of censure from the world. Alas! what can they do? How unfortunate are women? if they seek their diversion out of themselves and include the other sex, they must be Criminal? If in themselves (as those of the new Cabal) still they are criminal? Tho' censurers must carry their imaginations a much greater length than I am able to do mine, to explain this hypothesis with success, they pretend to find in these the vices of old Rome revived; and quote you certain detestable authors, who (to amuse posterity) have introduced you lasting monuments of vice, which could only subsist in imagination; and can in reality have no other foundation, than what are to be found in the dreams of poets, and the ill nature of those censurers, who will have no diversions innocent, but what themselves advance!

Oh how laudable! how extraordinary! how wonderful! is the uncommon happiness of the cabal? They have wisely excluded that rapacious sex, who making a prey of the honor of ladies, find their greatest satisfaction (some few excepted) in boasting of their good fortune. The very chocolate-houses being witnesses of their self-love, where promiscuously, among the known and unknown, they expose the letters of the fair, explain the mysterious, and refine upon the happy part, in their redundancy of vanity, consulting nothing but what may feed the insatiable hydra!

The Cabal run no such dangers, they have all of happiness in themselves! Two beautiful ladies joined in an excess of amity (no word is tender enough to express their new delight) innocently embrace! for how can they be guilty? They vow eternal tenderness, they exclude the men, and condition that they will always do so. What irregularity can there be in this? 'Tis true, some things may be strained a little too far, and that causes reflections to be cast upon the rest. One of the fair, could not defend herself from receiving an importunate visit from a person of the troublesome sex. The lady who was her favorite, came unexpectedly at the same time upon another. Armida heard her chair set down in the hall, and presently knew her voice, enquiring with precipitation who was above? Having observed a common coach at the gate without a livery: the lover become surprised to the last degree, to see Armida's; she trembled! she turned pale! she conjured him to pass into her closet, and consent to be concealed till the lady was gone! His curiosity made him as obliging as she could desire; he was no sooner withdrawn, but his fair rival entered the chamber enraged, her voice shrill, her tone inquisitive and menacing, the extremes of jealousy in her eyes and air. Where is this inconstant—where is this ungrateful girl—? what happy wretch is it upon whom you bestow my rites!

to whom do you deliver the possession of my kisses and embraces? upon whom bestow that heart so invaluable, and for which I have paid the equivalent!— Come let us see this monster to whom my happiness is sacrificed—? Are you not sufficiently warned by the ruin of so many? are you also eager to be exposed, to be undone, to be food for vanity, to fill the detestable creatures with vain glory! what recompense?—ah, what satisfaction!—Can there be in any heart of theirs, more than in mine—Have they more tenderness—more endearments—their truth cannot come in comparison! besides, they find their account in treachery and boasting, their pride is gratified; whilst our interest is in mutual secrecy, in mutual justice, and in mutual constancy.

Such excursions as these, have given occasion to the enemies of the cabal to refine, as much as they please, upon the mysteries of it; there are, who will not allow of innocency in any intimacies. Detestable censurers, who after the manner of the Athenians, will not believe so great a man as Socrates (him, whom the oracle delivered to be the wisest of all men) could see every hour the beauty of an Alcibiades without taxing his sensibility. How did they recriminate for his affection, for his cares, his tenderness, to the lovely youth? how have they delivered him down to posterity, as blamable for a too guilty passion, for his beautiful pupil?—Since then it is not in the fate of even so wise a man to avoid the censure of the busy and the bold, care ought to be taken by others (less fortified against occasion of detraction, in declining such unaccountable intimacies) to prevent the ill-natured world's refining upon their mysterious innocence.

The persons who passed us in those three coaches, were returning from one of their private, I was going to say silent meetings; but far be it from me to detract from any of the attributes of the sex. The Lady L—— and her daughters make four of the Cabal. They have taken a little lodging about twelve furlongs from Angela, in a place obscure and pleasant, with a magazine of good wine and necessary conveniences, as to chambers of repose, a tolerable garden, and the country in prospect. They wear away the indulgent happy hours according to their own taste; their coaches and people (of whom they always take as few with them as possible) are left to wait at the convenient distance of a field in length, an easy walk to their bower of bliss. The day and hour of their rendezvous is appointed before-hand; they meet, they caress, they swear inviolable secrecy and amity; the glass corroborates their endearments, they momently exclude the men, fortify themselves in the precepts of virtue and chastity against all their destestable undermining arts, arraign without pity or compassion those who have been so unfortunate as to fall into their snare: propagate their principles of exposing them without mercy—give rules to such of the Cabal who are not married, how to behave themselves to such who they think fit they should marry; no such weighty affair being to be accomplished without the mutual consent of the society: at the same time lamenting the custom of the world, that has made it convenient (nay, almost indispensable) for all ladies once to marry. To those that have husbands, they have other instructions, in which this is sure to be one; to reserve their heart, their tender amity for their fair friend: and article in this well-bred wilfully undistinguishing age, which the husband seems to be rarely solicitous of.

Those who are, in their opinion, so happy as to be released from the imposing matrimonial fetters, are thought the ornament of the Cabal, and by all most happy: they claim an ascendancy, a right of governing, of admitting or excluding, in both they are extremely nice; with particular reserve to the constitution of the novice, they strictly examine her genius, whether it have fitted her for the mysteries of the Cabal, as if she may be rendered insensible on the side of nature. Nature, who has the trick of making them dote on the opposite improving sex, for if her foible be found directed to what nature inspires, she is unanimously excluded, and particular injunctions bestowed upon all the members of this distinguishing society from admitting her to their bosom, or initiating her in the mysteries of their endearments.

Secrecy also is a material article; this they inviolably promise, nor is it the least part of the instruction given to a new bride, lest she let her husband into a mystery (however innocent) that may expose and ridicule the community, as it happened in the case of the beautiful virgin Euphelia. No sooner did she appear as attendant on the queen, but the eyes of all the circle were directed to her; the men adored: the ladies would have discovered something to destroy that adoration, if it had been possible, except the Marchioness de Lerma, who bold and masculine, loudly taxed these invidious spectators of ill nature and malice. She took the fair maid into especial consideration, sheltered her under her distinguishing protection; and, in short, introduced her into the Cabal, of which, they say, the Marchioness was one of the first founders in Atalantis. Having something so robust in her air and mien, that the other sex would have certainly claimed her for one of theirs, if she had not thought fit to declare her self by her habit (alone) to be of the other; insomuch, that I have often heard it lamented by the curious, who have taxed themselves of negligence, and were intimate with her Lord, when living, that they did not desire him to explain upon that query.

Euphelia flourished under the shine of so great a favorite; the Marquis de los Minos fell in love with her; there was nothing to obstruct his happiness but the Marchioness de Lerma's jealousy. Enraged to lose her beautiful pupil, she traversed her advancement all that lay in her power; but the honor of such a marriage being conspicuous on the young virgin's side, she was forced to give up the secrets of the Cabal, and sacrifice the Marchioness's honor, to preserve the opinion of her own.

Some few such discoveries, have happened to cast a taint upon the innocency of the cabal. How malicious is the world? Who would not avoid their censure if it were possible? We must do justice to the endeavors of the witty Marchioness of Sandomire, when she used to mask her diversions in the habit of the other sex, and with her female favorite Ianthe wander thro' the Gallant Quarter of Atalantis in search of adventures. But what adventures? Good Heaven! none that could in reality wound her chastity! Her virtue sacred to her Lord, and the marriage bed, was preserved inviolable! For what could reflect back upon it with any prejudice, in the little liberties she took with her own sex? Whom she used to cajole, with the affected seeming gallantry of the other. Engage and carry them to the public gardens, and the houses of entertainment with music, and all diversions. These creatures of hire, failed not to find their account, in obliging the Marchioness's and Ianthe's peculiar taste, by all the liberties that belonged to women of their loose character and indigence. Tho' I should look upon it as an excess of mortification, were I the Marchioness, to see the corruption of the sex, and to what extremes, vice may step by step, lead those who were born, and probably educated in the road of innocence. It may be surely counted an inhumane curiosity, and shows a height of courage, more blamable than otherwise, not to be dejected at the brutality, the degeneracy of those of our own species.

The Viceroy of Peru's Lady has a more extensive taste, her circle admitting the eminent of both sexes. None can doubt of her condescension to the men, and because she will leave nothing undiscovered or unattempted in the map of tenderness, she has encouraged the warbling Lindamire (low as is her rank) to explain to her the terra incognita of the Cabal. Not one of 'em but think themselves honored by a person of her distinction and agreeable merit. To complete their happiness they seem to wish (but I doubt[1] it is in vain) thàt it were possible to exclude the other sex, and engross her wholly to their own. But alas! what hopes? Her heart, her eyes, her air, call for other approbations, the admiration of the men! In her alone that diffusive vanity is pardonable, is taking. She undoubtedly knows herself born to a greater capacity of giving happiness, than ought to fall to the share of one mortal; and therefore in her just and equal distribution of beauty, she seems to leave none of her numerous favorites, solid reason of complaint, that they are not in their turn considered as they deserve.

One of the ladies of the Cabal, that was in the leading coach, is a writer. The Chevalier Pierro, without having much wit of his own, married her for hers. A strange paradox! for what is music to the deaf, beauty to the blind? or the best Italian strains to a person without ear or judgment? Yet this was the Chevalier's case, and he made an admirable husband; believing (as he ought) that his wife was never in the wrong, nor himself in the right, but when she said so. Her wit was the leading card, which he was sure to follow, and like a lover (rather than a husband) never renounced. Add to this his youth, good shape, and an air of the world, which might make him in most companies, be esteemed a genteel man. Tho' with the

---

[1] Suspect.

addition, even of gratitude, Zara could not find her happiness in him; but because she would do nothing against her duty, and was a slave professed to outward honor and virtue, she obliged the Marquis— (who did her the courtesy of some of his superficial gallantries) to dress in the habit of her own sex. Thus was the marine lover introduced into her very innermost apartment, the cabinet; sacred to the muses and her self, where her obsequious husband durst never approach uncalled, nor was, but upon eminent days of grace, admitted.

The Marquis, who had a thousand adventures in his head, could not rest long upon any one. Besides he had a left-hand wife that took up the real tenderness of his heart. What he bestowed upon others was but by way of comparison to endear her the more to him, and as a foil to set off the luster of her charms. He soon grew weary of Zara's affair, not finding it possible to come up to the height of her love-sick romantic expectations. She, who had all the muses in her head, wanted to be caressed in a poetical manner; her lover by her good will should not be less than Apollo in his attributes of flame and fancy. Thus would she have been adored, but that was not to be expected from the Marquis, whose heart was engaged. Nor could any but a poet answer the extravagances of a poetess's expectation. Seignior Mompellier was newly become the fashion (his very just and admirable poem, having with applause introduced him) this was a lover indeed worth ten thousand of the vulgar; nor was cruelty one of his defects, the fair sex never had reason to complain of him that way. Zara, to the utmost extent of her poetical capacity, gave him to know in printed heroics, that she did justice to his extreme merit, not doubting, after this advance, but he would be grateful to hers. But whether her not being a beauty, or the Seignior's having wit enough for himself and a mistress too, caused him to slight that talent, and to neglect his good fortune. 'Tis certain she now speaks of him in terms that no way answers her beginning admiration.

Thus, discouraged by the men, she fell into the taste of the Cabal.

There are others of the Cabal, that lavish vast sums upon their inamorettos, with the impressment, diligence and warmth of a beginning lover. I could name a widow or two, who have almost undone themselves by their profuseness: so sacred and invincible is their principle of amity, that misfortunes cannot shake. In this little commonwealth is no property; whatever a lady possesses, is, sans ceremony, at the service, and for the use of her fair friend, without the vain nice scruple of being obliged. 'Tis her right; the other disputes it not; no, not so much as in thought, they have no reserve; mutual love bestows all things in common; 'twould be against the dignity of the passion, and unworthy such exalted abstracted notions as theirs. How far laudable your divinities will conclude of these tender amities (with all possible submission) I refer to your better judgments, and undisputed prerogative of setting the stamp of approbation, or dislike, upon all things.

Astrea. It is something so new and uncommon, so laudable and blamable, that we don't know how to determine; especially wanting light even to guess at what you call the mysteries of the Cabal. If only tender friendship, inviolable and sincere, be the regard, what can be more meritorious, or a truer emblem of their happiness above? 'Tis by imitation, the nearest approach they can make; a feint, a distant landscape of immortal joys. But if they carry it a length beyond what nature designed, and fortify themselves by these new-formed amities against the hymeneal union, or give their husbands but a second place in their affection and cares; 'tis wrong and to be blamed. Thus far to the merit of the thing it self. But when we look with true regard to the world, if it permit a shadow of suspicion, a bare imagination, that the mysteries they pretend, have any thing in 'em contrary to kind, and that strict modesty and virtue do not adorn and support their conversation; 'tis to be avoided and condemned; lest they give occasion for obscene laughter, new invented satire, fanciful jealousies and impure distrusts, in that nice unforgiving sex: who arbitrarily decide, that woman was only created (with all her beauty, softness, passions and complete tenderness) to adorn the husband's reign, perfect his happiness, and propagate the kind.

Lady Mary Wortley Montagu

Lady Mary Wortley Montagu

(1689–1762)

Adventurous and learned, Lady Mary Wortley Montagu was a celebrated literary figure of the eighteenth century. She traveled in Europe, lived in Turkey for over a year and in Italy for some twenty years. A victim of smallpox, she helped to popularize smallpox inoculation in England by having her own children inoculated. She wrote poetry, published anonymous essays on feminism and politics, and wrote volumes of letters, in which she often described the obstacles faced by learned women. The following selections include letters describing her relationship with her husband, from whom she eventually separated; letters describing her travels and her observations about women in other countries; and a letter to her daughter on the education of Lady Montagu's granddaughter.

FROM THE LETTERS AND WORKS OF LADY MARY WORTLEY MONTAGU

TO MR. WORTLEY MONTAGU.

[*March 28, 1710* [1]]

Perhaps you'll be surprized at this letter; I have had many debates with myself before I could resolve on it. I know it is not acting in form, but I do not look upon you as I do upon the rest of the world, and by what I do for *you,* you are not to judge my manner of acting with others. You are brother to a woman I tenderly loved; my protestations of friendship are not like other people's, I never speak but what I mean, and when I say I love, 'tis for ever. I had that real concern for Mrs. Wortley, I look with some regard on every one that is related to her. This and my long acquaintance with you may in some measure excuse what I am now doing. I am surprised at one of the Tatlers you send me; is it possible to have any sort of esteem for a

---

[1] A copy in Mr. W.'s writing is indorsed "28 March, To Wortley."

person one believes capable of having such trifling inclinations? Mr. Bickerstaff[2] has very wrong notions of our sex. I can say there are some of us that despise charms of show, and all the pageantry of greatness, perhaps with more ease than any of the philosophers. In contemning the world, they seem to take pains to contemn it; we despise it, without taking the pains to read lessons of morality to make us do it. At least I know I have always looked upon it with contempt, without being at the expense of one serious reflection to oblige me to it. I carry the matter yet farther; was I to choose of two thousand pounds a year or twenty thousand, the first would be my choice. There is something of an unavoidable *embarras* in making what is called a great figure in the world; [it] takes off from the happiness of life; I hate the noise and hurry inseparable from great estates and titles, and look upon both as blessings that ought only to be given to fools, for 'tis only to them that they are blessings. The pretty fellows you speak of, I own entertain me sometimes; but is it impossible to be diverted with what one despises? I can laugh at a puppet-show; at the same time I know there is nothing in it worth my attention or regard. General notions are generally wrong. Ignorance and folly are thought the best foundations for virtue, as if not knowing what a good wife is was necessary to make one so. I confess that can never be my way of reasoning; as I always forgive an *injury* when I think it not done out of malice, I can never think myself *obliged* by what is done without design. Give me leave to say it, (I know it sounds vain,) I know how to make a man of sense happy; but then that man must resolve to contribute something towards it himself. I have so much esteem for you, I should be very sorry to hear you was unhappy; but for the world I would not be the instrument of making you so; which (of the humour you are) is hardly to be avoided if I am your wife. You distrust me—I can neither be easy, nor loved, where I am distrusted. Nor do I believe your passion for me is what you pretend it; at least I am sure was I in love I could not talk as you do. Few women would have spoke so plainly as I have done; but to dissemble is among the things I never do. I take more pains to approve my conduct to myself than to the world; and would not have to accuse

2 The Tatler appeared under the fictitious name of Isaac Bickerstaff.

myself of a minute's deceit. I wish I loved you enough to devote myself to be for ever miserable, for the pleasure of a day or two's happiness. I cannot resolve upon it. You must think otherwise of me, or not at all.

I don't enjoin you to burn this letter. I know you will. 'Tis the first I ever writ to one of your sex, and shall be the last. You must never expect another. I resolve against all correspondence of the kind; my resolutions are seldom made, and never broken.

TO MR. WORTLEY MONTAGU.

Saturday morning [*August, 1712*].

I writ you a letter last night in some passion. I begin to fear again; I own myself a coward.—You made no reply to one part of my letter concerning my fortune. I am afraid you flatter yourself that my F. [father] may be at length reconciled and brought to reasonable terms. I am convinced, by what I have often heard him say, speaking of other cases like this, he never will. The fortune he has engaged to give with me, was settled on my B. [brother's] marriage, on my sister and on myself; but in such a manner, that it was left in his power to give it all to either of us, or divide it as he thought fit. He has given it all to me. Nothing remains for my sister, but the free bounty of my F. [father] from what he can save; which, notwithstanding the greatness of his estate, may be very little. Possibly after I have disobliged him so much, he may be glad to have her so easily provided for, with money already raised; especially if he has a design to marry himself, as I hear. I do not speak this that you should not endeavour to come to terms with him, if you please; but I am fully persuaded it will be to no purpose. He will have a very good answer to make:—that I suffered this match to proceed; that I made him make a very silly figure in it; that I have let him spend 400*l.* in wedding-cloaths; all which I saw without saying any thing. When I first pretended to oppose this match, he told me he was sure I had some other design in my head; I denied it with truth. But you see how little appearance there is of that truth. He proceeded with telling me that he never

by a Woman writt

would enter into treaty with another man, &c., and that I should be sent immediately into the North to stay there; and, when he died, he would only leave me an annuity of 400*l*. I had not courage to stand this view, and I submitted to what he pleased. He will now object against me,—why, since I intended to marry in this manner, I did not persist in my first resolution; that it would have been as easy for me to run away from T. [Thoresby] as from hence; and to what purpose did I put him, and the gentleman I was to marry, to expences, &c.? He will have a thousand plausible reasons for being irreconcilable, and 'tis very probable the world will be of his side. Reflect now for the last time in what manner you must take me. I shall come to you with only a night-gown and petticoat, and that is all you will get with me. I told a lady of my friends what I intend to do. You will think her a very good friend when I tell you she has proffered to lend us her house if we would come there the first night. I did not accept of this till I had let you know it. If you think it more convenient to carry me to your lodgings, make no scruple of it. Let it be where it will: if I am your wife I shall think no place unfit for me where you are. I beg we may leave London next morning, wherever you intend to go. I should wish to go out of England if it suits with your affairs. You are the best judge of your father's temper. If you think it would be obliging to him, or necessary for you, I will go with you immediately to ask his pardon and his blessing. If that is not proper at first, I think the best scheme is going to the Spa. When you come back, you may endeavour to make your father admit of seeing me, and treat with mine (though I persist in thinking it will be to no purpose). But I cannot think of living in the midst of my relations and acquaintance after so unjustifiable a step:—unjustifiable to the world,—but I think I can justify myself to myself. I again beg you to hire a coach to be at the door early Monday morning, to carry us some part of our way, wherever you resolve our journey shall be. If you determine to go to that lady's house, you had better come with a coach and six at seven o'clock to-morrow. She and I will be in the balcony that looks on the road: you have nothing to do but to stop under it, and we will come down to you. Do in this what you like best. After all, think very seriously. Your letter, which will be waited for, is to determine every thing. I forgive you a coarse expression in

Lady Mary Wortley Montagu

your last, which, however, I wish had not been there. You might have said something like it without expressing it in that manner; but there was so much complaisance in the rest of it I ought to be satisfied. You can shew me no goodness I shall not be sensible of. However, think again, and resolve never to think of me if you have the least doubt, or that it is likely to make you uneasy in your fortune. I believe to travel is the most likely way to make a solitude agreeable, and not tiresome: remember you have promised it.

'Tis something odd for a woman that brings nothing to expect any thing; but after the way of my education, I dare not pretend to live but in some degree suitable to it. I had rather die than return to a dependancy upon relations I have disobliged. Save me from that fear if you love me. If you cannot, or think I ought not to expect it, be sincere and tell me so. 'Tis better I should not be yours at all, than, for a short happiness, involve myself in ages of misery. I hope there will never be occasion for this precaution; but, however, 'tis neces-sary to make it. I depend entirely on your honour, and I cannot sus-pect you of any way doing wrong. Do not imagine I shall be angry at any thing you can tell me. Let it be sincere; do not impose on a woman that leaves all things for you.

TO MR. WORTLEY MONTAGU.

Friday night [*15th Aug., 1712*].

I tremble for what we are doing.—Are you sure you will love me for ever? Shall we never repent? I fear and I hope. I foresee all that will happen on this occasion. I shall incense my family in the highest degree. The generality of the world will blame my conduct, and the relations and friends of—[3] will invent a thousand stories of me; yet, 'tis possible, you may recompense everything to me. In this letter, which I am fond of, you promise me all that I wish. Since I writ so far, I received your Friday letter. I will be only yours, and I will do what you please.

---

[3] So in the original. Who was the unfortunate lover does not appear. He is else-where spoken of as a "Mr. K.," and it appears that he had estates in Ireland.

by a Woman writt

You shall hear from me again to-morrow, not to contradict, but to give some directions. My resolution is taken. Love me and use me well.

TO MR. WORTLEY MONTAGU.

> Walling Wells,[4] Oct. 22 [1712], which is the first post I could write, Monday night being so fatigued and sick I went straight to bed from the coach.

I don't know very well how to begin; I am perfectly unacquainted with a proper matrimonial stile. After all, I think 'tis best to write as if we were not married at all. I lament your absence, as if you was still my lover, and I am impatient to hear you are got safe to Durham, and that you have fixed a time for your return.

I have not been very long in this family; and I fancy myself in that described in the Spectator. The good people here look upon their children with a fondness that more than recompenses their care of them. I don't perceive much distinction in regard to their merits; and when they speak sense or nonsense, it affects the parents with almost the same pleasure. My friendship for the mother, and kindness for Miss Biddy, make me endure the squalling of Miss Nanny and Miss Mary with abundance of patience: and my foretelling the future conquests of the eldest daughter, makes me very well with the family.—I don't know whether you will presently find out that this seeming impertinent account is the tenderest expressions of my love to you; but it furnishes my imagination with agreeable pictures of our future life; and I flatter myself with the hopes of one day enjoying with you the same satisfactions; and that, after as many years together, I may see you retain the same fondness for me as I shall certainly mine for you, and the noise of a nursery may have more charms for us than the music of an opera.

[*Torn*] as these are the sure effect of my sincere love, since 'tis the nature of that passion to entertain the mind with pleasures in pros-

---

[4] Near Worksop, in Nottinghamshire, and about eleven miles from Thoresby. Lady Mary was on a visit to her friends Mr. and Mrs. White, who lived at Walling Wells.

pect; and I check myself when I grieve for your absence, by remembering how much reason I have to rejoice in the hope of passing my whole life with you. A good fortune not to be valued!—I am afraid of telling you that I return thanks for it to Heaven, because you will charge me with hypocrisy; but you are mistaken: I assist every day at public prayers in this family, and never forget in my private ejaculations how much I owe to Heaven for making me yours. 'Tis candle-light, or I should not conclude so soon.

TO MR. WORTLEY MONTAGU.

[*Indorsed "24th November," 1714.*]

I have taken up and laid down my pen several times, very much unresolved in what stile I ought to write to you: for once I suffer my inclination to get the better of my reason. I have not oft opportunities of indulging myself, and I will do it in this one letter. I know very well that nobody was ever teized into a liking: and 'tis perhaps harder to revive a past one, than to overcome an aversion; but I cannot forbear any longer telling you, I think you use me very unkindly. I don't say so much of your absence, as I should do if you was in the country and I in London; because I would not have you believe I am impatient to be in town, when I say I am impatient to be with you; but I am very sensible I parted with you in July and 'tis now the middle of November. As if this was not hardship enough, you do not tell me you are sorry for it. You write seldom, and with so much indifference as shews you hardly think of me at all. I complain of ill health, and you only say you hope 'tis not so bad as I make it. You never enquire after your child. I would fain flatter myself you have more kindness for me and him than you express; but I reflect with grief a man that is ashamed of passions that are natural and reasonable, is generally proud of those that [are] shameful and silly.

You should consider solitude, and spleen the consequence of solitude, is apt to give the most melancholy ideas, and there needs at least tender letters and kind expressions to hinder uneasinesses almost inseparable from absence. I am very sensible, how far I ought to be contented when your affairs oblige you to be without me. I would not have you do them any prejudice; but a little kindness will cost you nothing. I do not bid you lose any thing by hasting to see me, but I would have you think it a misfortune when we are asunder. Instead of that, you seem perfectly pleased with our separation, and indifferent how long it continues. When I reflect on all your behaviour, I am ashamed of my own: I think I am playing the part of my Lady Winchester.[5] At least be as generous as my lord; and as he made her an early confession of his aversion, own to me your inconstancy, and upon my word I will give you no more trouble about it. I have concealed as long as I can, the uneasiness the nothingness of your letters has given me, under an affected indifference; but dissimulation always sits awkwardly upon me; I am weary of it; and must beg you to write to me no more, if you cannot bring yourself to write otherwise. Multiplicity of business or diversions may have engaged you, but all people find time to do what they have a mind to. If your inclination is gone, I had rather never receive a letter from you, than one which, in lieu of comfort for your absence, gives me a pain even beyond it. For my part, as 'tis my first, this is my last complaint, and your next of the kind shall go back enclosed to you in blank paper.

FROM LETTERS DURING THE EMBASSY TO CONSTANTINOPLE.

TO THE LADY R. [RICH].

Vienna, Sept. 20, O.S. [1716].

I am extremely pleased, but not at all surprised, at the long delightful letter you have had the goodness to send me. I know that you can think of an absent friend even in the midst of a court, and that you love to oblige, where you can have no view of a return; and I expect

---

[5] Lady Mary's early friend, Lady Anne Vaughan, daughter to the Earl of Carberry, was married to the Marquis of Winchester, afterwards Duke of Bolton, in July, 1713. They separated soon after their marriage.

from you that you should love me, and think of me, when you don't see me.

I have compassion for the mortifications that you tell me befall our little friend, and I pity her much more, since I know that they are only owing to the barbarous customs of our country. Upon my word, if she was here, she would have no other fault but being something too young for the fashion, and she has nothing to do but to transplant hither about seven years hence, to be again a young and blooming beauty. I can assure you that wrinkles, or a small stoop in the shoulders, nay, grey hair itself, is no objection to the making new conquests. I know you cannot easily figure to yourself a young fellow of five-and-twenty ogling my Lady Suff—[Suffolk] with passion, or pressing to lead the Countess of O—d [Oxford] from an opera. But such are the sights I see every day, and I don't perceive any body surprised at them but myself. A woman, till five-and-thirty, is only looked upon as a raw girl, and can possibly make no noise in the world till about forty. I don't know what your ladyship may think of this matter; but 'tis a considerable comfort to me, to know there is upon earth such a paradise for old women; and I am content to be insignificant at present, in the design of returning when I am fit to appear nowhere else. I cannot help lamenting upon this occasion, the pitiful case of too many good English ladies, long since retired to prudery and ratafia, whom if their stars had luckily conducted hither, would still shine in the first rank of beauties; and then that perplexing word reputation has quite another meaning here than what you give it at London; and getting a lover is so far from losing, that 'tis properly getting reputation; ladies being much more respected in regard to the rank of their lovers, than that of their husbands.

But what you'll think very odd, the two sects that divide our whole nation of petticoats, are utterly unknown. Here are neither coquettes nor prudes. No woman dares appear coquette enough to encourage two lovers at a time. And I have not seen any such prudes as to pretend fidelity to their husbands, who are certainly the best natured set of people in the world, and they look upon their wives' gallants as favourably as men do upon their deputies, that take the troublesome part of their business off of their hands; though they have not the less to do; for they are generally deputies in another place themselves; in

one word, 'tis the established custom for every lady to have two husbands, one that bears the name, and another that performs the duties.
And these engagements are so well known, that it would be a down-
right affront, and publicly resented, if you invited a woman of quality
to dinner, without at the same time inviting her two attendants of
lover and husband, between whom she always sits in state with great
gravity. These sub-marriages generally last twenty years together,
and the lady often commands the poor lover's estate even to the utter
ruin of his family; though they are as seldom begun by any passion
as other matches. But a man makes but an ill figure that is not in
some commerce of this nature; and a woman looks out for a lover as
soon as she's married, as part of her equipage, without which she
could not be genteel; and the first article of the treaty is establishing
the pension, which remains to the lady though the gallant should
prove inconstant; and this chargeable point of honour I look upon as
the real foundation of so many wonderful instances of constancy. I
really know several women of the first quality, whose pensions are as
well known as their annual rents, and yet nobody esteems them the
less; on the contrary, their discretion would be called in question, if
they should be suspected to be mistresses for nothing; and a great
part of their emulation consists in trying who shall get most; and
having no intrigue at all is so far a disgrace, that, I'll assure you, a
lady, who is very much my friend here, told me but yesterday, how
much I was obliged to her for justifying my conduct in a conversation on my subject, where is was publicly asserted that I could not
possibly have common sense, that I had been about town above a
fortnight, and had made no steps towards commencing an amour. My
friend pleaded for me that my stay was uncertain, and she believed
that was the cause of my seeming stupidity; and this was all she could
find to say in my justification.

But one of the pleasantest adventures I ever met in my life was last
night, and which will give you a just idea after what delicate manner
the *belles passions* are managed in this country. I was at the assembly
of the Countess of ——, and the young Count of —— led me down
stairs, and he asked me how long I intended to stay here? I made
answer that my stay depended on the emperor, and it was not in my
power to determine it. Well, madam, (said he,) whether your time

here is to be long or short, I think you ought to pass it agreeably, and to that end you must engage in a little affair of the heart.—My heart (answered I gravely enough) does not engage very easily, and I have no design of parting with it. I see, madam, (said he sighing,) by the ill nature of that answer, that I am not to hope for it, which is a great mortification to me that am charmed with you. But, however, I am still devoted to your service; and since I am not worthy of entertaining you myself, do me the honour of letting me know whom you like best among us, and I'll engage to manage the affair entirely to your satisfaction.—You may judge in what manner I should have received this compliment in my own country; but I was well enough acquainted with the way of this, to know that he really intended me an obligation, and thanked him with a grave courtesy for his zeal to serve me, and only assured him that I had no occasion to make use of it.

Thus you see, my dear, gallantry and good-breeding are as different, in different climates, as morality and religion. Who have the rightest notions of both, we shall never know till the day of judgment, for which great day of *éclaircissement*, I own there is very little impatience in your, &c.

FROM THE LETTERS
OF LADY MARY WORTLEY MONTAGU

TO LADY MAR, LADY MONTAGU'S SISTER.

Adrianople, April 1, O. S., 1717.

I wish, dear sister, that you were as regular in letting me know what passes on your side of the globe as I am careful in endeavoring to amuse you by the account of all I see here that I think worth your notice. You content yourself with telling me over and over, that the town is very dull: it may possibly be dull to you, when every day does not present you with something new; but for me, that am in arrears at least two months' news, all that seems very stale with you would be very fresh and sweet here. Pray let me into more particulars, and I will try to awaken your gratitude, by giving you a full and true relation of the novelties of this place, none of which would surprise you more than the sight of my person, as I am now in my Turkish habit, though I believe you would be of my opinion, that 'tis admirably becoming. I intend to send you my picture; in the mean time accept of it here.

The first part of my dress is a pair of drawers, very full, that reach to my shoes, and conceal the legs more modestly than your petticoats. They are of a thin rose-colored damask, brocaded with silver flowers. My shoes are of white kid leather, embroidered with gold. Over this hangs my smock, of a fine white silk gauze, edged with embroidery. This smock has wide sleeves, hanging half way down the arm, and is closed at the neck with a diamond button; but the shape and color of the bosom are very well to be distinguished through it. The *antery* is a waistcoat, made close to the shape, of white and gold damask, with very long sleeves falling back, and fringed with deep gold fringe, and should have diamond or pearl buttons. My *caftan*, of the same stuff with my drawers, is a robe exactly fitted to my shape, and reaching to my feet, with very long straight falling sleeves. Over this is my girdle, of about four fingers broad, which all that can afford it have entirely of diamonds or other precious stones; those who will not be at that expense, have it of exquisite embroidery on satin; but it must be fastened before with a clasp of diamonds. The *curdee* is a loose robe they throw off or put on according to the weather, being of a rich brocade (mine is green and gold), either lined with ermine or sables; the sleeves reach very little below the shoulders. The headdress is composed of a cap, called *talpock*, which is in winter of fine velvet embroidered with pearls or diamonds, and in summer of a light shining silver stuff. This is fixed on one side of the head, hanging a little way down with a gold tassel, and bound on either with a circle of diamonds (as I have seen several) or a rich embroidered handkerchief. On the other side of the head the hair is laid flat; and here the ladies are at liberty to show their fancies: some putting flowers, others a plume of heron's feathers, and, in short, what they please; but the most general fashion is a large *bouquet* of jewels, made like natural flowers: that is, the buds, of pearl; the roses, of different colored rubies; the jasmins, of diamonds; the jonquils, of topazes, etc., so well set and enameled, 'tis hard to imagine any thing of that kind so beautiful. The hair hangs at its full length behind, divided into tresses braided with pearl or ribbon, which is always in great quantity.

I never saw in my life so many fine heads of hair. In one lady's I have counted a hundred and ten of the tresses, all natural; but it must be owned that every kind of beauty is more common here than with us. 'Tis surprising to see a young woman that is not very handsome. They have naturally the most beautiful complexion in the world, and generally large black eyes. I can assure you with great truth, that the court of England (though I believe it is the fairest in Christendom) does not contain so many beauties as are under our protection here. They generally shape their eyebrows, and both Greeks and Turks have a custom of putting round their eyes a black tincture, that, at a distance, by candle-light, adds very much to the blackness of them. I fancy many of our ladies would be overjoyed to know this secret; but 'tis too visible by day. They dye their nails a rose-color; but, I own, I can not enough accustom myself to this fashion to find any beauty in it.

As to their morality or good conduct, I can say, like Harlequin, that 'tis just as it is with you; and the Turkish ladies don't commit one sin the less for not being Christians. Now that I am a little acquainted with their ways, I can not forbear admiring either the exemplary discretion or extreme stupidity of all the writers that have given accounts of them. 'Tis very easy to see they have in reality more liberty than we have. No woman, of what rank soever, is permitted to go into the streets without two *murlins*; one that covers her face all but her eyes, and another that hides the whole dress of her head, and hangs half way down her back. Their shapes are also wholly concealed by a thing they call a *ferigee*, which no woman of any sort appears without; this has straight sleeves, that reach to their finger-ends, and it laps all round them, not unlike a riding-hood. In winter 'tis of cloth, and in summer of plain stuff or silk. You may guess, then, how effectually this disguises them, so that there is no distinguishing the great lady from her slave. 'Tis impossible for the most jealous husband to know his wife when he meets her; and no man dare touch or follow a woman in the street.

This perpetual masquerade gives them entire liberty of following their inclinations without danger of discovery. The most usual method of intrigue is to send an appointment to the lover to meet the lady at a Jew's shop, which are as notoriously convenient as our Indian-houses; and yet, even those who don't make use of them, do not scruple to go buy pennyworths, and tumble over rich goods, which are chiefly to be found among that sort of people. The great ladies seldom let their gallants know who they are; and 'tis so difficult to find it out, that they can very seldom guess at her name, whom they have corresponded with for above half a year together. You may easily imagine the number of faithful wives very small in a country where they have nothing to fear from a lover's indiscretion, since we see so many have the courage to expose themselves to that in this world, and all the threatened punishment of the next, which is never preached to the Turkish damsels. Neither have they much to apprehend from the resentment of their husband; those ladies that are rich having all their money in their own hands.

Upon the whole, I look upon the Turkish women as the only free people in the empire: the very divan pays respect to them; and the Grand-Seignior himself, when a pasha is executed, never violates the privileges of the *harem* (or women's apartment), which remains unsearched and entire to the widow. They are queens of their slaves, whom the husband has no permission so much as to look upon, except it be an old woman or two that his lady chooses. 'Tis true their law permits them four wives; but there is no instance of a man of quality that makes use of this liberty, or of a woman of rank that would suffer it.

Lady Mary Wortley Montagu

FROM THE LETTERS AND WORKS
OF LADY MARY WORTLEY MONTAGU

TO THE COUNTESS OF BUTE, LADY MONTAGU'S DAUGHTER.

Jan. 28, N.S. [1753].

Dear Child,—You have given me a great deal of satisfaction by your account of your eldest daughter. I am particularly pleased to hear she is a good arithmetician; it is the best proof of understanding: the knowledge of numbers is one of the chief distinctions between us and the brutes. If there is anything in blood, you may reasonably expect your children should be endowed with an uncommon share of good sense. Mr. Wortley's family and mine have both produced some of the greatest men that have been born in England: I mean Admiral Sandwich, and my grandfather, who was distinguished by the name of Wise William. I have heard Lord Bute's father mentioned as an extraordinary genius, though he had not many opportunities of showing it; and his uncle, the present Duke of Argyll, has one of the best heads I ever knew. I will therefore speak to you as supposing Lady Mary not only capable, but desirous of learning: in that case by all means let her be indulged in it. You will tell me I did not make it a part of your education: your prospect was very different from hers. As you had no defect either in mind or person to hinder, and much in your circumstances to attract, the highest offers, it seemed your business to learn how to live in the world, as it is hers to know how to be easy out of it. It is the common error of builders and parents to follow some plan they think beautiful (and perhaps is so), without considering that nothing is beautiful that is displaced. Hence we see so many edifices raised that the raisers can never inhabit, being too large for their fortunes. Vistas are laid open over barren heaths, and apartments contrived for a coolness very agreeable in Italy, but killing in the north of Britain: thus every woman endeavours to breed her daughter a fine lady, qualifying her for a station in which she will never appear, and at the same time incapacitating her for that retirement to which she is destined. Learning, if she has a real taste for it, will not only make her contented, but happy in it. No entertainment is so cheap as reading, nor any pleasure so lasting. She will not want new fashions, nor regret the loss of expensive diversions, or variety of company, if she can be amused with an author in her closet. To render this amusement extensive, she should be permitted to learn the languages. I have it lamented that boys lose so many years in mere learning of words: this is no objection to a girl, whose time is not so precious: she cannot advance herself in any profession, and has therefore more hours to spare; and as you say her memory is good, she will be very agreeably employed this way. There are two cautions to be given on this subject: first, not to think herself learned when she can read Latin, or even Greek. Languages are more properly to be called vehicles of learning than learning itself, as may be observed in many school-masters, who, though perhaps critics in grammar, are the most ignorant fellows upon earth. True knowledge consists in knowing things, not words. I would wish her no further a linguist than to enable her to read books in their originals, that are often corrupted, and always injured, by translations. Two hours' application every morning will bring this about much sooner than you can imagine, and she will have leisure enough besides to run over the English poetry, which is a more important part of a woman's education than it is generally supposed. Many a young damsel has been ruined by a fine copy of verses, which she would have laughed at if she had known it had been stolen from Mr. Waller. I remember, when I was a girl, I saved one of my companions from destruction, who communicated to me an epistle she was quite charmed with. As she had a natural good taste, she observed the lines were not so smooth as Prior's or Pope's, but had more thought and spirit than any of theirs. She was wonderfully delighted with such a demonstration of her lover's sense and passion, and not a little pleased with her own charms, that had force enough to inspire such elegancies. In the midst of this triumph I showed her that they were taken from Randolph's poems, and the unfortunate transcriber was dismissed with the scorn he deserved. To say truth, the poor plagiary was very unlucky to fall into my hands; that author being no longer in fashion, would have escaped any one of less universal reading than myself.

Lady Mary Wortley Montagu

You should encourage your daughter to talk over with you what she reads; and, as you are very capable of distinguishing, take care she does not mistake pert folly for wit and humour, or rhyme for poetry, which are the common errors of young people, and have a train of ill consequences. The second caution to be given her (and which is most absolutely necessary) is to conceal whatever learning she attains, with as much solicitude as she would hide crookedness or lameness; the parade of it can only serve to draw on her the envy, and consequently the most inveterate hatred, of all he and she fools, which will certainly be at least three parts in four of all her acquaintance. The use of knowledge in our sex, besides the amusement of solitude, is to moderate the passions, and learn to be contented with a small expense, which are the certain effects of a studious life; and it may be preferable even to that fame which men have engrossed to themselves, and will not suffer us to share. You will tell me I have not observed this rule myself; but you are mistaken: it is only inevitable accident that has given me any reputation that way. I have always carefully avoided it, and ever thought it a misfortune. The explanation of this paragraph would occasion a long digression, which I will not trouble you with, it being my present design only to say what I think useful for the instruction of my granddaughter, which I have much at heart. If she has the same inclination (I should say passion) for learning that I was born with, history, geography, and philosophy will furnish her with materials to pass away cheerfully a longer life than is allotted to mortals. I believe there are few heads capable of making Sir I. Newton's calculations, but the result of them is not difficult to be understood by a moderate capacity. Do not fear this should make her affect the character of Lady ——, or Lady ——, or Mrs. ——. Those women are ridiculous, not because they have learning, but because they have it not. One thinks herself a complete historian, after reading Echard's Roman History; another a profound philosopher, having got by heart some of Pope's unintelligible essays; and a third an able divine, on the strength of Whitefield's sermons: thus you hear them screaming politics and controversy.

It is a saying of Thucydides, ignorance is bold, and knowledge reserved. Indeed, it is impossible to be far advanced in it without being more humbled by a conviction of human ignorance, than elated by learning. At the same time I recommend books, I neither exclude work nor drawing. I think it as scandalous for a woman not to know how to use a needle, as for a man not to know how to use a sword. I was once extreme fond of my pencil, and it was a great mortification to me when my father turned off my master, having made a considerable progress for a short time I learnt. My overeagerness in the pursuit of it had brought a weakness on my eyes, that made it necessary to leave it off; and all the advantage I got was the improvement of my hand. I see, by hers, that practice will make her a ready writer: she may attain it by serving you for a secretary, when your health or affairs make it troublesome to you to write yourself; and custom will make it an agreeable amusement to her. She cannot have too many for that station of life which will probably be her fate. The ultimate end of your education was to make you a good wife (and I have the comfort to hear that you are one): hers ought to be, to make her happy in a virgin state. I will not say it is happier; but it is undoubtedly safer than any marriage. In a lottery, where there are (at the lowest computation) ten thousand blanks to a prize, it is the most prudent choice not to venture. I have always been so thoroughly persuaded of this truth, that, notwithstanding the flattering views I had for you (as I never intended you a sacrifice to my vanity), I thought I owed you the justice to lay before you all the hazards attending matrimony; you may recollect I did so in the strongest manner. Perhaps you may have more success in the instructing your daughter: she has so much company at home, she will not need seeking it abroad, and will more readily take the notions you think fit to give her. As you were alone in my family, it would have been thought a great cruelty to suffer you no companions of your own age, especially having so many near relations, and I do not wonder their opinions influenced yours. I was not sorry to see you not determined on a single life, knowing it was not your father's intention, and contented myself with endeavouring to make your home so easy that you might not be in haste to leave it.

I am afraid you will think this a very long and insignificant letter. I hope the kindness of the design will excuse it, being willing to give you every proof in my power that I am

Your most affectionate mother.

Mary Wollstonecraft

Mary Wollstonecraft

(1759–1797)

When Mary Wollstonecraft wrote about women's oppression, she wrote out of personal experience. She was the daughter of an alcoholic and brutal father. She had helped her sister escape from an unhappy marriage and had watched a close friend die in childbirth. After vainly trying to earn a living at typically "feminine" occupations, Wollstonecraft turned to writing. She wrote novels, essays, reviews, letters, and books on education and on politics. With the publication of her *A Vindication of the Rights of Woman*, a reasoned and passionate appeal for women's independence, she became the most noted feminist of her time. Shortly after the publication of *A Vindication*, she began a love affair with an American, Gilbert Imlay, and bore him a child. When Imlay deserted her and their child, Mary Wollstonecraft unsuccessfully attempted suicide, by throwing herself from a bridge into the Thames. She later returned to writing, married the philosopher, William Godwin, and bore him a daughter, Mary Shelley. The following selection from Wollstonecraft's *A vindication* reveals the brilliance with which she could argue against women's oppression; the selection from her *Letters to Imlay* suggests the extent to which she herself was subject to that oppression.

FROM A VINDICATION
OF THE RIGHTS OF WOMAN.

From Chapter II.

THE PREVAILING OPINION OF A
SEXUAL CHARACTER DISCUSSED.

To account for, and excuse the tyranny of man, many ingenious arguments have been brought forward to prove, that the two sexes, in the acquirement of virtue, ought to aim at attaining a very different character: or, to speak explicitly, women are not allowed to have sufficient strength of mind to acquire what really deserves the name of virtue. Yet it should seem, allowing them to have souls, that there is but one way appointed by providence to lead *mankind* to either virtue or happiness.

If then women are not a swarm of ephemeron triflers, why should they be kept in ignorance under the specious name of innocence? Men complain, and with reason, of the follies and caprices of our sex, when they do not keenly satirize our headstrong passions and grovelling vices. Behold, I should answer, the natural effect of ignorance! The mind will ever be unstable that has only prejudices to rest on, and the current will run with destructive fury when there are no barriers to break its force. Women are told from their infancy, and taught by the example of their mothers, that a little knowledge of human weakness, justly termed cunning, softness of temper, *outward* obedience, and a scrupulous attention to a puerile kind of propriety, will obtain for them the protection of man; and should they be beautiful, every thing else is needless, for at least twenty years of their lives.

Thus Milton describes our first frail mother; though when he tells us that women are formed for softness and sweet attractive grace, I cannot comprehend his meaning, unless, in the true Mahometan strain, he meant to deprive us of souls, and insinuate that we were beings only designed by sweet attractive grace, and docile blind obedience, to gratify the senses of man when he can no longer soar on the wing of contemplation.

How grossly do they insult us, who thus advise us only to render ourselves gentle, domestic brutes! For instance, the winning softness, so warmly, and frequently recommended, that governs by obeying. What childish expressions, and how insignificant is the being—can it be an immortal one? who will condescend to govern by such sinister methods! "Certainly," says Lord Bacon, "man is of kin to the beasts by his body: and if he be not of kin to God by his spirit, he is a base and ignoble creature!" Men, indeed, appear to me to act in a very unphilosophical manner, when they try to secure the good conduct of women by attempting to keep them always in a state of childhood. Rousseau was more consistent when he wished to stop the progress of reason in both sexes, for if men eat of the tree of knowledge, women will come in for a taste; but, from the imperfect cultivation which their understandings now receive, they only attain a knowledge of evil.

Mary Wollstonecraft

Children, I grant, should be innocent; but when the epithet is applied to men, or women, it is but a civil term for weakness. For if it be allowed that women were destined by providence to acquire human virtues, and by the exercise of their understandings, that stability of character which is the firmest ground to rest our future hopes upon, they must be permitted to turn to the fountain of light, and not forced to shape their course by the twinkling of a mere satellite. Milton, I grant, was of a very different opinion; for he only bends to the indefeasible right of beauty, though it would be difficult to render two passages which I now mean to contrast consistent. But into similar inconsistencies are great men often led by their senses.

> "To whom thus Eve with perfect beauty adorn'd:
> My Author and Disposer, what thou bidst
> Unargued I obey; so God ordains;
> God is thy law, thou mine; to know no more
> Is Woman's happiest knowledge and her praise."

These are exactly the arguments that I have used to children; but I have added, your reason is now gaining strength, and, till it arrives at some degree of maturity, you must look up to me for advice, then you ought to *think*, and only rely on God.

Yet in the following lines Milton seems to coincide with me; when he makes Adam thus expostulate with his Maker.

> "Hast thou not made me here thy substitute,
> And these inferior far beneath me set?
> Among unequals what society
> Can sort, what harmony or true delight?
> Which must be mutual, in proportion due
> Giv'n and receiv'd; but in disparity
> The one intense, the other still remiss
> Cannot well suit with either, but soon prove
> Tedious alike: of fellowship I speak
> Such as I seek fit to participate
> All rational delight—"

In treating, therefore, of the manners of women, let us, disregarding sensual arguments, trace what we should endeavour to make them in order to co-operate, if the expression be not too bold, with the Supreme Being.

By individual education, I mean, for the sense of the word is not precisely defined, such an attention to a child as will slowly sharpen the senses, form the temper, regulate the passions, as they begin to ferment, and set the understanding to work before the body arrives at maturity; so that the man may only have to proceed, not to begin, the important task of learning to think and reason.

To prevent any misconstruction, I must add, that I do not believe that a private education can work the wonders which some sanguine writers have attributed to it. Men and women must be educated, in a great degree, by the opinions and manners of the society they live in. In every age there has been a stream of popular opinion that has carried all before it, and given a family character, as it were, to the century. It may then fairly be inferred, that, till society be differently constituted, much cannot be expected from education. It is, however, sufficient for my present purpose to assert, that, whatever effect circumstances have on the abilities, every being may become virtuous by the exercise of its own reason; for if but one being was created with vicious inclinations, that is positively bad, what can save us from atheism? or if we worship a God, is not that God a devil?

Consequently, the most perfect education, in my opinion is, such an exercise of the understanding as is best calculated to strengthen the body and form the heart. Or, in other words, to enable the individual to attain such habits of virtue as will render it independent. In fact, it is a farce to call any being virtuous whose virtues do not result from the exercise of its own reason. This was Rousseau's opinion respecting men: I extend it to women, and confidently assert, that they have been drawn out of their sphere by false refinement. and not by an endeavour to acquire masculine qualities. Still the regal homage which they receive is so intoxicating, that till the manners of the times are changed, and formed on more reasonable principles, it may be impossible to convince them, that the illegitimate power, which they obtain by degrading themselves, is a curse, and that they must return to nature and equality, if they wish to secure the placid satisfaction that unsophisticated affections impart. But for this epoch we must wait—wait, perhaps, till kings and nobles, enlightened by reason, and, preferring the real dignity of man to childish state, throw off their gaudy hereditary trappings; and if then women do not resign the arbitrary power of beauty, they will prove that they have *less* mind than man.

I may be accused of arrogance; still I must declare, what I firmly believe, that all the writers who have written on the subject of female education and manners, from Rousseau to Dr. Gregory, have contributed to render women more artificial, weaker characters, than they would otherwise have been; and, consequently, more useless members of society. I might have expressed this conviction in a lower key; but I am afraid it would have been the whine of affectation, and not the faithful expression of my feelings, of the clear result, which experience and reflection have led me to draw. When I come to that division of the subject, I shall advert to the passages that I more particularly disapprove of, in the works of the authors I have just alluded to; but it is first necessary to observe, that my objection extends to the whole purport of those books, which tend, in my opinion, to degrade one half of the human species, and render women pleasing at the expense of every solid virtue.

Though to reason on Rousseau's ground, if man did attain a degree of perfection of mind when his body arrived at maturity, it might be proper in order to make a man and his wife *one*, that she should rely entirely on his understanding; and the graceful ivy, clasping the oak that supported it, would form a whole in which strength and beauty would be equally conspicuous. But, alas! husbands, as well as their helpmates, are often only overgrown children; nay, thanks to early debauchery, scarcely men in their outward form, and if the blind lead the blind, one need not come from heaven to tell us the consequence.

Many are the causes that, in the present corrupt state of society, contribute to enslave women by cramping their understandings and sharpening their senses. One, perhaps, that silently does more mischief than all the rest, is their disregard of order.

To do every thing in an orderly manner, is a most important precept, which women, who, generally speaking, receive only a disorderly kind of education, seldom attend to with that degree of exactness that men, who from their infancy are broken into method, observe. This negligent kind of guesswork, for what other epithet can be used to point out the random exertions of a sort of instinctive common sense, never brought to the test of reason? prevents their generalizing matters of fact, so they do to-day what they did yesterday, merely because they did it yesterday.

This contempt of the understanding in early life has more baneful consequences than is commonly supposed; for the little knowledge which women of strong minds attain, is, from various circumstances, of a more desultory kind than the knowledge of men, and it is acquired more by sheer observations on real life, than from comparing what has been individually observed with the results of experience generalized by speculation. Led by their dependent situation and domestic employments more into society, what they learn is rather by snatches; and as learning is with them, in general, only a secondary thing, they do not pursue any one branch with that persevering ardour necessary to give vigour to the faculties, and clearness to the judgment. In the present state of society, a little learning is required to support the character of a gentleman; and boys are obliged to submit to a few years of discipline. But in the education of women the cultivation of the understanding is always subordinate to the acquirement of some corporeal accomplishment; even while enervated by confinement and false notions of modesty, the body is prevented from attaining that grace and beauty which relaxed half-formed limbs never exhibit. Besides, in youth their faculties are not brought forward by emulation; and having no serious scientific study, if they have natural sagacity it is turned too soon on life and manners. They dwell on effects, and modifications, without tracing them back to causes; and complicated rules to adjust behaviour are a weak substitute for simple principles.

As a proof that education gives this appearance of weakness to females, we may instance the example of military men, who are, like them, sent into the world before their minds have been stored with knowledge or fortified by principles. The consequences are similar; soldiers acquire a little superficial knowledge, snatched from the muddy current of conversation, and, from continually mixing with society, they gain, what is termed a knowledge of the world; and this acquaintance with manners and customs has frequently been con-

Mary Wollstonecraft

founded with a knowledge of the human heart. But can the crude fruit of casual observation, never brought to the test of judgment, formed by comparing speculation and experience, deserve such a distinction? Soldiers, as well as women, practice the minor virtues with punctilious politeness. Where is then the sexual difference, when the education has been the same; All the difference that I can discern, arises from the superior advantage of liberty which enables the former to see more of life.

It is wandering from my present subject, perhaps, to make a political remark; but as it was produced naturally by the train of my reflections, I shall not pass it silently over.

Standing armies can never consist of resolute, robust men; they may be well disciplined machines, but they will seldom contain men under the influence of strong passions or with very vigorous faculties. And as for any depth of understanding, I will venture to affirm, that it is as rarely to be found in the army as amongst women; and the cause I maintain, is the same. It may be further observed, that officers are also particularly attentive to their persons, fond of dancing, crowded rooms, adventures, and ridicule. Like the *fair* sex, the business of their lives is gallantry. They were taught to please, and they only live to please. Yet they do not lose their rank in the distinction of sexes, for they are still reckoned superior to women, though in what their superiority consists, beyond what I have just mentioned, it is difficult to discover.

The great misfortune is this, that they, both acquire manners before morals, and a knowledge of life before they have from reflection, any acquaintance with the grand ideal outline of human nature. The consequence is natural; satisfied with common nature, they become a prey to prejudices, and taking all their opinions on credit, they blindly submit to authority. So that if they have any sense, it is a kind of instinctive glance, that catches proportions, and decides with respect to manners; but fails when arguments are to be pursued below the surface or opinions analyzed.

May not the same remark be applied to women? Nay, the argument may be carried still further, for they are both thrown out of a useful station by the unnatural distinctions established in civilized life. Riches and hereditary honours have made cyphers of women to give consequence to the numerical figure; and idleness has produced a mixture of gallantry and despotism in society, which leads the very men who are the slaves of their mistresses, to tyrannize over their sisters, wives and daughters. This is only keeping them in rank and file, it is true. Strengthen the female mind by enlarging it, and there will be an end to blind obedience; but, as blind obedience is ever sought for by power, tyrants and sensualists are in the right when they endeavour to keep women in the dark, because the former only want slaves, and the latter a play-thing. The sensualist, indeed, has been the most dangerous of tyrants, and women have been duped by their lovers, as princes by their ministers, whilst dreaming that they reigned over them.

I now principally allude to Rousseau, for his character of Sophia, is, undoubtedly, a captivating one, though it appears to me grossly unnatural; however, it is not the superstructure, but the foundation of her character, the principles on which her education was built, that I mean to attack; nay, warmly as I admire the genius of that able writer, whose opinions I shall often have occasion to cite, indignation always takes place of admiration, and the rigid frown of insulted virtue effaces the smile of complacency, which his eloquent periods are wont to raise, when I read his voluptuous reveries. Is this the man, who, in his ardour for virtue, would banish all the soft arts of peace, and almost carry us back to Spartan discipline? Is this the man who delights to paint the useful struggles of passion, the triumphs of good dispositions, and the heroic flights which carry the glowing soul out of itself? How are these mighty sentiments lowered when he describes the pretty foot and enticing airs of his little favourite! But, for the present, I wave the subject, and, instead of severely reprehending the transient effusions of overweening sensibility, I shall only observe, that whoever has cast a benevolent eye on society, must often have been gratified by the sight of humble mutual love, not dignified by sentiment, nor strengthened by a union in intellectual pursuits. The domestic trifles of the day have afforded matter for cheerful converse, and innocent caresses have softened toils which did not require great exercise of mind, or stretch of thought: yet, has not the sight of this moderate felicity excited more tenderness than respect? An emotion similar to what we feel when children are playing, or animals sporting, whilst the contemplation of the noble struggles of suffering merit has raised admiration, and carried our thoughts to that world where sensation will give place to reason.

Women are, therefore, to be considered either as moral beings, or so weak that they must be entirely subjected to the superior faculties of men.

Let us examine this question. Rousseau declares, that a woman should never, for a moment feel herself independent, that she should be governed by fear to exercise her *natural* cunning, and made a coquetish slave in order to render her a more alluring object of desire, a *sweeter* companion to man, whenever he chooses to relax himself. He carries the arguments, which he pretends to draw from the indications of nature, still further, and insinuates that truth and fortitude the corner stones of all human virtue, shall be cultivated with certain restrictions, because with respect to the female character, obedience is the grand lesson which ought to be impressed with unrelenting rigour.

What nonsense! when will a great man arise with sufficient strength of mind to puff away the fumes which pride and sensuality have thus spread over the subject! If women are by nature inferior to men, their virtues must be the same in quality, if not in degree, or virtue is a relative idea; consequently, their conduct should be founded on the same principles and have the same aim.

Connected with man as daughters, wives, and mothers, their moral character may be estimated by their manner of fulfilling those simple duties; but the end, the grand end of their exertions should be to unfold their own faculties, and acquire the dignity of conscious virtue. They may try to render their road pleasant; but ought never to forget, in common with man, that life yields not the felicity which can satisfy an immortal soul. I do not mean to insinuate, that either sex should be so lost, in abstract reflections or distant views, as to forget the affections and duties that lie before them, and are in truth, the means appointed to produce the fruit of life; on the contrary, I would warmly recommend them, even while I assert, that they afford most satisfaction when they are considered in their true subordinate light.

Probably the prevailing opinion, that woman was created for man, may have taken its rise from Moses's poetical story; yet, as very few it is presumed, who have bestowed any serious thought on the subject, ever supposed that Eve was, literally speaking, one of Adam's ribs, the deduction must be allowed to fall to the ground; or only be so far admitted as it proves that man, from the remotest antiquity, found it convenient to exert his strength to subjugate his companion, and his invention to show that she ought to have her neck bent under the yoke; because she as well as the brute creation, was created to do his pleasure.

Let it not be concluded, that I wish to invert the order of things; I have already granted, that, from the constitution of their bodies, men seem to be designed by Providence to attain a greater degree of virtue. I speak collectively of the whole sex; but I see not the shadow of a reason to conclude that their virtues should differ in respect to their nature. In fact, how can they, if virtue has only one eternal standard? I must, therefore, if I reason consequentially, as strenuously maintain, that they have the same simple direction, as that there is a God.

It follows then, that cunning should not be opposed to wisdom, little cares to great exertions, nor insipid softness, varnished over with the name of gentleness, to that fortitude which grand views alone can inspire.

I shall be told, that woman would then lose many of her peculiar graces, and the opinion of a well known poet might be quoted to refute my unqualified assertions. For Pope has said, in the name of the whole male sex,

> "Yet ne'er so sure our passions to create,
> As when she touch'd the brink of all we hate."

Iᴛ what light this sally places men and women, I shall leave to the judicious to determine; meanwhile I shall content myself with observing, that I cannot discover why, unless they are mortal, females should always be degraded by being made subservient to love or lust.

To speak disrespectfully of love is, I know, high treason against sentiment and fine feelings; but I wish to speak the simple language of truth, and rather to address the head than the heart. To endeavour to reason love out of the world, would be to out Quixote Cervantes, and equally offend against common sense; but an endeavour to restrain this tumultuous passion, and to prove that it should not be allowed to dethrone superior powers, or to usurp the sceptre which the understanding should ever coolly wield, appears less wild.

Youth is the season for love in both sexes; but in those days of thoughtless enjoyment, provision should be made for the more important years of life, when reflection takes place of sensation. But Rousseau, and most of the male writers who have followed his steps, have warmly inculcated that the whole tendency of female education ought to be directed to one point to render them pleasing.

Let me reason with the supporters of this opinion, who have any knowledge of human nature, do they imagine that marriage can eradicate the habitude of life? The woman who has only been taught to please, will soon find that her charms are oblique sun-beams, and that they cannot have much effect on her husband's heart when they are seen every day, when the summer is past and gone. Will she then have sufficient native energy to look into herself for comfort and cultivate her dormant faculties? or, is it not more rational to expect, that she will try to please other men; and, in the emotions raised by the expectation of new conquests, endeavour to forget the mortification her love or pride has received? When the husband ceases to be a lover—and the time will inevitably come, her desire of pleasing will then grow languid, or become a spring of bitterness; and love, perhaps, the most evanescent of all passions, gives place to jealousy or vanity.

I now speak of women who are restrained by principle or prejudice; such women though they would shrink from an intrigue with real abhorrence, yet, nevertheless, wish to be convinced by the homage of gallantry, that they are cruelly neglected by their husbands; or, days and weeks are spent in dreaming of the happiness enjoyed by congenial souls, till the health is undermined and the spirits broken by discontent. How then can the great art of pleasing be such a necessary study? it is only useful to a mistress; the chaste wife, and serious mother, should only consider her power to please as the polish of her virtues, and the affection of her husband as one of the comforts that render her task less difficult, and her life happier. But, whether she be loved or neglected, her first wish should be to make herself respectable, and not rely for all her happiness on a being subject to like infirmities with herself.

FROM LETTERS TO IMLAY

LETTER V

[Paris, November, 1793.] Sunday Night.

I have just received your letter, and feel as if I could not go to bed tranquilly without saying a few words in reply, merely to tell you that my mind is serene, and my heart affectionate.

Ever since you last saw me inclined to faint, I have felt some gentle twitches, which make me begin to think that I am nourishing a creature who will soon be sensible of my care. This thought has not only produced an overflowing of tenderness to you, but made me very attentive to calm my mind and take exercise, lest I should destroy an object, in whom we are to have a mutual interest, you know. Yesterday—do not smile!—finding that I had hurt myself by lifting precipitately a large log of wood, I sat down in an agony, till I felt those said twitches again.

Are you very busy?

So you may reckon on its being finished soon, though not before you come home, unless you are detained longer than I now allow myself to believe you will.

Be that as it may, write to me, my best love, and bid me be patient —kindly—and the expressions of kindness will again beguile the time, as sweetly as they have done to-night. Tell me also over and over again, that your happiness (and you deserve to be happy!) is closely connected with mine, and I will try to dissipate, as they rise, the fumes of former discontent, that have too often clouded the sunshine which you have endeavoured to diffuse through my mind. God bless you! Take care of yourself, and remember with tenderness your affectionate

Mary.

I am going to rest very happy, and you have made me so. This is the kindest good-night I can utter.

LETTER XII

[*Paris, January, 1794.*] *Wednesday Morning.*

I will never, if I am not entirely cured of quarrelling, begin to encourage "quick-coming fancies," when we are separated. Yesterday, my love, I could not open your letter for some time; and, though it was not half as severe as I merited, it threw me into such a fit of trembling, as seriously alarmed me. I did not, as you may suppose, care for a little pain on my own account; but all the fears which I have had for a few days past, returned with fresh force. This morning I am better; will you not be glad to hear it? You perceive that sorrow has almost made a child of me, and that I want to be soothed to peace.

One thing you mistake in my character, and imagine that to be coldness, which is just the contrary. For, when I am hurt by the person most dear to me, I must let out a whole torrent of emotions, in which tenderness would be uppermost, or stifle them altogether; and it appears to me almost a duty to stifle them when I imagine *that I am treated with coldness.*

I am afraid that I have vexed you, my own love. I know the quickness of your feelings—and let me, in the sincerity of my heart, assure you, there is nothing I would not suffer to make you happy. My own happiness wholly depends on you; and, knowing you, when my reason is not clouded, I look forward to a rational prospect of as much felicity as the earth affords, with a little dash of rapture into the bargain, if you will look at me, when we meet again, as you have sometimes greeted your humbled, yet most affectionate

Mary.

LETTER XXVII

[Paris, 1794.] October 26.

My dear Love—I began to wish so earnestly to hear from you, that the sight of your letters occasioned such pleasurable emotions, I was obliged to throw them aside till the little girl and I were alone together; and this said little girl, our darling, is become a most intelligent little creature, and as gay as a lark, and that in the morning too, which I do not find quite so convenient. I once told you, that the sensations before she was born, and when she is sucking, were pleasant; but they do not deserve to be compared to the emotions I feel, when she stops to smile upon me, or laughs outright on meeting me unexpectedly in the street, or after a short absence. She has now the advantage of having two good nurses, and I am at present able to discharge my duty to her, without being the slave of it.

I have therefore employed and amused myself since I got rid of ——, and am making a progress in the language, amongst other things. I have also made some new acquaintance. I have almost *charmed* a judge of the tribunal, R——, who, though I should not have thought it possible, has humanity, if not *beaucoup d'esprit*. But let me tell you, if you do not make haste back, I shall be half in love with the author of the *Marseillaise*, who is a handsome man, a little too broad-faced or so, and plays sweetly on the violin.

What do you say to this threat? Why, *entre nous*, I like to give way to a sprightly vein when writing to you, that is, when I am pleased with you. "The devil," you know, is proverbially said to be "in a good humour when he is pleased." Will you not then be a good boy, and come back quickly to play with your girls? but I shall not allow you to love the new-comer best.

My heart longs for your return, my love, and only looks for, and seeks happiness with you; yet do not imagine that I childishly wish you to come back before you have arranged things in such a manner that it will not be necessary for you to leave us soon again, or to make exertions which injure your constitution.

Yours most truly and tenderly,

Mary.

P.S.—You would oblige me by delivering the inclosed to Mr. ——, and pray call for an answer. It is for a person uncomfortably situated.

LETTER XXX

[*Paris, 1794.*] *December 29.*

Though I suppose you have later intelligence, yet, as —— has just informed me that he has an opportunity of sending immediately to you, I take advantage of it to inclose you

How I hate this crooked business! This intercourse with the world, which obliges one to see the worst side of human nature! Why cannot you be content with the object you had first in view when you entered into this wearisome labyrinth? I know very well that you have imperceptibly been drawn on; yet why does one project, successful or abortive, only give place to two others? Is it not sufficient to avoid poverty? I am contented to do my part; and, even here, sufficient to escape from wretchedness is not difficult to obtain. And let me tell you, I have my project also, and if you do not soon return, the little girl and I will take care of ourselves; we will not accept any of your cold kindness—your distant civilities— no; not we.

This is but half jesting, for I am really tormented by the desire which —— manifests to have you remain where you are. Yet why do I talk to you? If he can persuade you, let him! for, if you are not happier with me, and your own wishes do not make you throw aside these eternal projects, I am above using any arguments, though rea- son as well as affection seems to offer them, if our affection be mutual, they will occur to you, and you will act accordingly.

Since my arrival here, I have found the German lady of whom

you have heard me speak. Her first child died in the month; but she has another about the age of my Fanny, a fine little creature. They are still but contriving to live—earning their daily bread— yet, though they are but just above poverty, I envy them. She is a tender, affectionate mother, fatigued even by her attention. However, she has an affectionate husband in her turn to render her care light, and to share her pleasure.

I will own to you that, feeling extreme tenderness for my little girl, I grow sad very often when I am playing with her, that you are not here to observe with me how her mind unfolds, and her little heart becomes attached! These appear to me to be true pleasures, and still you suffer them to escape you, in search of what we may never enjoy. It is your own maxim to "live in the present moment." *If you do*, stay, for God's sake; but tell me the truth—if not, tell me when I may expect to see you, and let me not be always vainly look- ing for you, till I grow sick at heart.

Adieu! I am a little hurt. I must take my darling to my bosom to comfort me.

LETTER XXXVI

[*Paris, 1795.*] *February 10.*

You talk of "permanent views and future comfort"—not for me, for I am dead to hope. The inquietudes of the last winter have finished the business, and my heart is not only broken, but my con- stitution destroyed. I conceive myself in a galloping consumption, and the continual anxiety I feel at the thought of leaving my child, feeds the fever that nightly devours me. It is on her account that I again write to you, to conjure you, by all that you hold sacred, to leave her here with the German lady you may have heard me men- tion! She has a child of the same age, and they may be brought up together as I wish her to be brought up. I shall write more fully on the subject. To facilitate this I shall give up my present lodgings, and go into the same house. I can live much cheaper there, which is now become an object. I have had 3,000 livres from ——, and

I shall take one more, to pay my servant's wages, &c., and then I shall endeavour to procure what I want by my own exertions. I shall entirely give up the acquaintance of the Americans.

—— and I have not been on good terms for a long time. Yesterday he very unmanlily exulted over me, on account of your determination to stay. I had provoked it, it is true, by some asperities against commerce which have dropped from me when we have argued about the propriety of your remaining where you are; and it is no matter, I have drunk too deep of the bitter cup to care about trifles.

When you first entered into these plans, you bounded your views to the gaining of a thousand pounds. It was sufficient to have procured a farm in America, which would have been an independence. You find now that you did not know yourself, and that a certain situation in life is more necessary to you than you imagine—more necessary than an uncorrupted heart. For a year or two you may procure yourself what you call pleasure; but, in the solitude of declining life, I shall be remembered with regret—I was going to say with remorse, but checked my pen.

As I have never concealed the nature of my connection with you, your reputation will not suffer. I shall never have a confident; I am content with the approbation of my own mind; and, if there be a searcher of hearts, mine will not be despised. Reading what you have written relative to the desertion of women, I have often wondered how theory and practice could be so different, till I recollected that the sentiments of passion, and the resolves of reason are very distinct. As to my sisters, as you are so continually hurried with business, you need not write to them; I shall, when my mind is calmer. God bless you! Adieu!

This has been such a period of barbarity and misery. I ought not to complain of having my share. I wish one moment that I had never heard of the cruelties that have been practised here, and the next, envy the mothers who have been killed with their children. Surely I had suffered enough in life, not to be cursed with a fondness, that burns up the vital stream I am imparting. You will think me mad: I would I were so, that I could forget my misery—so that my head or heart would be still.

LETTER XXXVII

[Paris, 1795.] February 19.

When I first received your letter, putting off your return to an indefinite time, I felt so hurt that I know not what I wrote. I am now calmer, though it was not the kind of wound over which time has the quickest effect; on the contrary, the more I think, the sadder I grow. Society fatigues me inexpressibly. So much so, that finding fault with everyone, I have only reason enough to discover that the fault is in myself. My child alone interests me, and, but for her, I should not take any pains to recover my health.

As it is, I shall wean her, and try if by that step (to which I feel a repugnance, for it is my only solace) I can get rid of my cough. Physicians talk much of the danger attending any complaint on the lungs, after a woman has suckled for some months. They lay a stress also on the necessity of keeping the mind tranquil—and, my God! how has mine been harrassed! But whilst the caprices of other women are gratified, "the wind of heaven not suffered to visit them too rudely," I have not found a guardian angel, in heaven or on earth, to ward off sorrow or care from my bosom.

What sacrifices have you not made for a woman you did not respect! But I will not go over this ground. I want to tell you that I do not understand you. You say that you have not given up all thoughts of returning here—and I know that it will be necessary—nay is. I cannot explain myself; but if you have not lost your memory, you will easily divine my meaning. What! is our life then only to be made up of separations? and am I only to return to a country, that has not merely lost all charms for me, but for which I feel a repugnance that almost amounts to horror, only to be left there a prey to it!

Why is it so necessary that I should return? brought up here, my girl would be freer. Indeed, expecting you to join us, I had formed some plans of usefulness that have now vanished with my hopes of happiness.

In the bitterness of my heart, I could complain with reason, that

I am left here dependent on a man, whose avidity to acquire a fortune has rendered him callous to every sentiment connected with social or affectionate emotions. With a brutal insensibility, he cannot help displaying the pleasure your determination to stay gives him, in spite of the effect it is visible it has had on me.

Till I can earn money, I shall endeavour to borrow some, for I want to avoid asking him continually for the sum necessary to maintain me. Do not mistake me, I have never been refused. Yet I have gone half a dozen times to the house to ask for it, and come away without speaking—you must guess why. Besides, I wish to avoid hearing of the eternal projects to which you have sacrificed my peace—not remembering—but I will be silent for ever—.

LETTER LXVIII

[Dover, 1795] Sunday, October 4.

I wrote to you by the packet, to inform you that your letter of the 18th of last month, had determined me to set out with Captain ——; but, as we sailed very quick, I take it for granted, that you have not received it.

You say, I must decide for myself. I have decided that it was most for the interest of my little girl, and for my own comfort, little as I expect, for us to live together; and I even thought that you would be glad, some years hence, when the tumult of business was over, to repose in the society of an affectionate friend, and mark the progress of our interesting child, whilst endeavouring to be of use in the circle you at last resolved to rest in; for you cannot run about for ever.

From the tenour of your last letter however, I am led to imagine that you have formed some new attachment. If it be so, let me earnestly request you to see me once more, and immediately. This is the only proof I require of the friendship you profess for me. I will then decide, since you boggle about a mere form.

I am labouring to write with calmness; but the extreme anguish I feel, at landing without having any friend to receive me, and even to be conscious that the friend whom I most wish to see, will feel a disagreeable sensation at being informed of my arrival, does not come under the description of common misery. Every emotion yields to an overwhelming flood of sorrow, and the playfulness of my child distresses me. On her account, I wished to remain a few days here, comfortless as is my situation. Besides, I did not wish to surprise you. You have told me, that you would make any sacrifice to promote my happiness—and, even in your last unkind letter, you talk of the ties which bind you to me and my child. Tell me that you wish it, and I will cut this Gordian knot.

I now most earnestly intreat you to write to me, without fail, by the return of the post. Direct your letter to be left at the post-office, and tell me whether you will come to me here, or where you will meet me. I can receive your letter on Wednesday morning.

Do not keep me in suspense. I expect nothing from you, or any human being: my die is cast! I have fortitude enough to determine to do my duty; yet I cannot raise my depressed spirits, or calm my trembling heart. That being who moulded it thus, knows that I am unable to tear up by the roots the propensity to affection which has been the torment of my life—but life will have an end!

Should you come here (a few months ago I could not have doubted it) you will find me at ——. If you prefer meeting me on the road, tell me where.

Yours affectionately,
Mary.

LETTER LXIX

[*London November, 1795*]

I write you now on my knees; imploring you to send my child and the maid with ——, to Paris, to be consigned to the care of Madame ——, Rue ——, Section de ——. Should they be removed, —— can give their direction.

Let the maid have all my clothes without distinction.

Pray pay the cook her wages, and do not mention the confession which I forced from her; a little sooner or later is of no consequence.

Mary Wollstonecraft

Nothing but my extreme stupidity could have rendered me blind so long. Yet, whilst you assured me that you had no attachment, I thought we might still have lived together.

I shall make no comments on your conduct or any appeal to the world. Let my wrongs sleep with me! Soon, very soon, I shall be at peace. When you receive this, my burning head will be cold.

I would encounter a thousand deaths, rather than a night like the last. Your treatment has thrown my mind into a state of chaos; yet I am serene. I go to find comfort, and my only fear is, that my poor body will be insulted by an endeavour to recall my hated existence. But I shall plunge into the Thames where there is the least chance of my being snatched from the death I seek.

God bless you! May you never know by experience what you have made me endure. Should your sensibility ever awake, remorse will find its way to your heart; and, in the midst of business and sensual pleasure, I shall appear before you, the victim of your deviation from rectitude.

LETTER LXX

[London November, 1795.] Sunday Morning.

I have only to lament, that, when the bitterness of death was past, I was inhumanly brought back to life and misery. But a fixed determination is not to be baffled by disappointment; nor will I allow that to be a frantic attempt which was one of the calmest acts of reason. In this respect, I am only accountable to myself. Did I care for what is termed reputation, it is by other circumstances that I should be dishonoured.

You say, "that you know not how to extricate ourselves out of the wretchedness into which we have been plunged." You are extricated long since. But I forbear to comment. If I am condemned to live longer, it is a living death.

It appears to me that you lay much more stress on delicacy than on principle; for I am unable to discover what sentiment of delicacy would have been violated by your visiting a wretched friend, if

by a Woman writt

indeed you have any friendship for me. But since your new attachment is the only sacred thing in your eyes, I am silent—Be happy! My complaints shall never more damp your enjoyment; perhaps I am mistaken in supposing that even my death could, for more than a moment. This is what you call magnanimity. It is happy for yourself, that you possess this quality in the highest degree.

Your continually asserting that you will do all in your power to contribute to my comfort, when you only allude to pecuniary assistance, appears to me a flagrant breach of delicacy. I want not such vulgar comfort, nor will I accept it. I never wanted but your heart— That gone, you have nothing more to give. Had I only poverty to fear, I should not shrink from life. Forgive me then, if I say, that I shall consider any direct or indirect attempt to supply my necessities, as an insult which I have not merited, and as rather done out of tenderness for your own reputation, than for me. Do not mistake me; I do not think that you value money, therefore I will not accept what you do not care for, though I do much less, because certain privations are not painful to me. When I am dead, respect for yourself will make you take care of the child.

I write with difficulty—probably I shall never write to you again. Adieu!

God bless you!

Mary Shelley

Mary Shelley

(1797–1851)

Mary Wollstonecraft died a short time after the birth of her daughter, Mary Shelley. Just as Mary Wollstonecraft's life was marked by renown and tragedy, so was the life of the daughter she never knew. Before Mary Shelley was twenty-one, she had run away to live with the poet, Percy Shelley, whom she later married, had borne three children, and had published her well known novel, *Frankenstein*. Part of a celebrated literary circle, she was also a victim of personal tragedy. Three of her four children died. She suffered a miscarriage. When she was not yet twenty-five, her husband died by drowning. To help support herself and her one remaining child and to regain her peace of mind, she turned even more to writing. She wrote novels, short stories, newspaper and scholarly articles, did editions of Shelley's works, and continued her *Journal*, which she kept for most of her life. The following selection from her *Journal* reveals how, having been dependent upon Shelley for guidance, for companionship, seemingly for her very identity, Mary Shelley felt isolated and helpless without him. And the selection from *The Last Man*, a novel she wrote a few years after Shelley's death, reveals how she conveyed her loneliness in fictional form and how—as if she believed a woman's loneliness was not an important enough subject for fiction—she chose for her main character, a man.

FROM MARY SHELLEY'S JOURNAL

ALBARO, ITALY, 1822

Oct. 2.—On the 8th of July I finished my journal. This is a curious coincidence. The date still remains—the fatal 8th—a monument to show that all ended then. And I begin again? Oh, never! But several motives induce me, when the day has gone down, and all is silent around me, steeped in sleep, to pen as occasion wills, my reflections and feelings. First, I have no friend. For eight years I communicated, with unlimited freedom, with one whose genius, far transcending mine, awakened and guided my thoughts. I conversed with him; rectified my errors of judgment; obtained new lights from him; and my mind was satisfied. Now I am alone—oh, how alone! The stars may behold my tears, and the winds drink my sighs; but my thoughts are a sealed treasure, which I can confide to none. But can I express all I feel? Can I give words to thoughts and feelings that, as a tempest, hurry me along? Is this the sand that the ever-flowing sea of thought would impress indelibly? Alas! I am alone. No eye answers mine; my voice can with none assume its natural modulation. What a change! O my beloved Shelley! how often during those happy days —happy, though chequered—I thought how superiorly gifted I had been in being united to one to whom I could unveil myself, and who could understand me! Well, then, now I am reduced to these white pages, which I am to blot with dark imagery. As I write, let me think what he would have said if, speaking thus to him, he could have answered me. Yes, my own heart, I would fain know what to think of my desolate state; what you think I ought to do, what to think. I guess you would answer thus:—"Seek to know your own heart, and, learning what it best loves, try to enjoy that." Well, I cast my eyes around, and, look forward to the bounded prospect in view; I ask myself what pleases me there? My child;—so many feelings arise when I think of him, that I turn aside to think no more. Those I most loved are gone for ever; those who held the second rank are absent; and among those near me as yet, I trust to the disinterested kindness of one alone. Beneath all this, my imagination never flags. Literary labours, the improvement of my mind, and the enlargement of my ideas, are the only occupations that elevate me from my lethargy; all events seem to lead me to that one point, and the courses of destiny having dragged me to that single resting-place, have left me. Father, mother, friend, husband, children—all made, as it were, the team that conducted me here; and now all, except you, my poor boy (and you are necessary to the continuance of my life), all are gone, and I am left to fulfil my task. So be it.

Oct. 19.—How painful all change becomes to one who, entirely and despotically engrossed by their own feelings, leads as it were an *internal* life, quite different from the outward and apparent one! Whilst my life continues its monotonous course within sterile banks, an under-current disturbs the smooth face of the waters, distorts all objects reflected in it, and the mind is no longer a mirror in which outward events may reflect themselves, but becomes itself the painter and creator. If this perpetual activity has power to vary with endless change the everyday occurrences of a most monotonous life, it appears to be animated with the spirit of tempest and hurricane when any real occurrence diversifies the scene. Thus, to-night, a few bars of a known air seemed to be as a wind to rouse from its depths every deep-seated emotion of my mind. I would have given worlds to have sat, my eyes closed, and listened to them for years. The restraint I was under caused these feelings to vary with rapidity; but the words of the conversation, uninteresting as they might be, seemed all to convey two senses to me, and, touching a chord within me, to form a music of which the speaker was little aware. I do not think that any person's voice has the same power of awakening melancholy in me as Albè's [Byron's]. I have been accustomed, when hearing it, to listen and to speak little; another voice, not mine, ever replied—a voice whose strings are broken. When Albè ceases to speak, I expect to hear *that other* voice, and when I hear another instead, it jars strangely with every association. I have seen so little of Albè since our residence in Switzerland, and, having seen him there every day, his voice—a peculiar one—is engraved on my memory with other sounds and objects from which it can never disunite itself. I have heard Hunt in company and conversation with many, when my own one was not there. Trelawney, perhaps, is associated in my mind with Edward [Williams] more than with Shelley. Even our older friends, Peacock and Hogg, might talk together, or with others, and their voices would suggest no change to me. But, since incapacity and timidity always prevented my mingling in the nightly conversations of Diodati, they were, as it were, entirely tête-à-tête between my Shelley and Albè; and thus, as I have said, when Albè speaks and Shelley does not answer, it is as thunder without rain—the form of the sun without heat or light—as any familiar object might be, shorn of its best attributes; and I listen with an unspeakable melancholy that yet is not all pain.

The above explains that which would otherwise be an enigma— why Albè, by his mere presence and voice, has the power of exciting such deep and shifting emotions within me. For my feelings have no analogy either with my opinion of him, or the subject of his conversation. With another I might talk, and not for the moment think of Shelley—at least not think of him with the same vividness as if I were alone; but, when in company with Albè, I can never cease for a second to have Shelley in my heart and brain with a clearness that mocks reality—interfering even by its force with the functions of life—until, if tears do not relieve me, the hysterical feeling, analogous to that which the murmur of the sea gives me, presses painfully upon me.

Well, for the first time for about a month, I have been in company with Albè for two hours, and, coming home, I write this, so necessary is it for me to express in words the force of my feelings. Shelley, beloved! I look at the stars and at all nature, and it speaks to me of you in the clearest accents. Why cannot you answer me, my own one? Is the instrument so utterly destroyed? I would endure ages of pain to hear one tone of your voice strike on my ear!

Nov. 11.—It is better to grieve than not to grieve. Grief at least tells me that I was not always what I am now. I was once selected for happiness; let the memory of that abide by me. You pass by an old ruined house in a desolate lane, and heed it not. But if you hear that that house is haunted by a wild and beautiful spirit, it acquires an interest and beauty of its own.

I shall be glad to be more alone again; one ought to see no one, or many; and, confined to one society, I shall lose all energy except that which I possess from my own resources; and I must be alone for those to be put in activity.

A cold heart! Have I a cold heart? God knows! But none need envy the icy region this heart encircles; and at least the tears are hot which the emotions of this cold heart forces me to shed. A cold heart! yes, it would be cold enough if all were as I wished it—cold, or burning in the flame for whose sake I forgive this, and would forgive every other imputation—that flame in which your heart, beloved, lay unconsumed. My heart is very full to-night.

I shall write his life, and thus occupy myself in the only manner from which I can derive consolation. That will be a task that may convey some balm. What though I weep? All is better than inaction and—not forgetfulness—that never is—but an inactivity of remembrance.

And you, my own Boy! I am about to begin a task which, if you live, will be an invaluable treasure to you in after times. I must collect my materials, and then, in the commemoration of the divine virtues of your Father, I shall fulfil the only act of pleasure there remains for me, and be ready to follow you, if you leave me, my task being fulfilled. I have lived; rapture, exultation, content—all the varied changes of enjoyment—have been mine. It is all gone; but still, the airy paintings of what it has gone through float by, and distance shall not dim them. If I were alone, I had already begun what I had determined to do; but I must have patience, and for those events my memory is brass, my thoughts a never-tired engraver. France—Poverty—A few days of solitude, and some uneasiness—A tranquil residence in a beautiful spot [Bishopsgate]—Switzerland—Bath—Marlow—Milan—The Baths of Lucca—Este—Venice—Rome—Naples—Rome and misery—Leghorn—Florence—Pisa—Solitude—The Williamses—The Baths—Pisa: these are the heads of chapters, and each containing a tale romantic beyond romance.

I no longer enjoy, but I love! Death cannot deprive me of that living spark which feeds on all given it, and which is now triumphant in sorrow. I love, and shall enjoy happiness again. I do not doubt that; but when?

ALBARO, ITALY, 1823

Feb. 2.—On the 21st of January those rites were fulfilled.[1] Shelley! my own beloved! You rest beneath the blue sky of Rome; in that, at least, I am satisfied.

What matters it that they cannot find the grave of my William? That spot is sanctified by the presence of his pure earthly vesture, and that is sufficient—at least, it must be. I am too truly miserable to dwell on what at another time might have made me unhappy. He is beneath the tomb of Cestius. I see the spot.

Feb. 3.—A storm has come across me; a slight circumstance has disturbed the deceitful calm of which I boasted. I thought I heard

[1] Shelley's ashes were buried in the Protestant Cemetery in Rome on January 21, 1823. The body of his son William could not be found.

my Shelley call me—not my Shelley in heaven—but my Shelley, my companion in my daily tasks. I was reading; I heard a voice say "Mary!" "It is Shelley," I thought; the revulsion was of agony. Never more—

But I have better hopes and other feelings. Your earthly shrine is shattered, but your spirit ever hovers over me, or awaits me when I shall be worthy to join it. To that spirit which, when imprisoned here, yet showed, by its exalted nature, its superior derivation—

Feb. 24.—Evils throng around me, my beloved, and I have indeed lost all in losing thee. Were it not for my Child, this would rather be a soothing reflection, and, if starvation were my fate, I should fulfil that fate without a sigh. But our Child demands all my care now that you have left us. I must be all to him: the Father, Death has deprived him of; the relations, the bad world permits him not to have. What is yet in store for me? Am I to close the eyes of our Boy, and then join you?

The last weeks have been spent in quiet. Study could not give repose to, but somewhat regulated, my thoughts. I said: "I lead an innocent life, and it may become a useful one. I have talent, I will improve that talent; and if, while meditating on the wisdom of ages, and storing my mind with all that has been recorded of it, any new light bursts upon me, or any discovery occurs that may be useful to my fellows, then the balm of utility may be added to innocence."

What is it that moves up and down in my soul, and makes me feel as if my intellect could master all but my fate? I fear it is only youthful ardour—the yet untamed spirit which, wholly withdrawn from the hopes, and almost from the affections, of life, indulges itself in the only walk free to it, and, mental exertion being all my thought except regret, would make me place my hopes in that. I am indeed become a recluse in thought and act; and my mind, turned heavenward, would, but for my only tie, lose all commune with what is around me. If I be proud, yet it is with humility that I am so. I am not vain. My heart shakes with its suppressed emotions, and I flag beneath the thoughts that possess me.

Each day, as I have taken my solitary walk, I have felt myself exalted with the idea of occupation, improvement, knowledge, and peace. Looking back to my past life as a delicious dream, I steeled myself as well as I could against such severe regrets as should over-throw my calmness. Once or twice, pausing in my walk, I have exclaimed in despair———"Is it even so?" Yet, for the most part resigned, I was occupied by reflection—on those ideas you, my beloved, planted in my mind—and meditated on our nature, our source, and our destination.

To-day, melancholy would invade me, and I thought the peace I enjoyed was transient. Then that letter[2] came to place its seal on my prognostications. Yet it was not the refusal, or the insult heaped upon me, that stung me to tears. It was their bitter words about our Boy. Why, I live only to keep him from their hands. How dared they dream that I held him not far more precious than all, save the hope of again seeing you, my lost one? But for his smiles, where should I now be?

Stars that shine unclouded, ye cannot tell me what will be! Yet I can tell you a part. I may have misgivings, weaknesses, and momentary lapses into unworthy despondency, but—save in devotion towards my Boy—fortune had emptied her quiver, and to all her future shafts I oppose courage, hopelessness of ought on this side, with a firm trust in what is beyond the grave.

Visit me in my dreams to-night, my beloved Shelley! kind, loving, excellent as thou wert! and the event of this day shall be forgotten.

Mar. 17.—Isabel [Booth], Friend of my youth, whom I have sometimes thought might now step upon the vacant scene and that we might both support each other, can you not hear and pity me?

Mar. 19.—As I have until now recurred to this book to discharge into it the overflowings of a mind too full of the bitterest waters of life, so will I to-night, now that I am calm, put down some of my milder reveries; that, when I turn it over, I may not only find a record of the most painful thoughts that ever filled a human heart even to distraction.

I am beginning seriously to educate myself; and in another place I have marked the scope of this somewhat tardy education, intellec-

---

[2] Sir Timothy Shelley's letter of February 6, 1823 to Byron. Sir Timothy wrote that Mary's "conduct was the very reverse of what it ought to have been." "As to her child," he added, "I am inclined to afford the means of a suitable protection and care of him in this country, if he shall be placed with a person I shall approve."

tually considered. In a moral point of view, this education is of some years' standing, and it only now takes the form of seeking its food in books. I have long accustomed myself to the study of my own heart, and have sought and found in its recesses that which cannot embody itself in words—hardly in feelings. I have found strength in the conception of its faculties; much native force in the understanding of them; and what appears to me not a contemptible penetration in the subtle divisions of good and evil. But I have found less strength of self-support, of resistance to what is vulgarly called temptation; yet I think also that I have found true humility (for surely no one can be less presumptuous than I), an ardent love for the immutable laws of right, much native goodness of emotion, and purity of thought.

Enough, if every day I gain a profounder knowledge of my defects and a more certain method of turning them to a good direction.

Study has become to me more necessary than the air I breathe. In the questioning and searching turn it gives to my thoughts, I find some relief to wild reverie; in the self-satisfaction I feel in commanding myself, I find present solace; in the hope that thence arises, that I may become more worthy of my Shelley, I find a consolation that even makes me less wretched than in my most wretched moments.

Mar. 30.—I have now finished part of the "Odyssey." I mark this. I cannot write. Day after day I suffer the most tremendous agitation. I cannot write, or read, or think. Whether it be the anxiety for letters that shakes a frame not so strong as hitherto—whether it be my annoyances here—whether it be my regrets, my sorrows, and despair, or all these—I know not; but I am a wreck.

May 31.—The lanes are filled with fireflies; they dart between the trunks of the trees, and people the land with earth-stars. I walked among them to-night, and descended towards the sea. I passed by the ruined church, and stood on the platform that overlooks the beach. The black rocks were stretched out among the blue waters, which dashed with no impetuous motion against them. The dark boats, with their white sails, glided gently over its surface, and the star-enlightened promontories closed in the bay: below, amid the crags, I heard the monotonous but harmonious, voices of the fishermen.

How beautiful these shores, and this sea! Such is the scene—such the waves within which my beloved vanished from mortality.

Mary Shelley

The time is drawing near when I must quit this country. It is
true that, in the situation I now am, Italy is but the corpse of the
enchantress that she was. Besides, if I had stayed here, the state of
things would have been different. The idea of our Child's advantage
alone enables me to keep fixed in my resolution to return to England.
It is best for him—and I go.

Four years ago, we lost our darling William; four years ago, in
excessive agony, I called for death to free me from all I felt that I
should suffer here. I continue to live, and *thou* art gone. I leave Italy
and the few that still remain to me. That, I regret less; for our intercourse is [so] much chequered with all of dross that this earth so
delights to blend with kindness and sympathy, that I long for solitude,
with the exercise of such affections as still remain to me. Away, I
shall be conscious that these friends love me, and none can then
gainsay the pure attachment which chiefly clings to them, because
they knew and loved you—because I knew them when with you, and
I cannot think of them without feeling your spirit beside me.

I cannot grieve for you, beloved Shelley; I grieve for thy friends—
for the world—for thy Child—most for myself, enthroned in thy
love, growing wiser and better beneath thy gentle influence, taught
by you the highest philosophy—your pupil, friend, lover, wife,
mother of your children! The glory of the dream is gone. I am a cloud
from which the light of sunset has passed. Give me patience in the
present struggle. *Meum cordium cor!* Good night!

> "I would give
> All that I am to be as thou now art;
> But I am chain'd to time, and cannot thence depart"[3]

LONDON, ENGLAND, 1824[4]

Jan. 18.—I have now been nearly four months in England and if
I am to judge of the future by the past and the present, I have small
delight in looking forward. I even regret those days and weeks of

---

[3] *Adonais*, XXVI.

[4] Mary left Albaro for England on July 22, 1823. On January 14, 1824, she was
living at 14 Speldhurst Street, Brunswick Square, London.

intense melancholy that composed my life at Genoa. Yes, solitary and unbeloved as I was there, I enjoyed a more pleasurable state of being than I do here. I was still in Italy, and my heart and imagination were both gratified by that circumstance. I awoke with the light and beheld the theatre of nature from my window; the trees spread their green beauty before me, the resplendent sky was above me, the mountains were invested with enchanting colours. I had even begun to contemplate painlessly the blue expanse of the tranquil sea, speckled by the snow-white sails, gazed upon by the unclouded stars. There was morning and its balmy air, noon and its exhilarating heat, evening and its wondrous sunset, night and its starry pageant. Then, my studies; my drawing, which soothed me; my Greek, which I studied with greater complacency as I stole every now and then a look on the scene near me; my metaphysics, that strengthened and elevated my mind. Then my solitary walks and my reveries; they were magnificent, deep, pathetic, wild, and exalted. I sounded the depths of my own nature; I appealed to the nature around me to corroborate the testimony that my own heart bore to its purity. I thought of *him* with hope; my grief was active, striving, expectant. I was worth something then in the catalogue of beings. I could have written something, been something. Now, I am exiled from these beloved scenes; its language is becoming a stranger to mine ears; my Child is forgetting it. I am imprisoned in a dreary town; I see neither fields, nor hills, nor trees, nor sky; the exhilaration of enrapt contemplation is no more felt by me; aspirations agonising, yet grand, from which the soul reposed in peace, have ceased to ascend from the quenched altar of my mind. Writing has become a task; my studies irksome; my life dreary. In this prison it is only in human intercourse that I can pretend to find consolation; and woe, woe, and triple woe, to whoever seeks pleasure in human intercourse when that pleasure is not founded on deep and intense affection; as for the rest—

> "The bubble floats before,
> The shadow stalks behind."

My Father's situation, his cares and debts, prevent my enjoying his society.

Mary Shelley

I love Jane [Williams] better than any other human being, but I am pressed upon by the knowledge that she but slightly returns this affection. I love her, and my purest pleasure is derived from that source—a capacious basin, and but a small rill flows into it. I love some one or two more, "with a degree of love," but I see them seldom. I am excited while with them, but the reaction of this feeling is dreadfully painful, but while in London I cannot forego this excitement. I know some clever men, in whose conversation I delight, but this is rare, like angels' visits. Alas! having lived day by day with one of the wisest, best, and most affectionate of spirits, how void, bare, and drear is the scene of life!

Oh, Shelley, dear, lamented, beloved! help me, raise me, support me; let me not feel ever thus fallen and degraded! My imagination is dead, my genius lost, my energies sleep. Why am I not beneath that weedgrown tower?[5] Seeing Coleridge last night reminded me forcibly of past times: his beautiful descriptions reminded me of Shelley's conversations. Such was the intercourse I once daily enjoyed, added to supreme and active goodness, sympathy, and affection, and a wild, picturesque mode of living that suited my active spirit and satisfied its craving for novelty of impression.

I will go into the country and philosophise; some gleams of past entrancement may visit me there.

May 14.—This, then, is my English life; and thus I am to drag on existence; confined in my small room, friendless. Each day I string me to the task. I endeavour to read and write; my ideas stagnate and my understanding refuses to follow the words I read; day after day passes while torrents fall from the dark clouds, and my mind is as gloomy as this odious day. Without human friends I must attach myself to natural objects; but though I talk of the country, what difference shall I find in this miserable climate. Italy, dear Italy, murderess of those I love and of all my happiness, one word of your soft language coming unawares upon me, has made me shed bitter tears. When shall I hear it again spoken, when see your skies, your trees, your streams? The imprisonment attendant on a succession of rainy days has quite overcome me. God knows I strive to be content,

[5] Shelley's grave was at the foot of a tower of the old Roman wall which enclosed one side of the Protestant Cemetery.

but in vain. Amidst all the depressing circumstances that weigh on me, none sinks deeper than the failure of my intellectual powers; nothing I write pleases me. Whether I am just in this, or whether the want of Shelley's (oh, my loved Shelley, it is some alleviation only to write your name!) encouragement, I can hardly tell, but it seems to me as if the lovely and sublime objects of nature had been my best inspirers, and wanting these I am lost. Although so utterly miserable at Genoa, yet what reveries were mine as I looked on the aspect of the ravine—the sunny deep and its boats—the promontories clothed in purple light—the starry heavens—the fireflies—the uprising of Spring! Then I could think, and my imagination could invent and combine, and self became absorbed in the grandeur of the universe I created. Now, my mind is a blank, a gulf filled with formless mist.

The last man!⁶ Yes, I may well describe that solitary being's feelings, feeling myself as the last relic of a beloved race, my companions extinct before me.

And thus has the accumulating sorrows of days and weeks been forced to find a voice, because the word *lucena* met my eyes, and the idea of lost Italy sprang in my mind. What graceful lamps those are, though of bare construction and vulgar use; I thought of bringing one with me; I am glad I did not. I will go back only to have a *lucena*. If I told people so they would think me mad, and yet not madder than they seem to be now, when I say that the blue skies and verdure-clad earth of that dear land are necessary to my existence.

If there be a kind spirit attendant on me, in compensation for these miserable days, let me only dream to-night that I am in Italy! Mine own Shelley, what a horror you had (fully sympathised in by me) of returning to this miserable country! To be here without you is to be doubly exiled, to be away from Italy is to lose you twice. Dearest, why is my spirit thus losing all energy? Indeed, indeed, I must go back, or your poor utterly lost Mary will never dare think herself worthy to visit you beyond the grave.

May 15.—This then was the coming event that cast its shadow on

⁶ Mary's novel, *The Last Man* (3 vols.), was published in February, 1826.

my last night's miserable thoughts. Byron had become one of the people of the grave[7]—that miserable conclave to which the beings I best loved belong. I knew him in the bright days of youth, when neither care nor fear had visited me—before death had made me feel my mortality, and the earth was the scene of my hopes. Can I forget our evening visits to Diodati? our excursions on the lake, when he sang the Tyrolese Hymn, and his voice was harmonized with winds and waves. Can I forget his attentions and consolations to me during my deepest misery? Never.

Beauty sat on his countenance and power beamed from his eye. His faults being, for the most part, weaknesses, induced one readily to pardon them.

Albè—the dear, capricious, fascinating Albè—has left this desert world! God grant I may die young! A new race is springing about me. At the age of twenty-six, I am in the condition of an aged person. All my old friends are gone. I have no wish to form new. I cling to the few remaining; but they slide away, and my heart fails when I think by how few ties I hold to the world. "Life is the desert and the solitude—how populous the grave,"—and that region—to the dearer and best beloved beings which it has torn from me, now adds that resplendent spirit whose departure leaves the dull earth dark as midnight.

June 8.—What a divine night it is! I have just returned from Kentish Town;[8] a calm twilight pervades the clear sky; the lamp-like moon is hung out in heaven, and the bright west retains the dye of sunset.

If such weather would continue, I should write again; the lamp of thought is again illumined in my heart, and the fire descends from heaven that kindles it. Such, my loved Shelley, now ten years ago, at this season, did we first meet, and there were the very scenes— that churchyard, with its sacred tomb, was the spot where first love shone in your dear eyes. The stars of heaven are now your country, and your spirit drinks beauty and wisdom in those spheres, and I, beloved, shall one day join you. Nature speaks to me of you. In

[7] Byron died on April 19, 1824, at Missolonghi, in Greece.
[8] Jane Williams had recently moved to 12 Mortimer Terrace. Kentish Town.

by a Woman writt

towns and society I do not feel your presence; but there you are with me, my own, my unalienable!

I feel my powers again, and this is, of itself, happiness; the eclipse of winter is passing from my mind. I shall again feel the enthusiastic glow of composition; again, as I pour forth my soul upon paper, feel the winged ideas arise, and enjoy the delight of expressing them. Study and occupation will be a pleasure, and not a task, and this I shall owe to sight and companionship of trees and meadows, flowers and sunshine.

England, I charge thee, dress thyself in smiles for my sake! I will celebrate thee, O England! and cast a glory on thy name, if thou wilt for me remove thy veil of clouds, and let me contemplate the country of my Shelley and feel in communion with him!

I have been gay in company before, but the inspiriting sentiment of the heart's peace I have not felt before to-night; and yet, my own, never was I so entirely yours. In sorrow and grief I wish sometimes (how vainly) for earthly consolation. At a period of pleasing excitement I cling to your memory alone, and you alone receive the overflowing of my heart.

Beloved Shelley, good night! One pang will seize me when I think, but I will only think, that thou art where I shall be, and conclude with my usual prayer—from the depth of my soul I make it—May I die young!

Sept. 3.[9]—With what hopes did I come to England? I pictured little of what was pleasurable; the feeling I had, could not be called hope; it was expectation. Yet, at that time, now a year ago, what should I have said if a prophet had told me, that after the whole revolution of the year, I should be as poor in all estimable treasures as when I arrived.

I have only seen two persons from whom I have hoped or wished for friendly feeling. One, a Poet,[10] who sought me at first, whose voice, laden with sentiment, passed as Shelley's, and who read with the same deep feeling as he; whose gentle manners were pleasing, and who seemed to a degree pleased; who once or twice listened to my

[9] On June 21, 1824, Mary moved to 5 Bartholomew Place, Kentish Town.

[10] Bryan Waller Procter (Barry Cornwall), who assisted with the publication of the *Posthumous Poems* (1824).

sad plaints, and bent his dark blue eyes upon me. Association, gratitude, esteem, made me take interest in his long though rare visits.

The other[11] was kind; sought me; was pleased with me. I could talk to him, that was much. He was attached to another, so that I felt at my ease with him. They have disappeared from my horizon. Jane alone remains; if she loved me as well as I do her, it would be much; she is all gentleness, and she is my only consolation, yet she does not console me.

I have just completed my 27th year; at such a time hope and youth are still in their prime, and the pains I feel, therefore, are ever alive and vivid within me. What shall I do? Nothing! I study, that passes the time. I write, at times that pleases me; though double sorrow comes when I feel that Shelley no longer reads and approves of what I write; besides, I have no great faith in my success. Composition is delightful, but if you do not expect the sympathy of your fellow creatures in what you write, the pleasure of writing is of short duration.

I have my lovely Boy, without him I could not live. I have Jane, in her society I forget time, but the idea of it does not cheer me in my griefful moods. It is strange that the religious feeling that exalted my emotions in happiness deserts me in my misery. I have little enjoyment, no hope. I have given myself ten years more of life. God grant that they may not be augmented. I should be glad that they were curtailed. Loveless beings surround me; they talk of my personal attractions, of my talents, my manners.

The wisest and best have loved me. The beautiful, and glorious, and noble have looked on me with the divine expression of love, till Death, the reaper, carried to his over-stocked barns my lamented harvest.

But now I am not loved! Never, oh, never more shall I love. Synonymous to such words are, never more shall I be happy, never more feel life sit triumphant in my frame. I am a wreck. By what do

[11] Possibly Vincent Novello, the musician, who was very much "attached," having a wife and several children. In her letter of October 20, [1823] to Hunt, Mary wrote (*Letters*, I, 277): "Mr. Novello is my *prediletto*. I like him better and better each time I see him—his excessive good nature, enthusiastic friendship for you—his kindness towards me and his playing have quite won my heart."

the fragments cling together? Why do they not part, to be borne away by the tide to the boundless ocean, where those are whom day and night I pray that I may rejoin?

I shall be happier, perhaps, in Italy; yet, when I sometimes think that she is the murderess, I tremble for my Boy. We shall see: if no change comes, I shall be unable to support the burthen of time, and no change, if it hurt not his dear head, can be for the worse.

Oct. 26.—Time rolls on, and what does it bring? What can I do? How change my destiny? Months change their names, years their cyphers. My brow is sadly trenched, the blossom of youth faded. My mind gathers wrinkles. What will become of me?

How long it is since an emotion of joy filled my once exulting heart, or beamed from my once bright eyes. I am young still, though age creeps on apace; but I may not love any but the dead. I think that an emotion of joy would destroy me, so new, so strange would it be to my widowed heart.

Shelley had said,

"Lift not the painted veil which men call life."[12]

Mine is not painted; dark and enshadowed, it curtains out all happiness, all hope. Tears fill my eyes; well may I weep, solitary girl! The dead know you not; the living heed you not. You sit in your lone room, and the howling wind, gloomy prognostic of winter, gives not forth so despairing a tone as the unheard sighs your ill-fated heart breathes.

I was loved once! still let me cling to the memory; but to live for oneself alone; to read and communicate your reflections to none; to write and be cheered by none; to weep, and in no bosom; no more on thy bosom, my Shelley, to spend my tears—this is misery!

Such is the Alpha and Omega of my tale. I can speak to none. Writing this is useless; it does not even soothe me; on the contrary, it irritates me by showing the pitiful expedient to which I am reduced.

I have been a year in England, and, ungentle England, for what

[12] The first line of one of Shelley's sonnets of 1818.

have I to thank you? For disappointment, melancholy, and tears; for unkindness, a bleeding heart, and despairing thoughts. I wish, England, to associate but one idea with thee—immeasurable distance and insurmountable barriers, so that I never, never might breathe thine air more.

Beloved Italy! you are my country, my hope, my heaven!

Dec. 3.—I endeavour to rouse my fortitude and calm of mind by high and philosophic thoughts, and my studies aid this endeavour. I have pondered for hours on Cicero's description of that power of virtue in the human mind which renders man's frail being superior to fortune.

"Eadem ratio habet in re quiddam amplum atque magnificum ad imperandum magis quam ad parendum accommodatum; omnia humana non tolerabilia solum sed etiam levia ducens; altum quiddam et excelsum, nihil timens, nemini cedens, semper invictum."

What should I fear? To whom cede? By what be conquered?

Little, truly, have I to fear. One only misfortune can touch me. That must be the last, for I should sink under it. At the age of seven-and-twenty, in the busy metropolis of native England, I find myself alone. The struggle is hard that can give rise to misanthropy in one, like me, attached to my fellow-creatures. Yet now, did not the memory of those matchless lost ones redeem their race, I should learn to hate men, who are strong only to oppress, moral only to insult. Oh, ye winged hours that fly fast, that, having first destroyed my happiness, now bear my swift-departing youth with you, being patience, wisdom, and content! I will not stoop to the world, or become like those who compose it, and be actuated by mean pursuits and petty ends. I will endeavour to remain unconquered by hard and bitter fortune; yet the tears that start in my eyes show pangs she inflicts upon me.

So much for philosophising. Shall I ever be a philosopher?

LONDON, ENGLAND, 1826

Sept. 5.—A month of peace—a whole month of happiness with my dearest friend [Jane Williams] at Brighton—and I have lived to hear her thank God that it is over . . .

Sept. 17.—Thy picture[13] is come, my only one! Thine those speaking eyes, that mild yet animated look, unlike aught earthly wert thou ever, and art now!

If thou hadst still lived, how different had been my life and feelings!

Thou are near to guard and save me, angelic one! Thy divine glance will be my protection and defence. I was not worthy of thee, and thou hast left me; yet that dear look assures me that thou wert mine, and recalls and narrates to my backward-looking mind a long tale of love and happiness.

My head aches. My heart—my hapless heart—is deluged in bitterness. Great God! if there be any pity for human suffering, tell me what I am to do. I strive to study, I strive to write, but I cannot live without loving and being loved, without sympathy; if this is denied to me, I must die. Would that the hour were come!

The end of September.—Charles Shelley died during this month [September 16]. Percy is now Shelley's only son.

LONDON, ENGLAND, 1827

June 26.—I have just made acquaintance with Tom Moore.[14] He reminds me delightfully of the past, and I like him much. There is something warm and genuine in his feelings and manner, which is very attractive, and redeems him from the sin of worldliness with which he has been charged.

July 2.—Moore breakfasted with me on Sunday [July 1]. We talked of past times—of Shelley and Lord Byron. He was very agreeable, and I never felt myself so perfectly at my ease with any one. I do not know why this is, he seems to understand and to like me. This is a new and unexpected pleasure. I have been so long exiled from the style of society in which I spent the better part of my life; it is an evanescent pleasure, but I will enjoy it while I can.

July 11.—Moore has left town; his singing is something new and

---

[13] The portrait of Shelley by Amelia Curran, which Mary had been trying since July, 1822, to get.

[14] Moore had sought Mary's assistance with his *Life of Byron.*

strange and beautiful. I have enjoyed his visits, and spent several happy hours in his society. That is much.

July 13.—My friend has proved false and treacherous![15] Miserable discovery. For four years I was devoted to her, and I earned only ingratitude. Not for worlds would I attempt to transfer the deathly blackness of my meditations to these pages. Let no trace remain save the deep bleeding hidden wound of my lost heart, of such a tale of horror and despair. Writing, study, quiet, such remedies I must seek. What deadly cold flows through my veins; my head weighed down; my limbs sink under me. I start at every sound as the messenger of fresh misery, and despair invests my soul with trembling horror.

Sept. 25.—Arundel.—. . . But now my desire is so innocent. Why may I not hover a good genius round my lovely friend's[16] path? It is my destiny, it would seem to form rather the ties of friendship than love—the grand evil that results from this is—that while the power of mutual Love is in itself a mighty destiny—friendship though true, yields to the adverse gale—and the vessels are divided far which ought never to part company. . . .

How dark—how very dark the future seems—I shrink in fear from the mere imagination of coming time. Is any evil about to approach me? Have I not suffered enough?

October 9.—Quanto bene mi rammento sette anni fa, in questa medesima stagione i pensieri, i sentimenti del mio cuore! Allora cominciai Valperga. Allora sola col mio Bene fui felice. Allora le nuvole furono spinte dal furioso vento davanti dalla luna, nuvole magnifiche, che in forme grandiose e bianche parevano stabili quanto le montagne e sotto la tirannia del vento si mostravano più fragili che un velo di seta minutissima, scendeva allor la pioggia, gli albori si spogliavano. Autunno bello fosti allora ed ora bello terribile, malinconico ci sei, ed io, dove sono?[17]

---

[15] Shortly before this date Jane Williams had "married" T. J. Hogg. She had told tales about Mary's deficiencies as Shelley's wife, and these had got back to Mary.

[16] Probably refers to Mary's close friend Isabel Robinson (Mrs. Sholto Douglas), whom Mary apparently was visiting on September 25, and with whom she was in a few days to make a trip to Dieppe.

[17] [Translation:] "How well do I remember seven years ago, in this same season, the thoughts, the feelings of my heart. Then I began *Valperga*. Then alone with my

Friday, Dec. 5.—I am alone in London—and very unhappy. I have lost one friend and am divided from another. I weep much and cannot be consoled.

LONDON, ENGLAND, 1838

Sunday, Oct. 21.—I have been so often abused by pretended friends for my lukewarmness in "the good cause," that, though I disdain to answer them, I shall put down here a few thoughts on this subject. I am much of a self-examiner. Vanity is not my fault, I think; if it is, it is uncomfortable vanity, for I have none that teaches me to be satisfied with myself; far otherwise,—and, if I use the word disdain, it is that I think my qualities (such as they are) not appreciated from unworthy causes.

In the first place, with regard to "the good cause"—the cause of the advancement of freedom and knowledge, of the rights of women, &c.—I am not a person of opinions. I have said elsewhere that human beings differ greatly in this. Some have a passion for reforming the world; others do not cling to particular opinions. That my parents and Shelley were of the former class, makes me respect it. I respect such when joined to real disinterestedness, toleration, and a clear understanding. My accusers, after such as these, appear to me mere drivellers. For myself, I earnestly desire the good and enlightenment of my fellow-creatures, and see all, in the present course, tending to the same, and rejoice; but I am not for violent extremes, which only bring on an injurious reaction. I have never written a word in disfavour of liberalism; that I have not supported it openly in writing, arises from the following causes, as far as I know:—

That I have not argumentative powers: I see things pretty clearly, but cannot demonstrate them. Besides, I feel the counter-arguments too strongly. I do not feel that I could say ought to support the cause efficiently; besides that, on some topics (especially with regard to my

---

Beloved I was happy. Then the clouds were driven by the furious wind before the moon,—magnificent clouds, which, grand and white, seemed as stable as the mountains, and under the tyranny of the wind appeared more fragile than a veil of finest silk. Came then the rain, despoiling the trees. Autumn, you were beautiful then, and now you are beautiful, terrible, and melancholy—and I, where am I?"

own sex), I am far from making up my mind. I believe we are sent here to educate ourselves, and that self-denial, and disappointment, and self-control, are a part of our education; that it is not by taking away all restraining law that our improvement is to be achieved; and, though many things need great amendment, I can by no means go so far as my friends would have me. When I feel that I can say what will benefit my fellow-creatures, I will speak: not before.

Then, I recoil from the vulgar abuse of the inimical press. I do more than recoil: proud and sensitive, I act on the defensive—an inglorious position.

To hang back, as I do, brings a penalty. I was nursed and fed with a love of glory. To be something great and good was the precept given me by my Father: Shelley reiterated it. Alone and poor, I could only be something by joining a party; and there was much in me—the woman's love of looking up, and being guided, and being willing to do anything if any one supported and brought me forward —which would have made me a good partisan. But Shelley died, and I was alone. My Father, from age and domestic circumstances, could not *"me faire valoir."* My total friendlessness, my horror of pushing, and inability to put myself forward unless led, cherished and supported,—all this has sunk me in a state of loneliness no other human being ever before, I believe, endured—except Robinson Crusoe. How many tears and spasms of anguish this solitude has cost me, lies buried in my memory.

If I had raved and ranted about what I did not understand; had I adopted a set of opinions, and propagated them with enthusiasm; had I been careless of attack, and eager for notoriety; then the party to which I belonged had gathered round me, and I had not been alone. But since I had lost Shelley I have no wish to ally myself to the Radicals—they are full of repulsion to me—violent without any sense of Justice—selfish in the extreme—talking without knowledge —rude, envious and insolent—I wish to have nothing to do with them.

It has been the fashion with these same friends to accuse me of worldliness. There, indeed, in my own heart and conscience, I take a high ground. I may distrust my own judgment too much—be too indolent and too timid; but in conduct I am above merited blame.

I like society; I believe all persons who have any talent (who are in good health) do. The soil that gives forth nothing, may lie ever fallow; but that which produces—however humble its product—needs cultivation, change of harvest, refreshing dews, and ripening sun. Books do much; but the living intercourse is the vital heat. Debarred from that, how have I pined and died!

My early friends chose the position of enemies. When I first discovered that a trusted friend had acted falsely by me, I was nearly destroyed. My health was shaken. I remembered thinking, with a burst of agonizing tears, that I should prefer a bed of torture to the unutterable anguish a friend's falsehood engendered. There is no resentment; but the world can never be to me what it was before. Trust, and confidence, and the heart's sincere devotion, are gone.

I sought at that time to make acquaintances—to divert my mind from this anguish. I got entangled in various ways through my ready sympathy and too eager heart; but I never crouched to society—never sought it unworthily. If I have never written to vindicate the rights of women, I have ever befriended women when oppressed. At every risk I have befriended and supported victims to the social system; but I make no boast, for in truth it is simple justice I perform; and so I am still reviled for being worldly.

God grant a happier and a better day is near! Percy—my all-in-all—will, I trust, by his excellent understanding, his clear, bright, sincere spirit and affectionate heart, repay me for sad long years of desolation. His career may lead me into the thick of life or only gild a quiet home. I am content with either, and, as I grow older I grow more fearless for myself—I become firmer in my opinions. The experienced, the suffering, the thoughtful may at last speak unrebuked. If it be the will of God that I live, I may ally my name yet to "the good cause," though I do not expect to please my accusers.

Thus have I put down my thoughts. I may have deceived myself; I may be in the wrong; I try to examine myself; and such as I have written appears to me the exact truth.

Enough of this! The great work of life goes on. Death draws near. To be better after death than in life is one's hope and endeavour—to be so through self-schooling. If I write the above, it is that those who love me may hereafter know that I am not all to blame, nor merit the heavy accusations cast on me for not putting myself forward. *I can-*

not do that; it is against my nature. As well cast me from a precipice and rail at me for not flying.

LONDON, ENGLAND, 1839

Feb. 12.—I almost think that my present occupation will end in a fit of illness. I am editing Shelley's Poems, and writing notes for them.[18] I desire to do Shelley honour in the notes to the best of my knowledge and ability; for the rest, they are not well written; it little matters to me which. Would that I had more literary vanity, or vanity of any kind, I were happier. As it is, I am torn to pieces by memory. Would that all were mute in the grave!

I *much* disliked the leaving out any of "Queen Mab." I dislike it still more than I can express, and I even wish I had resisted to the last; but when I was told that certain portions would injure the copyright of all the volumes to the publisher, I yielded. I had consulted Hunt, Hogg, and Peacock; they all said I had a right to do as I liked, and offered no one objection. Trelawney sent back the volume to Moxon in a rage at seeing parts left out. How very much he must enjoy the opportunity thus afforded him of doing a rude and insolent act! It was *almost* worth while to make the omission, if only to give him this pleasure.

Hogg has written me an insulting letter because I left out the dedication to Harriet. Poor Harriet, to whose sad fate I attribute so many of my own heavy sorrows, as the atonement claimed by fate for her death.

Little does Jefferson, how little does any one, know me! When Clarke's edition of "Queen Mab" came to us at the Baths of Pisa, Shelley expressed great pleasure that these verses were omitted. This recollection caused me to do the same. It was to do him honour. What could it be to me? There are other verses I should well like to obliterate for ever, but they will be printed; and any to her could in no way tend to my discomfort or gratify one ungenerous feeling. They shall be restored, though I do not feel easy as to the good I do

[18] *The Poetical Works of P. B. Shelley*, ed. by Mrs. Shelley (London, Edward Moxon, 1839, 4 vols.).

Shelley. I may have been mistaken. Jefferson might mistake me and been [sic] angry; that were nothing. He has done far more, and done his best to give another poke to the poisonous dagger which has long rankled in my heart. I cannot forgive any man that insults any woman. She cannot call him out, she disdains words of retort; she must endure, but it is never to be forgiven; not, indeed, cherished as matter of enmity—that I never feel—but of caution to shield oneself from the like again.

In so arduous a task others might hope for encouragement and kindness from their friends—I know mine better. I am unstable, sometimes melancholy, and have been called on some occasions imperious; but I never did an ungenerous act in my life. I sympathise warmly with others, and have wasted my heart in their love and service.

FROM THE LAST MAN

I awoke in the morning, just as the higher windows of the lofty houses received the first beams of the rising sun. The birds were chirping, perched on the window sills and deserted thresholds of the doors. I awoke, and my first thought was, Adrian and Clara are dead. I no longer shall be hailed by their good-morrow—or pass the long day in their society. I shall never see them more. The ocean has robbed me of them—stolen their hearts of love from their breasts, and given over to corruption what was dearer to me than light, or life, or hope.

I was an untaught shepherd boy, when Adrian deigned to confer on me his friendship. The best years of my life had been passed with him. All I had possessed of this world's goods, of happiness, knowledge, or virtue—I owed to him. He had, in his person, his intellect, and rare qualities, given a glory to my life, which without him it had never known. Beyond all other beings he had taught me, that goodness, pure and single, can be an attribute of man. It was a sight for angels to congregate to behold, to view him lead, govern, and solace, the last days of the human race.

Mary Shelley

My lovely Clara also was lost to me—she who last of the daughters of man, exhibited all those feminine and maiden virtues, which poets, painters, and sculptors, have in their various languages strove to express. Yet, as far as she was concerned, could I lament that she was removed in early youth from the certain advent of misery? Pure she was of soul, and all her intents were holy. But her heart was the throne of love, and the sensibility her lovely countenance expressed, was the prophet of many woes, not the less deep and drear, because she would have forever concealed them.

These two wondrously endowed beings had been spared from the universal wreck, to be my companions during the last year of solitude. I had felt, while they were with me, all their worth. I was conscious that every other sentiment, regret, or passion had by degrees merged into a yearning, clinging affection for them. I had not forgotten the sweet partner of my youth, mother of my children, my adored Idris; but I saw at least a part of her spirit alive again in her brother; and after, that by Evelyn's death I had lost what most dearly recalled her to me, I enshrined her memory in Adrian's form, and endeavored to confound the two dear ideas. I sound the depths of my heart, and try in vain to draw thence the expressions that can typify my love for these remnants of my race. If regret and sorrow came athwart me, as well it might in our solitary and uncertain state, the clear tones of Adrian's voice, and his fervent look, dissipated the gloom; or I was cheered unaware by the mild content and sweet resignation Clara's cloudless brow and deep blue eyes expressed. They were all to me—the suns of my benighted soul—repose in my weariness—slumber in my sleepless wo. Ill, most ill, with disjointed words, bare and weak, have I expressed the feeling with which I clung to them. I would have wound myself like ivy inextricably round them, so that the same blow might destroy us. I would have entered and been a part of them—so that

If the dull substance of my flesh were thought,

even now I had accompanied them to their new and incommunicable abode.

Never shall I see them more. I am bereft of their dear converse—

bereft of sight of them. I am a tree rent by lightning; never will the bark close over the bared fibres—never will their quivering life, torn by the winds, receive the opiate of a moment's balm. I am alone in the world—but that expression as yet was less pregnant with misery, than that Adrian and Clara are dead.

The tide of thought and feeling rolls on forever the same, though the banks and shapes around, which govern its course, and the reflection in the wave, vary. Thus the sentiment of immediate loss in some sort decayed, while that of utter, irremediable loneliness grew on me with time. Three days I wandered through Ravenna—now thinking only of the beloved beings who slept in the oozy caves of ocean—now looking forward on the dread blank before me; shuddering to make an onward step—writhing at each change that marked the progress of the hours.

For three days I wandered to and fro in this melancholy town. I passed whole hours in going from house to house, listening whether I could detect some lurking sign of human existence. Sometimes I rang at a bell; it tinkled through the vaulted rooms, and silence succeeded to the sound. I called myself hopeless, yet still I hoped; and still disappointment ushered in the hours, intruding the cold, sharp steel which first pierced me, into the aching festering wound. I fed like a wild beast, which seizes its food only when stung by intolerable hunger. I did not change my garb, or seek the shelter of a roof, during all those days. Burning heats, nervous irritation, a ceaseless, but confused flow of thought, sleepless nights, and days instinct with a frenzy of agitation, possessed me during that time.

As the fever of my blood increased, a desire of wandering came upon me. I remember, that the sun had set on the fifth day after my wreck, when, without purpose or aim, I quitted the town of Ravenna. I must have been very ill. Had I been possessed by more or less of delirium, that night had surely been my last; for, as I continued to walk on the banks of the Mantone, whose upward course I followed, I looked wistfully on the stream, acknowledging to myself that its pellucid waves could medicine my woes for ever, and was unable to account to myself for my tardiness in seeking their shelter from the poisoned arrows of thought, that were piercing me through and through. I walked a considerable part of the night, and excessive weariness at length conquered my repugnance to the availing myself of the deserted habitations of my species. The waning moon, which had just risen, showed me a cottage, whose neat entrance and trim garden reminded me of my own England. I lifted up the latch of the door and entered. A kitchen first presented itself, where, guided by the moon beams, I found materials for striking a light. Within this was a bed room; the couch was furnished with sheets of snowy whiteness; the wood piled on the hearth, and an array as for a meal, might almost have deceived me into the dear belief that I had here found what I had so long sought—one survivor, a companion for my loneliness, a solace to my despair. I steeled myself against the delusion; the room itself was vacant: it was only prudent, I repeated to myself, to examine the rest of the house. I fancied that I was proof against the expectation; yet my heart beat audibly, as I laid my hand on the lock of each door, and it sunk again, when I perceived in each the same vacancy. Dark and silent they were as vaults; so I returned to the first chamber, wondering what sightless host had spread the materials for my repast, and my repose. I drew a chair to the table, and examined what the viands were of which I was to partake. In truth it was a death feast! The bread was blue and mouldy; the cheese lay a heap of dust. I did not dare examine the other dishes; a troop of ants passed in a double line across the table cloth; every utensil was covered with dust, with cobwebs, and myriads of dead flies: these were objects each and all betokening the fallaciousness of my expectations. Tears rushed into my eyes; surely this was a wanton display of the power of the destroyer. What had I done, that each sensitive nerve was thus to be anatomized? Yet why complain more now than ever? This vacant cottage revealed no new sorrow—the world was empty; mankind was dead—I knew it well—why quarrel therefore with an acknowledged and stale truth? Yet, as I said, I had hoped in the very heart of despair, so that every new impression of the hardcut reality on my soul brought with it a fresh pang, telling me the yet unstudied lesson, that neither change of place nor time could bring alleviation to my misery, but that, as I now was, I must continue, day after day, month after month, year after year, while I lived. I hardly dared conjecture what space of time that expression implied. It is true, I was no longer in the first blush of manhood; neither had

I declined far in the vale of years—men have accounted mine the prime of life: I had just entered my thirty-seventh year; every limb was as well knit, every articulation as true, as when I had acted the shepherd on the hills of Cumberland; and with these advantages I was to commence the train of solitary life. Such were the reflections that ushered in my slumber on that night.

The shelter, however, and less disturbed repose which I enjoyed, restored me the following morning to a greater portion of health and strength, than I had experienced since my fatal shipwreck. Among the stores I had discovered on searching the cottage the preceding night, was a quantity of dried grapes; these refreshed me in the morning, as I left my lodging and proceeded towards a town which I discerned at no great distance. As far as I could divine, it must have been Forli. I entered with pleasure its wide and grassy streets. All, it is true, pictured the excess of desolation; yet I loved to find myself in those spots which had been the abode of my fellow creatures. I delighted to traverse street after street, to look up at the tall houses, and repeat to myself, Once they contained beings similar to myself— I was not always the wretch I am now. The wide square of Forli, the arcade around it, its light and pleasant aspect cheered me. I was pleased with the idea, that, if the earth should be again peopled, we, the lost race, would, in the relics left behind, present no contemptible exhibition of our powers to the new comers.

I entered one of the palaces, and opened the door of a magnificent saloon. I started—I looked again with renewed wonder. What wild-looking, unkempt, half-naked savage was that before me? The surprise was momentary.

I perceived that it was I myself whom I beheld in a large mirror at the end of the hall. No wonder that the lover of the princely Idris should fail to recognize himself in the miserable object there portayed. My tatterred dress was that in which I had crawled half alive from the tempestuous sea. My long and tangled hair hung in elf locks on my brow—my dark eyes, now hollow and wild, gleamed from under them—my cheeks were discolored by the jaundice, which (the effect of misery and neglect) suffused my skin, and were half hid by a beard of many days' growth.

Yet why should I not remain thus, I thought; the world is dead, and this squalid attire is a fitter mourning garb than the foppery of a black suit. And thus, methinks, I should have remained, had not hoped, without which I do not believe man could exist, whispered to me, that, in such a plight, I should be an object of fear and aversion to the being, preserved I knew not where, but I fondly trusted, at length to be found by me. Will my readers scorn the vanity, that made me attire myself with some care, for the sake of this visionary being? Or will they forgive the freaks of a half-crazed imagination? I can easily forgive myself—for hope, however vague, was so dear to me, and a sentiment of pleasure of so rare occurrence, that I yielded readily to any idea that cherished the one, or promised any recurrence of the former to my sorrowing heart.

After such occupation, I visited every street, alley, and nook of Forli. These Italian towns presented an appearance of still greater desolation, than those of England or France. Plague had appeared here earlier—it had finished its course, and achieved its work much sooner than with us. Probably the last summer had found no human being alive, in all the track included between the shores of Calabria and the northern Alps. My search was utterly vain, yet I did not despond. Reason methought was on my side; and the chances were by no means contemptible, that there should exist in some part of Italy a survivor like myself—of a wasted, depopulate land. As therefore I rambled through the empty town, I formed my plan for future operations. I would continue to journey on towards Rome. After I should have satisfied myself, by a narrow search, that I left behind no human being in the towns through which I passed, I would write up in a conspicuous part of each, with white paint, in three languages, that "Verney, the last of the race of Englishmen, had taken up his abode in Rome."

In pursuance of this scheme, I entered a painter's shop, and procured myself the paint. It is strange that so trivial an occupation should have consoled, and even enlivened me. But grief renders one childish, despair fantastic. To this simple inscription, I merely added the adjuration, "Friend, come! I wait for thee!—*Deh, vieni! ti aspetto!*"

On the following morning, with something like hope for my companion, I quitted Forli on my way to Rome. Until now, agonizing retrospect, and dreary prospects for the future, had stung me when awake, and cradled me to my repose. Many times I had delivered myself up to the tyranny of anguish—many times I resolved a speedy end to my woes; and death by my own hands was a remedy, whose practicability was even cheering to me. What could I fear in the other world? If there were an hell, and I were doomed to it, I should come an adept to the sufferance of its tortures—the act were easy, the speedy and certain end of my deplorable tragedy. But now these thoughts faded before the new born expectation. I went on my way, not as before, feeling each hour, each minute, to be an age instinct with incalculable pain.

As I wandered along the plain, at the foot of the Appenines— through their vallies, and over their bleak summits, my path led me through a country which had been trodden by heroes, visited and admired by thousands. They had, as a tide, receded, leaving me blank and bare in the midst. But why complain? Did I not hope?--so I schooled myself, even after the enlivening spirit had really deserted me, and thus I was obliged to call up all the fortitude I could command, and that was not much, to prevent a recurrence of that chaotic and intolerable despair, that had succeeded to the miserable shipwreck, that had consummated every fear, and dashed to annihilation every joy.

I rose each day with the morning sun, and left my desolate inn. As my feet strayed through the unpeopled country, my thoughts rambled through the universe, and I was least miserable when I could, absorbed in reverie, forget the passage of the hours. Each evening, in spite of weariness, I detested to enter any dwelling, there to take up my nightly abode—I have sat, hour after hour, at the door of the cottage I had selected, unable to lift the latch, and meet face to face blank desertion within. Many nights, though autumnal mists were spread around, I passed under an ilex—many times I have supped on arbutus berries and chesnuts, making a fire, gypsy-like, on the ground—because wild natural scenery reminded me less acutely of my hopeless state of loneliness. I counted the days, and bore with me a peeled willow wand, on which, as well as I could remember, I had notched the days that had elapsed since my wreck, and each night I added another unit to the melancholy sum.

Mary Shelley

I had toiled up a hill which led to Spoleto. Around was spread a plain, encircled by the chesnut-covered Appenines. A dark ravine was on one side, spanned by an aqueduct, whose tall arches were rooted in the dell below, and attested that man had once deigned to bestow labor and thought here; to adorn and civilize nature. Savage, ungrateful nature, which in wild sport defaced his remains, protruding her easily renewed, and fragile growth of wild flowers and parasite plants around his eternal edifices. I sat on a fragment of rock, and looked round. The sun had bathed in gold the western atmosphere, and in the east the clouds caught the radiance, and budded into transient loveliness. I set on a world that contained me alone for its inhabitant. I took out my wand—I counted the marks. Twenty-five were already traced—twenty-five days had already elapsed, since human voice had gladdened my ears, or human countenance met my gaze. Twenty-five long, weary days, succeeded by dark and lonesome nights, had mingled with foregone years, and had become a part of the past—the never to be recalled—a real, undeniable portion of my life—twenty-five long, long days.

Why this was not a month!—Why talk of days—or weeks—or months—I must grasp years in my imagination, if I would truly picture the future to myself—three, five, ten, twenty, fifty anniversaries of that fatal epoch might elapse—every year containing twelve months, each of more numerous calculation in a diary, than the twenty-five days gone by—Can it be? Will it be?—We had been used to look forward to death tremulously—wherefore, but because its place was obscure? But more terrible, and far more obscure, was the unveiled course of my lone futurity. I broke my wand; I threw it from me. I needed no recorder of the inch and barleycorn growth of my life, while my unquiet thoughts created other divisions, than those ruled over by the planets—and, in looking back on the age that had elapsed since I had been alone, I disdained to give the name of days and hours to the throes of agony which had in truth portioned it out.

I hid my face in my hands. The twitter of the young birds going to rest, and their rustling among the trees, disturbed the still evening air—the crickets chirped—the aziolo cooed at intervals. My thoughts had been of death—these sounds spoke to me of life. I lifted up my eyes—a bat wheeled round—the sun had sunk behind the jagged line of mountains, and the paly, crescent moon was visible, silver white, amidst the orange sunset, and accompanied by one bright star, prolonged thus the twilight. A herd of cattle passed along in the dell below, untended, toward their watering place—the grass was rustled by a gentle breeze, and the olive-woods, mellowed into soft masses by the moonlight, contrasted their sea-green with the dark chesnut foliage. Yes, this is the earth; there is no change—no ruin—no rent made in her verdurous expanse; she continues to wheel round and round, with alternate night and day, through the sky, though man is not her adorner or inhabitant. Why could I not forget myself like one of those animals, and no longer suffer the wild tumult of misery that I endure? Yet, ah! what a deadly breach yawns between their state and mine! Have not they companions? Have not they each their mate—their cherished young, their home, which, though unexpressed to us, is, I doubt not, endeared and enriched, even in their eyes, by the society which kind nature has created for them? It is I only that am alone—I, on this little hill top, gazing on plain and mountain recess—on sky, and its starry population, listening to every sound of earth, and air, and murmuring wave,—I only cannot express to any companion my many thoughts, nor lay my throbbing head on any loved bosom, nor drink from meeting eyes and intoxicating dew, that transcends the fabulous nectar of the gods. Shall I not then complain? Shall I not curse the murderous engine which has mowed down the children of men, by brethren? Shall I not bestow a malediction on every other of nature's offspring, which dares live and enjoy, while I live and suffer?

Ah, no! I will discipline my sorrowing heart to sympathy in your joys; I will be happy, because ye are so. Live on, ye innocents, nature's selected darlings; I am not much unlike to you. Nerves, pulse, brain, joint, and flesh, of such am I composed, and ye are organized by the same laws. I have something beyond this, but I will call it a defect, not an endowment, if it leads me to misery, while ye are happy. Just then, there emerged from a near copse two goats and a little kid, by the mother's side; they began to browze the herbage of the hill. I approached near to them, without their perceiving me; I gathered a handful of fresh grass, and held it out; the little one nestled close to its mother, while she timidly withdrew. The male

Mary Shelley

stepped forward, fixing his eyes on me: I drew near, still holding out my lure, while he, depressing his head, rushed at me with his horns. I was a very fool; I knew it, yet I yielded to my rage. I snatched up a huge fragment of rock; it would have crushed my rash foe. I poised it—aimed it—then my heart failed me. I hurled it wide of the mark; it rolled clattering among the bushes into the dell. My little visitants, all aghast, galloped back into the covert of the wood; while I, my very heart bleeding and torn, rushed down the hill, and by the violence of bodily exertion, sought to escape from my miserable self.

Harriet Martineau

Harriet Martineau

(1802–1876)

Harriet Martineau's struggle to publish her first book, *Illustrations of Political Economy*, tested her belief in her own work. She was rejected by publisher after publisher. When she finally found a publisher for the work, his terms were so unfavorable that they seemed to bode certain failure. Leaving him, Martineau began the four-mile walk back to her lodgings. As she later described it in her *Autobiography*, she "became too giddy to stand without support; and I leaned over some dirty palings, pretending to look at a cabbage bed, but saying to myself, as I stood with closed eyes, 'My book will do yet.' " *Illustrations of Political Economy*, a fictionalized account of economics, brought her international fame. She went on to write books on economics, culture, history, philosophy, and travel, as well as novels, short stories, and an extensive autobiography. Already an established writer, Martineau traveled to the Middle East and recorded her impressions in *Eastern Life, Present and Past*. Again, she had difficulties in publishing the work; again, it was highly acclaimed when it appeared. The following selection from *Eastern Life* describes Martineau's view of the harem, a view that contrasts strikingly with the romanticized picture male writers often give.

FROM EASTERN LIFE: PRESENT AND PAST

THE HAREEM.

I saw two Hareems in the East; and it would be wrong to pass them over in an account of my travels; though the subject is as little agreeable as any I can have to treat. I cannot now think of the two mornings thus employed without a heaviness of heart greater than I have ever brought away from Deaf and Dumb Schools, Lunatic Asylums, or even Prisons. As such are my impressions of hareems, of course I shall not say whose they were that I visited. Suffice it that one was at Cairo and the other at Damascus.

The royal hareems were not accessible while I was in Egypt. The

Pasha's eldest daughter, the widow of Defterdar Bey, was under her father's displeasure, and was, in fact, a prisoner in her own house. While her father did not visit her, no one else could: and while she was secluded, her younger sister could not receive visitors: and thus, their hareems were closed. The one which I saw was that of a gentleman of high rank; and as good a specimen as could be seen. The misfortune was that there was a mistake about the presence of an interpreter. A lady was to have met us who spoke Italian or French: but she did not arrive; and the morning therefore passed in dumb show: and we could not repeat our visit on a subsequent day, as we were invited to do. We lamented this much at the time: but our subsequent experience of what is to be learned in a hareem with the aid of an intelligent and kind interpretess convinced us that we had not lost much.

Before I went abroad, more than one sensible friend had warned me to leave behind as many prejudices as possible; and especially on this subject, on which the prejudices of Europeans are the strongest. I was reminded of the wide extent, both of time and space, in which Polygamy had existed; and that openness of mind was as necessary to the accurate observation of this institution as of every other. I had really taken this advice to heart: I had been struck by the view taken by Mr. Milnes in his beautiful poem of "the Hareem"; and I am sure I did meet this subject with every desire to investigate the ideas and general feelings involved in it. I learned a very great deal about the working of the institution; and I believe I apprehend the thoughts and feelings of the persons concerned in it: and I declare that if we are to look for a hell upon earth, it is where polygamy exists: and that, as polygamy runs riot in Egypt, Egypt is the lowest depth of this hell. I always before believed that every arrangement and prevalent practice had some one fair side—some one redeeming quality: and diligently did I look for this fair side in regard to polygamy: but there is none. The longer one studies the subject, and the deeper one penetrates into it—the more is one's mind confounded with the intricacy of its iniquity, and the more does one's heart feel as if it would break.

I shall say but little of what I know. If there were the slightest chance of doing any good, I would speak out at all hazards; I would

Harriet Martineau

meet all the danger, and endure all the disgust. But there is no reaching the minds of any who live under the accursed system. It is a system which belongs to a totally different region of ideas from ours: and there is nothing to appeal to in the minds of those who, knowing the facts of the institution, can endure it: and at home, no one needs appealing to and convincing. Any plea for liberality that we meet at home proceeds from some poetical fancy, or some laudable desire for impartiality in the absence of knowledge of the facts. Such pleas are not operative enough to render it worth while to shock and sadden many hearts by statements which no one should be required needlessly to endure. I will tell only something of what I saw, and but little of what I thought and know.

At ten o'clock, one morning, Mrs. Y. and I were home from our early ride, and dressed for our visit to a hareem of a high order. The lady to whose kindness we mainly owed this opportunity, accompanied us, with her daughter. We had a disagreeable drive in the carriage belonging to the hotel, knocking against asses, horses and people all the way. We alighted at the entrance of a paved passage leading to a court which we crossed: and then, in a second court, we were before the entrance of the hareem.

A party of eunuchs stood before a faded curtain, which they held aside when the gentlemen of our party and the dragoman had gone forward. Retired some way behind the curtain stood, in a half circle, eight or ten slave girls, in an attitude of deep obeisance. Two of them then took charge of each of us, holding us by the arms above the elbows, to help us upstairs. After crossing a lobby at the top of the stairs, we entered a handsome apartment, where lay the chief wife— at that time an invalid. The ceiling was gaily painted; and so were the walls—the latter with curiously bad attempts at domestic perspective. There were four handsome mirrors; and the curtains in the doorway were of a beautiful shawl fabric, fringed and tasselled. A Turkey carpet not only covered the whole floor, but was turned up at the corners. Deewáns extended round nearly the whole room—a lower one for ordinary use, and a high one for the seat of honour. The windows, which had a sufficient fence of blinds, looked upon a pretty garden, where I saw orange trees and many others, and the fences were hung with rich creepers.

On cushions on the floor lay the chief lady, ill and miserable-looking. She rose as we entered; but we made her lie down again: and she was then covered with a silk counterpane. Her dress was, as we saw when she rose, loose trowsers of blue striped cotton under her black silk jacket: and the same blue cotton appeared at the wrists, under her black sleeves. Her headdress was of black net, bunched out curiously behind. Her hair was braided down the sides of this headdress behind, and the ends were pinned over her forehead. Some of the black net was brought round her face, and under the chin, showing the outline of a face which had no beauty in it, nor traces of former beauty, but which was interesting to-day from her manifest illness and unhappiness. There was a strong expression of wayward-ness and peevishness about the mouth, however. She wore two handsome diamond rings; and she and one other lady had watches and gold chains. She complained of her head; and her left hand was bound up: she made signs by pressing her bosom, and imitating the dandling of a baby, which, with her occasional tears, persuaded my companions that she had met with some accident and had lost her infant. On leaving the hareem, we found that it was not a child of her own that she was mourning, but that of a white girl in the hareem: and that the wife's illness was wholly from grief for the loss of this baby; a curious illustration of the feelings and manners of the place! The children born in large hareems are extremely few: and they are usually idolised, and sometimes murdered. It is known that in the houses at home which morally most resemble these hareems (though little enough externally) when the rare event of the birth of a child happens, a passionate joy extends over the wretched household: jars are quieted, drunkenness is moderated, and there is no self-denial which the poor creatures will not undergo during this gratification of their feminine instincts. They will nurse the child all night in illness, and pamper it all day with sweetmeats and toys; they will fight for the possession of it, and be almost heartbroken at its loss: and lose it they must; for the child always dies—killed with kindness, even if born healthy. This natural outbreak of feminine instinct takes place in the too populous hareem, when a child is given to any one of the many who are longing for the gift: and if it dies naturally, it is mourned as we saw through a wonderful conquest of personal

jealousy by this general instinct. But when the jealousy is uppermost
—what happens then?—why, the strangling the innocent in its
sleep—or the letting it slip from the window into the river below—or
the mixing poison with its food; the mother and the murderess, always
rivals and now fiends, being shut up together for life. If the child
lives, what then? If a girl, she sees before her from the beginning the
nothingness of external life, and the chaos of interior existence, in
which she is to dwell for life. If a boy, he remains among the women
till ten years old, seeing things when the eunuchs come in to romp,
and hearing things among the chatter of the ignorant women which
brutalise him for life before the age of rationality comes. But I will
not dwell on these hopeless miseries.

A sensible looking old lady, who had lost an eye, sat at the head of
the invalid: and a nun-like elderly woman, whose head and throat
were wrapped in unstarched muslin, sat behind for a time, and then
went away, after an affectionate salutation to the invalid. Towards
the end of the visit, the husband's mother came in—looking like a
little old man in her coat trimmed with fur. Her countenance was
cheerful and pleasant. We saw, I think, about twenty more women—
some slaves—most or all young—some good-looking, but none
handsome. Some few were black; and the rest very light: Nubians or
Abyssinians and Circassians, no doubt. One of the best figures, as a
picture, in the hareem, was a Nubian girl, in an amber-coloured
watered silk, embroidered with black, looped up in festoons, and
finished with a black boddice. The richness of the gay printed cotton
skirts and sleeves surprised us: the finest shawls could hardly have
looked better. One graceful girl had her pretty figure well shown by
a tight-fitting black dress. Their heads were dressed much like the
chief lady's. Two, who must have been sisters, if not twins, had
patches between the eyes. One handsmaid was barefoot, and several
were without shoes. Though there were none of the whole large
number who could be called particularly pretty individually, the
scene was, on the whole, exceedingly striking, as the realisation of
what one knew before, but as in a dream. The girls went out and
came in, but, for the most part, stood in a half circle. Two sat on
their heels for a time: and some went to play in the neighbouring
apartments.

Coffee was handed to us twice, with all the well-known apparatus of jewelled cups, embroidered tray cover, and gold-flowered napkins. There were chibouques, of course: and sherbets in cut glass cups. The time was passed in attempts to have conversation by signs; attempts which are fruitless among people of the different ideas which belong to different races. How much they made out about us, we do not know: but they inquired into the mutual relationships of the party, and put the extraordinary questions which are always put to ladies who visit the hareems. A young lady of my acquaintance, of the age of eighteen, but looking younger, went with her mother to a hareem in Cairo (not the one I have been describing) and excited great amazement when obliged to confess that she had not either children or a husband. One of the wives threw her arms about her, intreated her to stay for ever, said she should have any husband she liked, but particularly recommended her own, saying that she was sure he would soon wish for another wife, and she had so much rather it should be my young friend, who would amuse her continually, than anybody else that she could not be so fond of. Everywhere they pitied us European women heartily, that we had to go about travelling, and appearing in the streets without being properly taken care of—that is watched. They think us strangely neglected in being left so free, and boast of their spy system and imprisonment as tokens of the value in which they are held.

The mourning worn by the lady who went with us was the subject of much speculation: and many questions were asked about her home and family. To appease the curiosity about her home, she gave her card. As I anticipated, this did not answer. It was the great puzzle of the whole interview. At first the poor lady thought it was to do her head good: then, she fidgetted about it, in the evident fear of omitting some observance: but at last, she understood that she was to keep it. When we had taken our departure, however, a eunuch was sent after us to inquire of the dragoman what "the letter" was which our companion had given to the lady.

The difficulty is to get away, when one is visiting a hareem. The poor ladies cannot conceive of one's having anything to do; and the only reason they can understand for the interview coming to an end is the arrival of sunset, after which it would, they think, be improper for any woman to be abroad. And the amusement to them of such a visit is so great that they protract it to the utmost, even in such a case as ours to-day, when all intercourse was conducted by dumb show. It is certainly very tiresome; and the only wonder is that the hostesses can like it. To sit hour after hour on the deewán, without any exchange of ideas, having our clothes examined, and being plied with successive cups of coffee and sherbet, and pipes, and being gazed at by a half-circle of girls in brocade and shawls, and made to sit down again as soon as one attempts to rise, is as wearisome an experience as one meets with in foreign lands. The weariness of heart is, however, the worst part of it. I noted all the faces well during our constrained stay; and I saw no trace of mind in any one except in the homely one-eyed old lady. All the younger ones were dull, soul-less, brutish, or peevish. How should it be otherwise, when the only idea of their whole lives is that which, with all our interests and engagements, we consider too prominent with us? There cannot be a woman of them all who is not dwarfed and withered in mind and soul by being kept wholly engrossed with that one interest—detained at that stage in existence which, though most important in its place, is so as a means to ulterior ends. The ignorance is fearful enough; but the grossness is revolting.

At the third move, and when it was by some means understood that we were waited for, we were permitted to go—after a visit of above two hours. The sick lady rose from her cushions, notwith-standing our opposition, and we were conducted forth with much observance. On each side of the curtain which overhung the outer entrance stood a girl with a bottle of rose water, some of which was splashed in our faces as we passed out.

We had reached the carriage when we were called back: his Excellency was waiting for us. So we visited him in a pretty apart-ment, paved with variegated marbles, and with a fountain in the centre. His Excellency was a sensible-looking man, with gay, easy and graceful manners. He lamented the mistake about the interpreter, and said we must go again, when we might have conversation. He insisted upon attending us to the carriage, actually passing between the files of beggars which lined the outer passage. The dragoman was so excessively shocked by this degree of condescension, that we felt obliged to be so too, and remonstrated: but in vain. He stood till the door was shut, and the whip was cracked. He is a liberal-minded man; and his hareem is nearly as favorable a specimen as could be selected for a visit; but what is this best specimen? I find these words written down on the same day, in my journal: written, as I well remember, in heaviness of heart. "I am glad of the opportunity of seeing a hareem: but it leaves an impression of discontent and uneasiness which I shall be glad to sleep off. And I am not conscious that there is prejudice in this. I feel that a visit to the worst room in the Rookery in St. Giles's would have affected me less painfully. There are there at least the elements of a rational life, however perverted; while here humanity is wholly and hopelessly baulked. It will never do to look on this as a case for cosmopolitan philosophy to regard complacently, and require a good construction for. It is not a phase of natural early manners. It is as pure a conventionalism as our representative monarchy, or German heraldry, or Hindoo caste; and the most atrocious in the world."

And of this atrocious system, Egypt is the most atrocious example. It has unequalled facilities for the importation of black and white slaves; and these facilities are used to the utmost; yet the population is incessantly on the decline. But for the importation of slaves, the upper classes, where polygamy runs riot, must soon die out—so few are the children born, and so fatal to health are the arrangements of society. The finest children are those born of Circassian or Georgian mothers; and but for these, we should soon hear little more of an upper class in Egypt. Large numbers are brought from the south— the girls to be made attendants or concubines in the hareem, and the boys to be made, in a vast proportion, those guards to the female part of the establishment whose mere presence is a perpetual insult and shame to humanity. The business of keeping up the supply of these miserable wretches—of whom the Pasha's eldest daughter has fifty for her exclusive service—is in the hands of the Christians of Asyoot. It is these Christians who provide a sufficient supply, and cause a sufficient mortality to keep the number of the sexes pretty equal: in consideration of which we cannot much wonder that Christianity does not appear very venerable in the eyes of Mohammedans.

These eunuchs are indulged in regard to dress, personal liberty, and often the possession of office, domestic, military, or political. When retained as guards of the hareem, they are in their master's confidence—acting as his spies, and indispensable to the ladies, as a medium of communication with the world, and as furnishing their amusements—being at once playmates and servants. It is no unusual thing for the eunuchs to whip the ladies away from a window, whence they had hoped for amusement; or to call them opprobrious names; or to inform against them to their owner: and it is also no unusual thing for them to romp with the ladies, to obtain their confidence, and to try their dispositions. Cases have been known of one of them becoming the friend of some poor girl of higher nature and tendencies than her companions; and even of a closer attachment, which is not objected to by the proprietor of both. It is a case too high for his jealousy, so long as he knows that the cage is secure. It has become rather the fashion to extenuate the lot of the captive of either sex: to point out how the Nubian girl, who would have ground corn and woven garments, and nursed her infants in comparative poverty all her days, is now surrounded by luxury, and provided for for life: and how the Circassian girl may become a wife of the son of her proprietor, and hold a high rank in the hareem: and how the wretched brothers of these slaves may rise to posts of military command or political confidence; but it is enough to see them to be disabused of all impressions of their good fortune. It is enough to see the dull and gross face of the handmaid of the hareem, and to remember at the moment the cheerful, modest countenance of the Nubian girl busy about her household tasks, or of the Nubian mother, with her infants hanging about her as she looks, with face open to the sky, for her husband's return from the field, or meets him on the river bank. It is enough to observe the wretched health and abject, or worn, or insolent look of the guard of the hareem, and to remember that he ought to have been the head of a household of his own, however humble: and in this contrast of what is with what ought to have been, slavery is seen to be fully as detestable here as anywhere else. These two hellish practices, slavery and polygamy, which, as practices, can clearly never be separated, are here avowedly connected; and in that connexion, are exalted into a double institution, whose working is such as to make one almost wish that the

Nile would rise to cover the tops of the hills, and sweep away the whole abomination. Till this happens, there is, in the condition of Egypt, a fearful warning before the eyes of all men. The Egyptians laugh at the marriage arrangements of Europe, declaring that virtual polygamy exists everywhere, and is not improved by hypocritical concealment. The European may see, when startled by the state of Egypt, that virtual slavery is indispensably required by the practice of polygamy; virtual proprietorship of the women involved, without the obligations imposed by actual proprietorship; and cruel oppression of the men who should have been the husbands of these women. And again, the Carolina planter, who knows as well as any Egyptian that polygamy is a natural concomitant of slavery, may see in the state of Egypt and the Egyptians what his country and his children must come to, if either of those vile arrangements is permitted which necessitates the other.

It is scarcely needful to say that those benevolent persons are mistaken who believe that Slavery in Egypt has been abolished by the Pasha, and the importation of slaves effectually prohibited. Neither the Pasha nor any other human power can abolish slavery while Polygamy is an institution of the country, the proportion of the sexes remaining in Egypt what it is, there and everywhere else.

The reason assigned by Montesquieu for polygamy throughout the East has no doubt something in it: that women become so early marriageable that the wife cannot satisfy the needs of the husband's mind and heart: and that therefore he must have both a bride and a companion of whom he may make a friend. How little there is in this to excuse the polygamy of Egypt may be seen by an observation of the state of things there and in Turkey, where the same religion and natural laws prevail as in Egypt. In Egypt, the difficulty would be great of finding a wife of any age who could be the friend of a man of any sense: and in Turkey, where the wives are of a far higher order, polygamy is rare, and women are not married so young. It is not usual there to find such disparity of years as one finds in Egypt between the husband and his youngest wife. The cause assigned by Montesquieu is true in connexion with a vicious state of society: but it is not insuperable, and it will operate only as long as it is wished for. If any influence could exalt the ideas of marriage, and improve the training of women in Egypt, it would soon be seen that men would prefer marrying women of nearly their own age, and would naturally remain comparatively constant: but before this experiment can be tried, parents must have ceased to become restless when their daughter reaches eleven years old, and afraid of disgrace if she remains unmarried long after that.

I was told, while at Cairo, of one extraordinary family where there is not only rational intercourse and confidence at home, and some relaxation of imprisonment, but the young ladies read!—and read French and Italian! I asked what would be the end of this: and my informant replied that whether the young ladies married or not, they would sooner or later sink down, he thought, into a state even less contented than the ordinary. There could be no sufficient inducement for secluded girls, who never saw anybody wiser than themselves, to go on reading French and Italian books within a certain range. For want of stimulus and sympathy, they would stop; and then, finding themselves dissatisfied among the nothings which fill the life of other women, they would be very unhappy. The exceptional persons under a bad state of things, and the beginners under an improving system must ever be sufferers— martyrs of their particular reformation. To this they may object less than others would for them, if they are conscious of the personal honour and general blessing of their martyrdom.

The youngest wife I ever saw (except the swathed and veiled brides we encountered in the streets of Egyptian cities) was in a Turkish hareem which Mrs. Y. and I visited at Damascus. I will tell that story now, that I may dismiss the subject of this chapter. I heartily dreaded this second visit to a hareem, and braced myself up to it as one does to an hour at the dentist's, or to an expedition into the City to prove a debt. We had the comfort of a good and pleasant interpreter; and there was more mirth and nonsense than in the Cairo hareem; and therefore somewhat less disgust and constraint: but still it was painful enough. We saw the seven wives of three gentlemen, and a crowd of attendants and visitors. Of the seven, two had been the wives of the head of the household, who was dead: three were the wives of his eldest son, aged twenty-two;

and the remaining two were the wives of his second son, aged fifteen.
The youngest son, aged thirteen, was not yet married; but he would
be thinking about it soon. The pair of widows were elderly women,
as merry as girls, and quite at their ease. Of the other five, three
were sisters: that is, we conclude, half-sisters; children of different
mothers in the same hareem. It is evident at a glance what a tragedy
lies under this; what the horrors of jealousy must be among sisters
thus connected for life; three of them between two husbands in the
same house! And we were told that the jealousy had begun, young
as they were, and the third having been married only a week. This
young creature, aged twelve, was the bride of the husband of fifteen.
She was the most conspicuous person in the place, not only for the
splendour of her dress, but because she sat on the deewán, while the
others sat or lounged on cushions on the raised floor. The moment
we took our seats I was struck with compassion for this child—
she looked so grave, and sad and timid. While the others romped
and giggled, pushing and pulling one another about, and laughing
at jokes among themselves, she never smiled, but looked on listlessly.
I was determined to make her laugh before we went away; and at
last she relaxed somewhat—smiling, and growing grave again in a
moment: but at length she really and truly laughed; and when we
were shown the whole hareem, she also slipped her bare and dyed
feet into her pattens inlaid with mother-of-pearl, and went into the
courts with us, nestling to us, and seeming to lose the sense of her
new position for the time: but there was far less of the gaiety of a
child about her than in the elderly widows. Her dress was superb;
a full skirt and boddice of geranium-coloured brocade, embossed
with gold flowers and leaves; and her frill and ruffles were of
geranium-coloured gauze. Her eyebrows were frightful—joined and
prolonged by black paint. Her head was covered with a silk net, in
almost every mesh of which were stuck jewels or natural flowers:
so that her head was like a bouquet sprinkled with diamonds. Her
nails were dyed black; and her feet were dyed black in chequers.
Her complexion, called white, was of an unhealthy yellow: and
indeed we did not see a healthy complexion among the whole company; nor anywhere among women who were secluded from exercise,
while pampered with all the luxuries of eastern living.

Harriet Martineau

Besides the seven wives, a number of attendants came in to look at us, and serve the pipes and sherbet; and a few ladies from a neighbouring hareem; and a party of Jewesses, with whom we had some previous acquaintance. Mrs. Y. was compelled to withdraw her lace veil, and then to take off her bonnet: and she was instructed that the street was the place for her to wear her veil down, and that they expected to see her face. Then her bonnet went round, and was tried on many heads—one merry girl wearing it long enough to surprise many new comers with the joke. My gloves were stretched and pulled all manner of ways, in their attempts to thrust their large, broad brown hands into them, one after another. But the great amusement was my trumpet. The eldest widow, who sat next me, asked for it, and put it to her ear; when I said "Bo!" When she had done laughing, she put it into her next neighbour's ear, and said "Bo!" and in this way it came round to me again. But in two minutes, it was asked for again, and went round a second time—everybody laughing as loud as ever at each "Bo!"—and then a third time! Could one have conceived it!—The next joke was on behalf of the Jewesses, four or five of whom sat in a row on the deewán. Almost everybody else was puffing away at a chibouque or a nargeeleh, and the place was one cloud of smoke. The poor Jewesses were obliged to decline joining us; for it happened to be Saturday: they must not smoke on the sabbath. They were naturally much pitied: and some of the young wives did what was possible for them. Drawing in a long breath of smoke, they puffed it forth in the faces of the Jewesses, who opened mouth and nostrils eagerly to receive it. Thus was the sabbath observed, to shouts of laughter.

A pretty little blue-eyed girl of seven was the only child we saw. She nestled against her mother; and the mother clasped her closely, lest we should carry her off to London. She begged we would not wish to take her child to London, and said she "would not sell her for much money." One of the wives was pointed out to us as particularly happy in the prospect of becoming a mother; and we were taken to see the room in which she was to lie in, which was all in readiness, though the event was not looked for for more than half a year. She was in the gayest spirits, and sang and danced. While she was lounging on her cushions, I thought her the handsomest and most graceful, as well as the happiest, of the party: but when she rose to dance, the charm was destroyed for ever. The dancing is utterly disgusting. A pretty Jewess of twelve years old danced, much in the same way; but with downcast eyes and an air of modesty. While the dancing went on, and the smoking, and drinking coffee and sherbet, and the singing, to the accompaniment of a tambourine, some hideous old hags came in successively, looked and laughed, and went away again. Some negresses made a good back ground to this thoroughly Eastern picture. All the while, romping, kissing and screaming went on among the ladies, old and young. At first, I thought them a perfect rabble; but when I recovered myself a little, I saw that there was some sense in the faces of the elderly women. In the midst of all this fun, the interpretess assured us that "there is much jealousy every day"; jealousy of the favoured wife; that is, in this case, of the one who was pointed out to us by her companions as so eminently happy, and with whom they were romping and kissing, as with the rest. Poor thing! even the happiness of these her best days is hollow: for she cannot have, at the same time, peace in the hareem and her husband's love.

They were so free in their questions about us, and so evidently pleased when we used a similar impertinence about them, that we took the opportunity of learning a good deal of their way of life. Mrs. Y. and I were consulting about noticing the bride's dress, when we found we had put off too long: we were asked how we liked her dress, and encouraged to handle the silk. So I went on to examine the bundles of false hair that some of them wore; the pearl bracelets on their tattooed arms, and their jewelled and inlaid pattens. In answer to our question what they did in the way of occupation, they said "nothing": but when we inquired whether they never made clothes or sweetmeats, they replied "yes." They earnestly wished us to stay always; and they could not understand why we should not. My case puzzled them particularly. I believe they took me for a servant; and they certainly pitied me extremely for having to go about without being taken care of. They asked what I did: and Mrs. Y., being anxious to do me all honour, told them I had written many books: but the information was thrown away, because they did not know what a book was. Then we informed them that I lived in

Olive Schreiner

Olive Schreiner

(1855–1920)

At twenty-six, after years of writing and of working as a governess in the farmland of her native South Africa, Olive Schreiner traveled to England. With her she carried the novel that was to make her one of the most noted feminists and novelists of her time—*The Story of an African Farm*. (Ironically, the novel was first published under a man's name.) Schreiner wrote novels, short stories, allegories, "dreams," articles, a book on women, and a book on South Africa. In her writings, she foresaw many of the problems that would confront the modern woman, modern South Africa, and the modern world. *The Story of an African Farm* is about three young people, growing up on a farm in South Africa. Em is domestic and conventional. Waldo is a simple man, who loves nature. Lyndall, the novel's central character, is rebellious and intellectual. The following selection focuses on Lyndall, just returned from boarding school and painfully aware of some of the problems she will face as a woman.

FROM THE STORY
OF AN AFRICAN FARM

LYNDALL.

She was more like a princess, yes, far more like a princess, than the lady who still hung on the wall in Tant' Sannie's bedroom. So Em thought. She leaned back in the little armchair; she wore a gray dressing-gown, and her long hair was combed out and hung to the ground. Em, sitting before her, looked up with mingled respect and admiration.

Lyndall was tired after her long journey, and had come to her room early. Her eyes ran over the familiar objects. Strange to go away for four years, and come back, and find that the candle standing on the dressing-table still cast the shadow of an old crone's head in the corner beyond the clothes-horse. Strange that even a shadow should last longer than man! She looked about among the old familiar objects; all was there, but the old self was gone.

"What are you noticing?" asked Em.

"Nothing, and everything. I thought the windows were higher. If I were you, when I get this place I should raise the walls. There is not room to breathe here; one suffocates."

"Gregory is going to make many alterations," said Em; and drawing nearer to the gray dressing-gown, respectfully, "Do you like him, Lyndall? Is he not handsome?"

"He must have been a fine baby," said Lyndall, looking at the white dimity curtain that hung above the window.

Em was puzzled.

"There are some men," said Lyndall, "whom you never can believe were babies at all; and others you never see without thinking how very nice they must have looked when they wore socks and pink sashes."

Em remained silent; then she said with a little dignity, "When you know him you will love him as I do. When I compare other people with him, they seem so weak and little. *Our* hearts are so cold, our loves are mixed up with so many other things. But he— no one is worthy of his love. I am not. It is so great and pure."

"You need not make yourself unhappy on that point—your poor return for his love, my dear," said Lyndall. "A man's love is a fire of olive-wood. It leaps higher every moment; it roars, it blazes, it shoots out red flames; it threatens to wrap you round and devour you—you who stand by like an icicle in the glow of its fierce warmth. You are self-reproached at your own chilliness and want of reciprocity. The next day, when you go to warm your hands a little, you find a few ashes. 'Tis a long love and cool against a short love and hot; men, at all events, have nothing to complain of."

"You speak so because you do not know men," said Em, instantly assuming the dignity of superior knowledge so universally affected by affianced and married women in discussing man's nature with their uncontracted sisters. "You will know them too some day, and then you will think differently," she said, with the condescending magnanimity which superior knowledge can always afford to show to ignorance.

Lyndall's little lip quivered in a manner indicative of intense amusement. She twirled a massive ring upon her forefinger—a ring more suitable for the hand of a man, and noticeable in design— a diamond cross let into gold, with the initials *R.R.* below it.

"Ah, Lyndall," Em cried, "perhaps you are engaged yourself— that is why you smile. Yes; I am sure you are. Look at this ring!"

Lyndall drew the hand quickly from her.

"I am not in so great a hurry to put my neck beneath any man's foot; and I do not so greatly admire the crying of babies," she said, as she closed her eyes half wearily and leaned back in the chair. "There are other women glad of such work."

Em felt rebuked and ashamed. How could she take Lyndall, and show her the white linen and the wreath and the embroidery? She was quiet for a little while, and then began to talk about Trana and the old farm-servants, till she saw her companion was weary; then she rose and left her for the night. But after Em was gone Lyndall sat on, watching the old crone's face in the corner, and with a weary look, as though the whole world's weight rested on these frail young shoulders.

The next morning, Waldo, starting off before breakfast with a bag of mealies slung over his shoulder to feed the ostriches, heard a light step behind him.

"Wait for me; I am coming with you," said Lyndall, adding as she came up to him, "if I had not gone to look for you yesterday you would not have come to greet me till now. Do you not like me any longer, Waldo?"

"Yes—but—you are changed."

It was the old clumsy, hesitating mode of speech.

"You liked the pinafores better?" she said quickly. She wore a dress of a simple cotton fabric, but very fashionably made, and on her head was a broad white hat. To Waldo she seemed superbly attired. She saw it. "My dress has changed a little," she said, "and I also; but not to you. Hang the bag over your other shoulder, that I may see your face. You say so little that if one does not look at you, you are an uncomprehended cipher." Waldo changed the bag, and they walked on side by side. "You have improved," she said. "Do you know that I have sometimes wished to see you while I was away; not often, but still sometimes."

They were at the gate of the first camp now. Waldo partly

emptied his bag of mealies, and they walked on over the dewy ground.

"Have you learned much?" he asked her simply, remembering how she had once said, "When I come back again I shall know everything that a human being can."

She laughed—

"Are you thinking of my old boast? Yes; I have learned something, though hardly what I expected, and not *quite* so much. In the first place, I have learned that one of my ancestors must have been a very great fool; for they say nothing comes out in a man but one of his forefathers possessed it before him. In the second place, I have discovered that of all cursed places under the sun, where the hungriest soul can hardly pick up a few grains of knowledge, a girls' boarding-school is the worst. They are called finishing-schools, and the name tells accurately what they are. They finish everything but imbecility and weakness, and that they cultivate. They are nicely adapted machines for experimenting on the question, 'Into how little space can a human soul be crushed?' I have seen some souls so compressed that they would have fitted into a small thimble, and found room to move there—wide room. A woman who has been for many years at one of those places carries the mark of the beast on her till she dies, though she may expand a little afterwards, when she breathes in the free world."

"Were you miserable?" he asked, looking at her with quick anxiety.

"I?—No. I am never miserable, and never happy. I wish I were. But I should have run away from the place on the fourth day, and hired myself to the first Boer-woman whose farm I came to, to make fire under her soap-pot, if I had had to live as the rest of the drove did. Can you form an idea, Waldo, of what it must be to be shut up with cackling old women, who are without knowledge of life, without love of the beautiful, without strength, to have your soul cultured by them? It is suffocation only to breathe the air they breathe; but I made them give me room. I told them I should leave, and they knew I came there on my own account; so they gave me a bedroom without the companionship of one of those things that were having their brains slowly diluted and squeezed out of them.

Olive Schreiner

I did not learn music, because I had no talent; and when the drove made cushions, and hideous flowers that the roses laugh at, and a footstool in six weeks that a machine would have made better in five minutes, I went to my room. With the money saved from such work I bought books and newspapers, and at night I sat up. I read and epitomized what I read; and I found time to write some plays, and find out how hard it is to make your thoughts look anything but imbecile fools when you paint them with ink on paper. In the holidays I learned a great deal more. I made acquaintances, saw a few places and many people, and some different ways of living, which is more than any books can show one. On the whole I am not dissatisfied with my four years. I have not learned what I expected; but I have learned something else. What have you been doing?"

"Nothing."

"That is not possible. I shall find out by-and-by."

They still stepped on side by side over the dewy bushes. Then suddenly she turned on him.

"Don't you wish you were a woman, Waldo?"

"No," he answered readily.

She laughed.

"I thought not. Even you are too worldly-wise for that. I never met a man who did. This is a pretty ring," she said, holding out her little hand, that the morning sun might make the diamonds sparkle. "Worth fifty pounds at least. I will give it to the first man who tells me he would like to be a woman. There might be one on Robben Island[1] who would win it perhaps, but I doubt it even there. It is delightful to be a woman; but every man thanks the Lord devoutly that he isn't one."

She drew her hat to one side to keep the sun out of her eyes as she walked. Waldo looked at her so intently that he stumbled over the bushes. Yes, this was his little Lyndall who had worn the check pinafores; he saw it now, and he walked closer beside her. They reached the next camp.

"Let us wait at this camp and watch the birds," she said, as an ostrich hen came bounding towards them, with velvety wings out-

[1] Lunatics at the Cape are sent to Robben Island.

by a Woman writt

stretched, while far away over the bushes the head of the cock was visible as he sat brooding on the eggs.

Lyndall folded her arms on the gate bar, and Waldo threw his empty bag on the wall, and leaned beside her.

"I like these birds," she said; "they share each other's work, and are companions. Do you take an interest in the position of women, Waldo?"

"No."

"I thought not. No one does, unless they are in need of a subject upon which to show their wit. And as for you, from of old you can see nothing that is not separated from you by a few millions of miles, and strewed over with mystery. If women were the inhabitants of Jupiter, of whom you had happened to hear something, you would pore over us and our condition night and day; but because we are before your eyes you never look at us. You care nothing that *this* is ragged and ugly," she said, putting her little finger on his sleeve; "but you strive mightily to make an imaginary leaf on an old stick beautiful. I'm sorry you don't care for the position of women; I should have liked us to be friends; and it is the only thing about which I think much, or feel much—if, indeed, I have any feeling about anything," she added flippantly, readjusting her dainty little arms. "When I was a baby, I fancy my parents left me out in the frost one night, and I got nipped internally; it feels so!"

"I have only a few old thoughts," he said, "and I think them over and over again, always beginning where I left off. I never get any further; I am weary of them."

"Like an old hen that sits on its eggs month after month, and they never come out?" she said quickly. "I am so pressed in upon by new things that, lest they should trip one another up, I have to keep forcing them back. My head swings sometimes. But this one thought stands, never goes—if I might but be one of those born in the future; then, perhaps, to be born a woman will not be to be born branded."

Waldo looked at her. It was hard to say whether she were in earnest or mocking.

"I know it is foolish. Wisdom never kicks at the iron walls it can't bring down," she said. "But we are cursed, Waldo; born

Olive Schreiner

cursed from the time our mothers bring us into the world till the shrouds are put on us. Do not look at me as though I were talking nonsense. Everything has two sides—the outside that is ridiculous, and the inside that is solemn."

"I am not laughing," said the boy, sedately enough; "but what curses you?"

He thought she would not reply to him she waited so long.

"It is not what is done to us, but what is made of us," she said at last, "that wrongs us. No man can be really injured but by what modifies himself. We all enter the world little plastic beings, with so much natural force, perhaps, but for the rest—blank; and the world tells us what we are to be, and shapes us by the ends it sets before us. To you it says, *Work!* and to us it says, *Seem!* To you it says, As you approximate to man's highest ideal of God, as your arm is strong and your knowledge great, and the power to labor is with you, so you shall gain all that human heart desires. To us it says, Strength shall not help you, nor knowledge, nor labor. You shall gain what men gain, but by other means. And so the world makes men and women.

"Look at this little chin of mine, Waldo, with the dimple in it. It is but a small part of my person; but though I had a knowledge of all things under the sun, and the wisdom to use it, and the deep loving heart of an angel, it would not stead me through life like this little chin. I can win money with it, I can win love; I can win power with it, I can win fame. What would knowledge help me? The less a woman has in her head the lighter she is for climbing. I once heard an old man say that he never saw intellect help a woman so much as a pretty ankle; and it was the truth. They begin to shape us to our cursed end," she said, with her lips drawn in to look as though they smiled, "when we are tiny things in shoes and socks. We sit with our little feet drawn up under us in the window, and look out at the boys in their happy play. We want to go. Then a loving hand is laid on us. 'Little one, you cannot go,' they say; 'your little face will burn, and your nice white dress be spoiled.' We feel it must be for our good, it is so lovingly said; but we cannot understand, and we kneel still with one little cheek wistfully pressed against the pane. Afterwards we go and thread blue beads, and make a string for our neck; and we go and stand before the glass. We see the complexion we were not to spoil, and the white frock, and we look into our own great eyes. Then the curse begins to act on us. It finishes its work when we are grown women, who no more look out wistfully at a more healthy life; we are contented. We fit our sphere as a Chinese woman's foot fits her shoe, exactly as though God had made both; and yet he knows nothing of either. In some of us the shaping to our end has been quite completed. The parts we are not to use have been quite atrophied, and have even dropped off; but in others—and we are not less to be pitied—they have been weakened and left. We wear the bandages, but our limbs have not grown to them; we know that we are compressed, and chafe against them.

"But what does it help? A little bitterness, a little longing when we are young, a little futile searching for work, a little passionate striving for room for the exercise of our powers—and then we go with the drove. A woman must march with her regiment. In the end she must be trodden down or go with it; and if she is wise she goes.

"I see in your great eyes what you are thinking," she said, glancing at him; "I always know what the person I am talking to is thinking of. How is this woman who makes such a fuss worse off than I? I will show you by a very little example. We stand here at this gate this morning, both poor, both young, both friendless; there is not much to choose between us. Let us turn away just as we are, to make our way in life. This evening you will come to a farmer's house. The farmer, albeit you come alone and on foot, will give you a pipe of tobacco and a cup of coffee and a bed. If he has no dam to build and no child to teach, to-morrow you can go on your way with a friendly greeting of the hand. I, if I come to the same place to-night, will have strange questions asked me, strange glances cast on me. The Boer-wife will shake her head and give me food to eat with the Kaffirs, and a right to sleep with the dogs. That would be the first step in our progress—a very little one, but every step to the end would repeat it. We were equals once when we lay newborn babes on our nurse's knees. We shall be equals again when they tie up our jaws for the last sleep."

Waldo looked in wonder at the little quivering face; it was a glimpse into a world of passion and feeling wholly new to him.

Olive Schreiner

"Mark you," she said, "we have always this advantage over you—we can at any time step into ease and competence, where you must labor patiently for it. A little weeping, a little wheedling, a little self-degradation, a little careful use of our advantages, and then some man will say, 'Come, be my wife!' With good looks and youth marriage is easy to attain. There are men enough; but a woman who has sold herself, even for a ring and a new name, need hold her skirt aside for no creature in the street. They both earn their bread in one way. Marriage for love is the beautifulest external symbol of the union of souls; marriage without it is the uncleanliest traffic that defiles the world." She ran her little finger savagely along the topmost bar, shaking off the dozen little dew-drops that still hung there. "And they tell us we have men's chivalrous attention!" she cried. "When we ask to be doctors, lawyers, lawmakers, anything but ill-paid drudges, they say, 'No; but you have men's chivalrous attention; now think of that and be satisfied! What would you do without it?' "

The bitter little silvery laugh, so seldom heard, rang out across the bushes. She bit her little teeth together.

"I was coming up in Cobb and Co.'s the other day. At a little wayside hotel we had to change the large coach for a small one. We were ten passengers, eight men and two women. As I sat in the house the gentlemen came and whispered to me, 'There is not room for all in the new coach, take your seat quickly.' We hurried out, and they gave me the best seat, and covered me with rugs, because it was drizzling. Then the last passenger came running up to the coach—an old woman with a wonderful bonnet, and a black shawl pinned with a yellow pin.

" 'There is no room,' they said; 'you must wait till next week's coach takes you up;' but she climbed on to the step, and held on at the window with both hands.

" 'My son-in-law is ill, and I must go and see him,' she said.

" 'My good woman,' said one, 'I am really exceedingly sorry that your son-in-law is ill; but there is absolutely no room for you here.'

" 'You had better get down,' said another, 'or the wheel will catch you.'

"I got up to give her my place.

" 'Oh, no, no!' they cried, 'we will not allow that.'

" 'I will rather kneel,' said one, and he crouched down at my feet; so the woman came in.

"There were nine of us in that coach, and only one showed chivalrous attention—and that was a woman to a woman.

"I shall be old and ugly too one day, and I shall look for men's chivalrous help, but I shall not find it.

"The bees are very attentive to the flowers till their honey is done, and then they fly over them. I don't know if the flowers feel grateful to the bees; they are great fools if they do."

"But some women," said Waldo, speaking as though the words forced themselves from him at that moment, "some women have power."

She lifted her beautiful eyes to his face.

"Power! Did you ever hear of men being asked whether other souls should have power or not? It is born in them. You may dam up the fountain of water, and make it a stagnant marsh, or you may let it run free and do its work; but *you* cannot say whether it shall be there; *it is there.* And it will act, if not openly for good, then covertly for evil; but it will act. If Goethe had been stolen away a child, and reared in a robber horde in the depths of a German forest, do you think the world would have had Faust and Iphigenie? But he would have been Goethe still—stronger, wiser than his fellows. At night, round their watch-fire, he would have chanted wild songs of rapine and murder, till the dark faces about him were moved and trembled. His songs would have echoed on from father to son, and nerved the heart and arm—for evil. Do you think if Napoleon had been born a woman that he would have been contented to give small tea-parties and talk small scandal? He would have risen; but the world would not have heard of him as it hears of him now—a man great and kingly, with all his sins; he would have left one of those names that stain the leaf of every history—the names of women, who, having power, but being denied the right to exercise it openly, rule in the dark, covertly, and by stealth, through the men whose passions they feed on and by whom they climb.

"Power!" she said suddenly, smiting her little hand upon the rail. "Yes, we have power; and since we are not to expend it in tunnelling mountains, nor healing diseases, nor making laws, nor money, nor on any extraneous object, we expend it on *you.* You are our goods, our merchandise, our material for operating on; we buy you, we sell you, we make fools of you, we act the wily old Jew with you, we keep six of you crawling to our little feet, and praying only for a touch of our little hand; and they say truly, there was never an ache or pain or a broken heart but a woman was at the bottom of it. We are not to study law, nor science, nor art, so we study you. There is never a nerve or fibre in your man's nature but we know it. We keep six of you dancing in the palm of one little hand," she said, balancing her outstretched arm gracefully, as though tiny beings disported themselves in its palm. "There—we throw you away, and you sink to the devil," she said, folding her arms composedly. "There was never a man who said one word for woman but he said two for man, and three for the whole human race."

She watched the bird pecking up the last yellow grains; but Waldo looked only at her.

When she spoke again it was very measuredly.

"They bring weighty arguments against us when we ask for the perfect freedom of women," she said; "but, when you come to the objections, they are like pumpkin devils with candles inside—hollow, and can't bite. They say that women do not wish for the sphere and freedom we ask for them, and would not use it.

"If the bird *does* like its cage, and *does* like its sugar, and will not leave it, why keep the door so very carefully shut? Why not open it, only a little? Do they know, there is many a bird will not break its wings against the bars, but would fly if the doors were open." She knit her forehead, and leaned farther over the bars.

"Then they say, 'If the women have the liberty you ask for, they will be found in positions for which they are not fitted!' If two men climb one ladder, did you ever see the weakest anywhere but at the foot? The surest sign of fitness is success. The weakness never wins but where there is handicapping. Nature left to herself will as beautifully apportion a man's work to his capacities as long ages ago she graduated the colors on the bird's breast. If we are not fit, you give us to no purpose the right to labor; the work will fall out of our hands into those that are wiser."

She talked more rapidly as she went on, as one talks of that over which they have brooded long, and which lies near their hearts.

Waldo watched her intently.

"They say women have one great and noble work left them, and they do it ill. That is true; they do it execrably. It is the work that demands the broadest culture, and they have not even the narrowest. The lawyer may see no deeper than his law-books, and the chemist see no further than the windows of his laboratory, and they may do their work well. But the woman who does woman's work needs a many-sided, multiform culture; the heights and depths of human life must not be beyond the reach of her vision; she must have knowledge of men and things in many states, a wide catholicity of sympathy, the strength that springs from knowledge, and the magnanimity which springs from strength. *We* bear the world, and *we* make it. The souls of little children are marvellously delicate and tender things, and keep forever the shadow that first falls on them, and that is the mother's, or at best a woman's. There was never a great man who had not a great mother—it is hardly an exaggeration. The first six years of our life make us; all that is added later is veneer; and yet some say, if a woman can cook a dinner or dress herself well she has culture enough.

"The mightiest and noblest of human work is given to us, and we do it ill. Send a navvy into an artist's studio to work, and see what you will find there! And yet, thank God, we have this work," she added quickly; "it is the one window through which we see into the great world of earnest labor. The meanest girl who dances and dresses becomes something higher when her children look up into her face, and ask her questions. It is the only education we have, and this they cannot take from us."

She smiled slightly; "They say that we complain of woman's being compelled to look upon marriage as a profession; but that she is free to enter upon it or leave it as she pleases.

"Yes, and a cat set afloat in a pond is free to sit in the tub till it dies there, it is under no obligation to wet its feet; and a drowning man may catch at a straw or not, just as he likes; it is a glorious liberty! Let any man think for five minutes of what old maidenhood means to a woman, and then let him be silent. Is it easy to bear through life a name that in itself signifies defeat; to dwell, as nine out of ten unmarried women must, under the finger of another woman? Is it easy to look forward to an old age without honor, without the

Olive Schreiner

reward of useful labor, without love? I wonder how many men there are who would give up everything that is dear in life for the sake of maintaining a high ideal purity."

She laughed a little laugh that was clear without being pleasant. "And then, when they have no other argument against us, they say, 'Go on; but when you have made women what you wish, and her children inherit her culture, you will defeat yourself. Man will gradually become extinct from excess of intellect, the passions which replenish the race will die.' Fools!" she said, curling her pretty lip. "A Hottentot sits at the roadside, and feeds on a rotten bone he has found there, and takes out his bottle of Cape-smoke, and swills at it, and grunts with satisfaction; and the cultured child of the nineteenth century sits in his armchair, and sips choice wines with the lip of a connoisseur, and tastes delicate dishes with a delicate palate, and with a satisfaction of which the Hottentot knows nothing. Heavy jaw and sloping forehead—all have gone with increasing intellect; but the animal appetites are there still—refined, discriminative, but immeasurably intensified. Fools! Before men forgave or worshipped, while they still were weak on their hind legs, did they not eat and drink, and fight for wives? When all the later additions to humanity have vanished, will not the foundation on which they are built remain?"

She was silent then for a while, and said somewhat dreamily, more as though speaking to herself than to him—

"They ask, 'What will you gain, even if man does not become extinct? You will have brought justice and equality on to the earth, and sent love from it. When men and women are equals they will love no more. Your highly-cultured women will not be loveable, will not love.'

"Do they see nothing, understand nothing? It is Tant' Sannie who buries husbands one after another, and folds her hands resignedly— 'The Lord gave, and the Lord hath taken away, and blessed be the name of the Lord'—and she looks for another. It is the hard-headed, deep thinker who, when the wife who has thought and worked with him goes, can find no rest, and lingers near her till he finds sleep beside her.

"A great soul draws and is drawn with a more fierce intensity than any small one. By every inch we grow in intellectual height our love strikes down its roots deeper, and spreads out its arms wider. It is for love's sake yet more than for any other that we look for that new time." She had leaned her head against the stones, and watched with her sad, soft eyes the retreating bird. "Then when that time comes," she said lowly, "when love is no more bought or sold, when it is not a means of making bread, when each woman's life is filled with earnest, independent labor—then love will come to her, a strange sudden sweetness breaking in upon her earnest work; not sought for, but found. Then, but not now—"

Waldo waited for her to finish the sentence, but she seemed to have forgotten him.

"Lyndall," he said, putting his hand upon her—she started—"if you think that that new time will be so great, so good, you who speak so easily—"

She interrupted him.

"Speak! speak!" she said; "the difficulty is not to speak; the difficulty is to keep silence."

"But why do you not try to bring that time?" he said with pitiful simplicity. "When you speak I believe all you say; other people would listen to you also."

"I am not so sure of that," she said with a smile.

Then over the small face came the weary look it had worn last night as it watched the shadow in the corner. Ah, so weary!

"I, Waldo, I?" she said. "I can do nothing good for myself, nothing for the world, till some one wakes me. I am asleep, swathed, shut up in self; till I have been delivered I can deliver no one."

He looked at her wondering, but she was not looking at him.

"To see the good and the beautiful," she said, "and to have no strength to live it, is only to be Moses on the mountain of Nebo, with the land at your feet and no power to enter. It would be better not to see it. Come," she said, looking up into his face, and seeing its uncomprehending expression, "let us go, it is getting late. Doss is anxious for his breakfast also," she added, wheeling round and calling to the dog, who was endeavoring to unearth a mole, an occupation to which he had been zealously addicted from the third month, but in which he had never on any single occasion proved successful.

Olive Schreiner

Waldo shouldered his bag, and Lyndall walked on before in silence, with the dog close to her side. Perhaps she thought of the narrowness of the limits within which a human soul may speak and be understood by its nearest of mental kin, of how soon it reaches that solitary land of the individual experience, in which no fellow footfall is ever heard. Whatever her thoughts may have been, she was soon interrupted. Waldo came close to her, and standing still, produced with awkwardness from his breast-pocket a small carved box.

"I made it for you," he said, holding it out.

"I like it," she said, examining it carefully.

The workmanship was better than that of the grave-post. The flowers that covered it were delicate, and here and there small conical protuberances were let in among them. She turned it round critically. Waldo bent over it lovingly.

"There is one strange thing about it," he said earnestly, putting a finger on one little pyramid. "I made it without these, and I felt something was wrong; I tried many changes, and at last I let these in, and then it was right. But why was it? They are not beautiful in themselves."

"They relieve the monotony of the smooth leaves, I suppose."

He shook his head as over a weighty matter.

"The sky is monotonous," he said, "when it is blue, and yet it is beautiful. I have thought of that often; but it is not monotony and it is not variety makes beauty. What is it? The sky, and your face, and this box—the same thing is in them all, only more in the sky and in your face. But what is it?"

She smiled—

"So you are at your old work still. Why, why, why? What is the reason? It is enough for me," she said, "if I find out what is beautiful and what is ugly, what is real and what is not. Why it is there, and over the final cause of things in general, I don't trouble myself; there must be one, but what is it to me? If I howl to all eternity, I shall never get hold of it; and if I did, I might be no better off. But you Germans are born with an aptitude for burrowing; you can't help yourselves. You must sniff after reasons, just as that dog must after a mole. He knows perfectly well he will never catch it, but he's under the imperative necessity of digging for it."

"But he *might* find it."

"*Might;* but he never has and never will. Life is too short to run after 'mights'; we must have certainties."

She tucked the box under her arm and was about to walk on, when Gregory Rose, with shining spurs, an ostrich feather in his hat, and a silver-headed whip, careered past. He bowed gallantly as he went by. They waited till the dust of the horse's hoofs had laid itself.

"There," said Lyndall, "goes a true woman—one born for the sphere that some women have to fill without being born for it. How happy he would be sewing frills into his little girl's frocks, and how pretty he would look sitting in a parlor, with a rough man making love to him! Don't you think so?"

"I shall not stay here when he is master," Waldo answered, not able to connect any kind of beauty with Gregory Rose.

"I should imagine not. The rule of a woman is tyranny; but the rule of a man-woman grinds fine. Where are you going?"

"Anywhere."

"What to do?"

"See—see everything."

"You will be disappointed."

"And were you?"

"Yes; and you will be more so. I want some things that men and the world give; you do not. If you have a few yards of earth to stand on, and a bit of blue over you, and something that you cannot see to dream about, you have all that you need, all that you know how to use. But I like to see real men. Let them be as disagreeable as they please, they are more interesting to me than flowers, or trees, or stars, or any other thing under the sun. Sometimes," she added, walking on, and shaking the dust daintily from her skirts, "when I am not too busy trying to find a new way of doing my hair that will show my little neck to better advantage, or over other work of that kind, sometimes it amuses me intensely to trace out the resemblance between one man and another; to see how Tant' Sannie and I, you and Bonaparte, Saint Simon on his pillar and the Emperor dining off larks' tongues, are one and the same compound, merely mixed in different proportions. What is microscopic in one is largely developed in another; what is a rudimentary in one man is an active organ in another; but all things are in all men, and one soul is the model of all. We shall find nothing new in human nature after we have once carefully dissected and analyzed the one being we ever shall truly know— ourself. The Kaffir girl threw some coffee on my arm in bed this morning; I felt displeased, but said nothing. Tant' Sannie would have thrown the saucer at her and sworn for an hour; but the feeling would be the same irritated displeasure. If a huge animated stomach like Bonaparte were put under a glass by a skilful mental micro- scopist, even he would be found to have an embryonic doubling somewhere indicative of a heart, and rudimentary buddings that might have become conscience and sincerity. Let me take your arm, Waldo. How full you are of mealie dust. No, never mind; it will brush off. And sometimes what is more amusing still than tracing the like- ness between man and man is to trace the analogy there always is between the progress and development of one individual and of a whole nation; or again, between a single nation and the entire human race. It is pleasant when it dawns on you that the one is just the other written out in large letters; and very odd to find all the little follies and virtues, and developments and retrogressions, written out in the big world's book that you find in your little internal self. It is the most amusing thing I know of; but of course being a woman, I have not often time for such amusements. Professional duties always first, you know. It takes a great deal of time and thought always to look perfectly exquisite, even for a pretty woman. Is the old buggy still in existence, Waldo?"

"Yes; but the harness is broken."

"Well, I wish you would mend it. You must teach me to drive. I must learn something while I am here. I got the Hottentot girl to show me how to make 'sarsarties' this morning; and Tant' Sannie is going to teach me to make kappjes. I will come and sit with you this afternoon while you mend the harness."

"Thank you."

"No, don't thank me; I come for my own pleasure. I never find any one I can talk to. Women bore me, and men, I talk so to, 'Going to the ball this evening? Nice little dog that of yours. Pretty little ears. So fond of pointer pups!' And they think me fascinating, charm- ing! Men are like the earth and we are the moon; we turn always one side to them, and they think there is no other, because they don't see it—but there is."

They had reached the house now.

"Tell me when you set to work," she said, and walked towards the door.

Waldo stood to look after her, and Doss stood at his side, a look of painful uncertainty depicted on his small countenance, and one little foot poised in the air. Should he stay with his master or go? He looked at the figure with the wide straw hat moving towards the house, and he looked up at his master; then he put down the little paw and went. Waldo watched them both in at the door, and then walked away alone. He was satisfied that at least his dog was with her.

Kate Chopin

Kate Chopin

(1851–1904)

Kate Chopin was described by a friend as a woman who "told a story well." Her short stories, incisive, realistic, and rich with the local color of Louisiana Creole and Acadian life, were highly praised by her contemporaries. But her best known novel, *The Awakening*, about a married woman who discovers her sexuality through her attraction to other men, met a storm of criticism that stunned and embittered Chopin. Like *The Awakening*, many of her short stories are about women who "awaken" to new understandings of themselves. As the following stories indicate, Chopin did not view women simplistically. She saw their need both for rebellion and for conformity, for independence and for marriage and children, and she wrote with compassion about women struggling with these conflicting needs.

THE GOING AWAY OF LIZA

The south-bound mail and express had just pulled away from Bludgitt station. There had been an exchange of mail bags; sundry freight marked "Abner Rydon, Bludgitt Station, Missouri" had been deposited upon the platform and that was all. It was Christmas eve, a raw, chill, Christmas eve, and the air was thick with promise of snow.

A few weazened, shivering men stood with hands plunged in their trouser pockets, watching the train come and go. When the station-master dragged the freight under shelter, depositing some of it within the waiting-room, they all tramped into the room too and proceeded to lounge round the rusty red-hot stove.

Presently a light cart drove up along-side the platform, and one of this leisurely band craning his neck to peer through the begrimed window panes, remarked:

"Thur's Abner, now."

Abner Rydon was a stalwart fellow of thirty. He was stern-visaged, with stubborn determination in the set of his square jaw. The casual glance which he offered the assembled group was neither friendly nor inviting.

"It's a wonder you wouldn't of took the two horse wagon, Ab, with them roads." He paid no attention to the insinuation.

"Seems to me you'd fix that thur road and throw a bridge acrost Bludgitt creek," suggested a second. "If I had your money—"

"If you had my money you wouldn't run the county with it more 'an you do your own," replied Abner as he quitted the room, bearing an armful of freight. Returning for more he was met by further friendly advances:

"I seen a man the other day, Ab, says he run acrost Liza-Jane a couple o' weeks ago in town."

Abner turned quickly upon the speaker, and with a sharp blow of his clenched fist sent him sprawling to the floor. He then continued towards the cart, mounted it, and drove rapidly away over the rough and fast-hardening road, and into the woods beyond.

A burst of hilarity greeted the discomfiture of this too daring speaker.

"Oh, Whillikens! *you* seen a man that run acrost Liza-Jane, did you!" "Anything more to say on the subject of Liza-Jane, Si? Ab ain't got so fur you can't ketch up with him."

Si had risen and was rubbing his injured back as best he could.

"The plague-on-it-fool," he muttered; "if he thinks so much o' that red-cheeked huzzy, what in tarnation did he want to turn her loose to Satan fur!"

When the mirth occasioned by this quickly acted scene had subsided, it left the assembly in a pleasant, reminiscent mood that led naturally to the quiet discussion of Abner Rydon's domestic affairs.

"I always said thet harm would come o' the match," remarked the traditional prophet, "time Almiry told me thet Liza-Jane was goin' to marry Abner Rydon. Why, a blind un could 'a seen they wasn't a matched team. First place, thet gal was all fur readin'—constant readin' in them paper-covered books thet come to her through the mail, an' readin's boun' to fill the mind up with one thing another in time.

"When she'd come an' see Almiry she'd out en' tell by the hour how folks lives in town. How the ladies sets in rockin' cheers by the winders all day imbroidryin' things with their white, jewel fingers;

an' how they walks up an' down drawin' rooms disdainful; an' rides
in open karridges along the boulyvards, bowin' languid to gents a
horseback. She got it all out o' them books, an' she called it the
higher life, an' said she hankered fur it, to Almiry."

"I was down here to Bludgitt the mornin' she left," interrupted
one whose information was more to the point. "Time I seen her I
knowed somthin' was up. Her black eyes was fairly snappin' fire,
an' her cheeks was blazin' most as red as the ribband round her nake.
She never were back'ard with her talk, an' when I ast whur she was
bound fur, she up an' let loose again' Ab, an' mother Rydon, an'
thur life of drudgery what was no ixistence."

"Ab never turned her out, did he?"

"Turn her out! Abner Rydon ain't the man to turn a dog from his
door. No; they had one o' them everlastin' quarrels what's been a
imbitterin' their married life. She out with the hull thing that day
down here to Bludgitt. How they fussed, an' how she endid by tellin'
him that no woman born could keep on lovin' a man that hadn't no
soul above the commonplaces. How he flung back at her that a woman
better quit livin' with a man when she quit kerrin' fur him. She said
she didn't ask no better, 'fur,' sa' she, 'I hev that within me, Mr.
MicBride, thet craves to taste the joys of ixistence. I hev gathered
my belongings; my own incompetence is in my pocket, an' I hev
shook the dust of the Rydon threshold from off of my feet forever,'
was her own words. An' Si Smith might's well learn to-day as
tomorrow that Ab Rydon's goin' to knock any man down that
mentions the name o' Liza-Jane to him."

At every fresh gust of wind that struck the north-west angle of the
old Rydon farm-house that night, mother Rydon would give a little
jump and clasp the arms of her comfortable chair that she occupied
at the fire-side.

"Lands, Abner! I hain't hered the wind a blowin' so since the night
the pasture fence was laid low, what's it a doin' out o' doors, anyway.
Before dark the hull country was covered with snow. Now the sleet's
a strikin' like pebbles again' the window panes."

"That's just it, mother; sleet an' snow an' wind a tryin' to outdo thurselves," said Abner, throwing upon the fire a fresh stick that he had brought from the porch, where a pile of evenly-cut fire wood was stacked.

He sat down beside the table upon which a lamp burned brightly, and opened his newspaper. His features seemed much less harsh than when he faced the roomful of loafers down at Bludgitt. There was a kind ring in his voice.

The two seated so cozily together amid their homely surroundings, resembled each other closely. Only the steadfast look in the eyes of the woman had grown patient with age.

"It's a mercy you went fur the goods to-day, Abner, what with Moll's lame foot, an' the mules loaned fur old man Buckthorn's funeral, you never would hev got the cart through them roads tomorrow. Who'd you see down to Bludgitt?"

"The same old lot at the station, a settin' round the stove. It's a puzzle to me how they live. That McBride don't do work enough to keep him in tobacco. Old Joseph—I guess he ain't able to work. But that Si Smith—why!" he exclaimed excitedly, "the government ought to take holt of it."

"That's thur business, Abner; 'tain't none o' ours," his mother replied rebukingly. "I'd like if you'd read me the noos, now. An' read about them curious animals."

Abner stretched his fine legs out towards the blaze and began to read from the conglomerate contents of his weekly paper. Old Mother Rydon sat upright, knitting and listening. Abner was reading slowly and carefully:

"This singular animal has seldom been seen by the eye of civilized man, familiar as are the native blacks with his habits and peculiar haunts. The writer—fortunately armed with his trusty—"

"Hold, Abner! Hark!"

"What is it, mother?"

"Seems like I heard something at the door latch, and a movin' on the porch."

"The dogs would bark if any one as much as opened the gate, mother. This talk about the animals has got you worked up."

"No such thing. Thur! I hered it again. Go see, Abner; 'tain't goin' to hurt nothin' to look."

Kate Chopin

Abner approached the door and opened it abruptly. A wild gust of wind came blowing into the room; beating and lashing as it did so, the bedraggled garments of a young woman who was clinging to the door-post.

"My God!" cried Abner starting back. Mother Rydon in astonishment could only utter: "Liza-Jane! for the land sakes!"

The wind literally drove the woman into the room. Abner stayed there with his hand upon the latch, shaken at what seemed this apparition before him.

Liza-Jane stood like a hunted and hungry thing in the great glow of the firelight, her big dark eyes greedily seizing upon every detail of homely and honest comfort that surrounded her. Her cheeks were not round nor red as they had been. Whatever sin or suffering had swept over her had left its impress upon her plastic being.

As Abner looked at her, of all the voices that clamored in his soul to be heard, that of the outraged husband was the loudest.

When mother Rydon endeavored to remove Liza-Jane's wet and tattered shawl the woman clutched it firmly, turning a frightened and beseeching face upon her husband.

"Abner, son, what air you a waitin' fur?" demanded mother Rydon, standing back.

Mother and son looked for a long instant into each other's eyes. Then Abner approached his wife. With unsteady hands he lifted the soaking garment from her shoulders. When he saw that Liza-Jane's arms fell to her side at his approach, and that two shining tears hung beneath the half closed lids, he knelt upon the floor and took the wet and torn shoes from off her feet.

A SHAMEFUL AFFAIR

I

Mildred Orme, seated in the snuggest corner of the big front porch of the Kraummer farmhouse, was as content as a girl need hope to be.

by a Woman writt

This was no such farm as one reads about in humorous fiction. Here were swelling acres where the undulating wheat gleamed in the sun like a golden sea. For silver there was the Meramec—or, better, it was pure crystal, for here and there one might look clean through it down to where the pebbles lay like green and yellow gems. Along the river's edge trees were growing to the very water, and in it, sweeping it when they were willows.

The house itself was big and broad, as country houses should be. The master was big and broad, too. The mistress was small and thin, and it was always she who went out at noon to pull the great clanging bell that called the farmhands in to dinner.

From her agreeable corner where she lounged with her Browning or her Ibsen, Mildred watched the woman do this every day. Yet when the clumsy farmhands all came tramping up the steps and crossed the porch in going to their meal that was served within, she never looked at them. Why should she? Farmhands are not so very nice to look at, and she was nothing of an anthropologist. But once when the half dozen men came along, a paper which she had laid carelessly upon the railing was blown across their path. One of them picked it up, and when he had mounted the steps restored it to her. He was young, and brown, of course, as the sun had made him. He had nice blue eyes. His fair hair was dishevelled. His shoulders were broad and square and his limbs strong and clean. A not unpicturesque figure in the rough attire that bared his throat to view and gave perfect freedom to his every motion.

Mildred did not make these several observations in the half second that she looked at him in courteous acknowledgment. It took her as many days to note them all. For she signaled him out each time that he passed her, meaning to give him a condescending little smile, as she knew how. But he never looked at her. To be sure, clever young women of twenty, who are handsome, besides, who have refused their half dozen offers and are settling down to the conviction that life is a tedious affair, are not going to care a straw whether farmhands look at them or not. And Mildred did not care, and the thing would not have occupied her a moment if Satan had not intervened, in offering the employment which natural conditions had failed to supply. It was summer time; she was idle; she was piqued, and that was the beginning of the shameful affair.

"Who are these men, Mrs. Kraummer, that work for you? Where do you pick them up?"

"Oh, ve picks 'em up everyvere. Some is neighbors, some is tramps, and so."

"And that broad-shouldered young fellow—is he a neighbor? The one who handed me my paper the other day—you remember?"

"Gott, no! You might yust as well say he vas a tramp. Aber he vorks like a steam ingine."

"Well, he's an extremely disagreeable-looking man. I should think you'd be afraid to have him about, not knowing him."

"Vat you vant to be 'fraid for?" laughed the little woman. "He don't talk no more un ven he vas deef und dumb. I didn't t'ought you vas sooch a baby."

"But, Mrs. Kraummer, I don't want you to think I'm a baby, as you say—a coward, as you mean. Ask the man if he will drive me to church to-morrow. You see, I'm not so very much afraid of him," she added with a smile.

The answer which this unmannerly farmhand returned to Mildred's request was simply a refusal. He could not drive her to church because he was going fishing.

"Aber," offered good Mrs. Kraummer, "Hans Platzfeldt will drive you to church, oder vereever you vants. He vas a goot boy vat you can trust, dat Hans."

"Oh, thank him very much. But I find I have so many letters to write to-morrow, and it promises to be hot, too. I shan't care to go to church after all."

She could have cried for vexation. Snubbed by a farmhand! a tramp, perhaps. She, Mildred Orme, who ought really to have been with the rest of the family at Narragansett—who had come to seek in this retired spot the repose that would enable her to follow exalted lines of thought. She marvelled at the problematic nature of farmhands.

After sending her the uncivil message already recorded, and as he passed beneath the porch where she sat, he did look at her finally, in a way to make her positively gasp at the sudden effrontery of the man.

But the inexplicable look stayed with her. She could not banish it.

II

It was not so very hot after all, the next day, when Mildred walked down the long narrow footpath that led through the bending wheat to the river. High above her waist reached the yellow grain. Mildred's brown eyes filled with a reflected golden light as they caught the glint of it, as she heard the trill that it answered to the gentle breeze. Anyone who has walked through the wheat in midsummer-time knows that sound.

In the woods it was sweet and solemn and cool. And there beside the river was the wretch who had annoyed her, first, with his indifference, then with the sudden boldness of his glance.

"Are you fishing?" she asked politely and with kindly dignity, which she supposed would define her position toward him. The inquiry lacked not pertinence, seeing that he sat motionless, with a pole in his hand and his eyes fixed on a cork that bobbed aimlessly on the water.

"Yes, madam," was his brief reply.

"It won't disturb you if I stand here a moment, to see what success you will have?"

"No, madam."

She stood very still, holding tight to the book she had brought with her. Her straw hat had slipped disreputably to one side, over the wavy bronze-brown bang that half covered her forehead. Her cheeks were ripe with color that the sun had coaxed there; so were her lips.

All the other farmhands had gone forth in Sunday attire. Perhaps this one had none better than these working clothes that he wore. A feminine commiseration swept her at the thought. He spoke never a word. She wondered how many hours he could sit there, so patiently waiting for fish to come to his hook. For her part, the situation began to pall, and she wanted to change it at last.

Kate Chopin

"Let me try a moment, please? I have an idea—"

"Yes, madam."

"The man is surely an idiot, with his monosyllables," she commented inwardly. But she remembered that monosyllables belong to a boor's equipment.

She laid her book carefully down and took the pole gingerly that he came to place in her hands. Then it was his turn to stand back and look respectfully and silently on at the absorbing performance.

"Oh!" cried the girl, suddenly, seized with excitement upon seeing the line dragged deep in the water.

"Wait, wait! Not yet."

He sprang to her side. With his eyes eagerly fastened on the tense line, he grasped the pole to prevent her drawing it, as her intention seemed to be. That is, he meant to grasp the pole, but instead, his brown hand came down upon Mildred's white one.

He started violently at finding himself so close to a bronze-brown tangle that almost swept his chin—to a hot cheek only a few inches away from his shoulder, to a pair of young, dark eyes that gleamed for an instant unconscious things into his own.

Then, why ever it happened, or how ever it happened, his arms were holding Mildred and he kissed her lips. She did not know if it was ten times or only once.

She looked around—her face milk-white—to see him disappear with rapid strides through the path that had brought her there. Then she was alone.

Only the birds had seen, and she could count on their discretion. She was not wildly indignant, as many would have been. Shame stunned her. But through it she gropingly wondered if she should tell the Kraummers that her chaste lips had been rifled of their innocence. Publish her own confusion? No! Once in her room she would give calm thought to the situation, and determine then how to act. The secret must remain her own: a hateful burden to bear alone until she could forget it.

III

And because she feared not to forget it, Mildred wept that night. All day long a hideous truth had been thrusting itself upon her that made her ask herself if she could be mad. She feared it. Else why was that kiss the most delicious thing she had known in her twenty years of life? The sting of it had never left her lips since it was pressed into them. The sweet trouble of it banished sleep from her pillow.

But Mildred would not bend the outward conditions of her life to serve any shameful whim that chanced to visit her soul, like an ugly dream. She would avoid nothing. She would go and come as always.

In the morning she found in her chair upon the porch the book she had left by the river. A fresh indignity! But she came and went as she intended to, and sat as usual upon the porch amid her familiar surroundings. When the Offender passed her by she knew it, though her eyes were never lifted. Are there only sight and sound to tell such things? She discerned it by a wave that swept her with confusion and she knew not what besides.

She watched him furtively, one day, when he talked with Farmer Kraummer out in the open. When he walked away she remained like one who has drunk much wine. Then unhesitatingly she turned and began her preparations to leave the Kraummer farmhouse.

When the afternoon was far spent they brought letters to her. One of them read like this:

"My Mildred, deary! I am only now at Narragansett, and so broke up not to find you. So you are down at that Kraummer farm, on the Iron Mountain. Well! What do you think of that delicious crank, Fred Evelyn? For a man must be a crank who does such things. Only fancy! Last year he chose to drive an engine back and forth across the plains. This year he tills the soil with laborers. Next year it will be something else as insane—because he likes to live more lives than one kind, and other Quixotic reasons. We are great chums. He writes me he's grown as strong as an ox. But he hasn't mentioned that you are there. I know you don't get on with him, for he isn't a

Kate Chopin

bit intellectual—detests Ibsen and abuses Tolstoi. He doesn't read 'in books'—says they are spectacles for the short-sighted to look at life through. Don't snub him, dear, or be too hard on him; he has a heart of gold, if he is the first crank in America."

Mildred tried to think—to feel that the intelligence which this letter brought to her would take somewhat of the sting from the shame that tortured her. But it did not. She knew that it could not.

In the gathering twilight she walked again through the wheat that was heavy and fragrant with dew. The path was very long and very narrow. When she was midway she saw the Offender coming toward her. What could she do? Turn and run, as a little child might? Spring into the wheat, as some frightened four-footed creature would? There was nothing but to pass him with the dignity which the occasion clearly demanded.

But he did not let her pass. He stood squarely in the pathway before her, hat in hand, a perturbed look upon his face.

"Miss Orme," he said, "I have wanted to say to you, every hour of the past week, that I am the most consummate hound that walks the earth."

She made no protest. Her whole bearing seemed to indicate that her opinion coincided with his own.

"If you have a father, or brother, or any one, in short, to whom you may say such things—"

"I think you aggravate the offense, sir, by speaking of it. I shall ask you never to mention it again. I want to forget that it ever happened. Will you kindly let me by."

"Oh," he ventured eagerly, "you want to forget it! Then, maybe, since you are willing to forget, you will be generous enough to forgive the offender some day?"

"Some day," she repeated, almost inaudibly, looking seemingly through him, but not at him—"some day—perhaps; when I shall have forgiven myself."

He stood motionless, watching her slim, straight figure lessening by degrees as she walked slowly away from him. He was wondering what she meant. Then a sudden, quick wave came beating into his brown throat and staining it crimson, when he guessed what it might be.

A VISIT TO AVOYELLES

Every one who came up from Avoyelles had the same story to tell of Mentine. *Cher Maître!* but she was changed. And there were babies, more than she could well manage; as good as four already. Jules was not kind except to himself. They seldom went to church, and never anywhere upon a visit. They lived as poorly as pine-woods people. Doudouce had heard the story often, the last time no later than that morning.

"Ho-a!" he shouted to his mule plumb in the middle of the cotton row. He had staggered along behind the plow since early morning, and of a sudden he felt he had had enough of it. He mounted the mule and rode away to the stable, leaving the plow with its polished blade thrust deep in the red Cane River soil. His head felt like a windmill with the recollections and sudden intentions that had crowded it and were whirling through his brain since he had heard the last story about Mentine.

He knew well enough Mentine would have married him seven years ago had not Jules Trodon come up from Avoyelles and captivated her with his handsome eyes and pleasant speech. Doudouce was resigned then, for he held Mentine's happiness above his own. But now she was suffering in a hopeless, common, exasperating way for the small comforts of life. People had told him so. And somehow, to-day, he could not stand the knowledge passively. He felt he must see those things they spoke of with his own eyes. He must strive to help her and her children if it were possible.

Doudouce could not sleep that night. He lay with wakeful eyes watching the moonlight creep across the bare floor of his room; listening to sounds that seemed unfamiliar and weird down among the rushes along the bayou. But towards morning he saw Mentine as he had seen her last in her white wedding gown and veil. She looked at him with appealing eyes and held out her arms for protection—for rescue, it seemed to him. That dream determined him. The following day Doudouce started for Avoyelles.

Kate Chopin

Jules Trodon's home lay a mile or two from Marksville. It consisted of three rooms strung in a row and opening upon a narrow gallery. The whole wore an aspect of poverty and dilapidation that summer day, towards noon, when Doudouce approached it. His presence outside the gate aroused the frantic barking of dogs that dashed down the steps as if to attack him. Two little brown barefooted children, a boy and girl, stood upon the gallery staring stupidly at him. "Call off you' dogs," he requested; but they only continued to stare.

"Down, Pluto! down, Achille!" cried the shrill voice of a woman who emerged from the house, holding upon her arm a delicate baby of a year or two. There was only an instant of unrecognition.

"*Mais* Doudouce, that ent you, *comment!* Well, if any one would tole me this mornin'! Git a chair, 'Tit Jules. That's Mista Doudouce, f'om 'way yonda Natchitoches w'ere yo' maman use' to live. *Mais*, you ent change'; you' lookin' well, Doudouce."

He shook hands in a slow, undemonstrative way, and seated himself clumsily upon the hide-bottomed chair, laying his broad-rimmed felt hat upon the floor beside him. He was very uncomfortable in the cloth Sunday coat which he wore.

"I had business that call' me to Marksville," he began, "an' I say to myse'f, '*Tiens*, you can't pass by without tell' 'em all howdy.' "

"*Par exemple!* w'at Jules would said to that! *Mais*, you' lookin' well; you ent change', Doudouce."

"An' you' lookin' well, Mentine. Jis' the same Mentine." He regretted that he lacked talent to make the lie bolder.

She moved a little uneasily, and felt upon her shoulder for a pin with which to fasten the front of her old gown where it lacked a button. She had kept the baby in her lap. Doudouce was wondering miserably if he would have known her outside her home. He would have known her sweet, cheerful brown eyes, that were not changed; but her figure, that had looked so trim in the wedding gown, was sadly misshapen. She was brown, with skin like parchment, and piteously thin. There were lines, some deep as if old age had cut them, about the eyes and mouth.

"An' how you lef' 'em all, yonda?" she asked, in a high voice that had grown shrill from screaming at children and dogs.

"They all well. It 's mighty li'le sickness in the country this yea'. But they been lookin' fo' you up yonda, straight along, Mentine."

"Don't talk, Doudouce, it 's no chance; with that po' wo' out piece o' lan' w'at Jules got. He say, anotha yea' like that, he 's goin' sell out, him."

The children were clutching her on either side, their persistent gaze always fastened upon Doudouce. He tried without avail to make friends with them. Then Jules came home from the field, riding the mule with which he had worked, and which he fastened outside the gate.

"Yere 's Doudouce f'om Natchitoches, Jules," called out Mentine, "he stop' to tell us howdy, *en passant.*" The husband mounted to the gallery and the two men shook hands; Doudouce listlessly, as he had done with Mentine; Jules with some bluster and show of cordiality.

"Well, you' a lucky man, you," he exclaimed with his swagger air, "able to broad like that, *encore!* You could n't do that if you had half a dozen mouth' to feed, *allez!*"

"Non, j'te grantis!" agreed Mentine, with a loud laugh. Doudouce winced, as he had done the instant before at Jules's heartless implication. This husband of Mentine surely had not changed during the seven years, except to grow broader, stronger, handsomer. But Doudouce did not tell him so.

After the mid-day dinner of boiled salt pork, corn bread and molasses, there was nothing for Doudouce but to take his leave when Jules did.

At the gate, the little boy was discovered in dangerous proximity to the mule's heels, and was properly screamed at and rebuked.

"I reckon he likes hosses," Doudouce remarked. "He take' afta you, Mentine. I got a li'le pony yonda home," he said, addressing the child, "w'at ent no use to me. I'm goin' sen' 'im down to you. He's a good, tough li'le mustang. You jis' can let 'im eat grass an' feed 'im a han'ful o' co'n, once a w'ile. An' he 's gentle, yes. You an' yo' ma can ride 'im to church, Sundays. *Hein!* you want?"

"W'at you say, Jules?" demanded the father. "W'at you say?" echoed Mentine, who was balancing the baby across the gate. " 'Tit sauvage, va!"

Doudouce shook hands all around, even with the baby, and walked off in the opposite direction to Jules, who had mounted the mule. He was bewildered. He stumbled over the rough ground because of tears that were blinding him, and that he had held in check for the past hour.

He had loved Mentine long ago, when she was young and attractive, and he found that he loved her still. He had tried to put all disturbing thought of her away, on that wedding-day, and he supposed he had succeeded. But he loved her now as he never had. Because she was no longer beautiful, he loved her. Because the delicate bloom of her existence had been rudely brushed away; because she was in a manner fallen; because she was Mentine, he loved her; fiercely, as a mother loves an afflicted child. He would have liked to thrust that man aside, and gather up her and her children, and hold them and keep them as long as life lasted.

After a moment or two Doudouce looked back at Mentine, standing at the gate with her baby. But her face was turned away from him. She was gazing after her husband, who went in the direction of the field.

THE STORY OF AN HOUR

Knowing that Mrs. Mallard was afflicted with a heart trouble, great care was taken to break to her as gently as possible the news of her husband's death.

It was her sister Josephine who told her, in broken sentences; veiled hints that revealed in half concealing. Her husband's friend Richards was there, too, near her. It was he who had been in the newspaper office when intelligence of the railroad disaster was received, with Brently Mallard's name leading the list of "killed." He had only taken the time to assure himself of its truth by a second telegram, and had hastened to forestall any less careful, less tender friend in bearing the sad message.

She did not hear the story as many women have heard the same, with a paralyzed inability to accept its significance. She wept at once, with sudden, wild abandonment, in her sister's arms. When the storm of grief had spent itself she went away to her room alone. She would have no one follow her.

There stood, facing the open window, a comfortable, roomy arm-chair. Into this she sank, pressed down by a physical exhaustion that haunted her body and seemed to reach into her soul.

She could see in the open square before her house the tops of trees that were all aquiver with the new spring life. The delicious breath of rain was in the air. In the street below a peddler was crying his wares. The notes of a distant song which some one was singing reached her faintly, and countless sparrows were twittering in the eaves.

There were patches of blue sky showing here and there through the clouds that had met and piled one above the other in the west facing her window.

She sat with her head thrown back upon the cushion of the chair, quite motionless, except when a sob came up into her throat and shook her, as a child who has cried itself to sleep continues to sob in its dreams.

She was young, with a fair, calm face, whose lines bespoke repression and even a certain strength. But now there was a dull stare in her eyes, whose gaze was fixed away off yonder on one of those patches of blue sky. It was not a glance of reflection, but rather indicated a suspension of intelligent thought.

There was something coming to her and she was waiting for it, fearfully. What was it? She did not know; it was too subtle and elusive to name. But she felt it, creeping out of the sky, reaching toward her through the sounds, the scents, the color that filled the air.

Now her bosom rose and fell tumultuously. She was beginning to recognize this thing that was approaching to possess her, and she was striving to beat it back with her will—as powerless as her two white slender hands would have been.

When she abandoned herself a little whispered word escaped her slightly parted lips. She said it over and over under her breath: "free, free, free!" The vacant stare and the look of terror that had followed it went from her eyes. They stayed keen and bright. Her pulses beat fast, and the coursing blood warmed and relaxed every inch of her body.

She did not stop to ask if it were or were not a monstrous joy that held her. A clear and exalted perception enabled her to dismiss the suggestion as trivial.

She knew that she would weep again when she saw the kind, tender hands folded in death; the face that had never looked save with love upon her, fixed and gray and dead. But she saw beyond that bitter moment a long procession of years to come that would belong to her absolutely. And she opened and spread her arms out to them in welcome.

There would be no one to live for her during those coming years; she would live for herself. There would be no powerful will bending hers in that blind persistence with which men and women believe they have a right to impose a private will upon a fellow-creature. A kind intention or a cruel intention made the act seem no less a crime as she looked upon it in that brief moment of illumination.

And yet she had loved him—sometimes. Often she had not. What did it matter! What could love, the unsolved mystery, count for in face of this possession of self-assertion which she suddenly recognized as the strongest impulse of her being!

"Free! Body and soul free!" she kept whispering.

Josephine was kneeling before the closed door with her lips to the keyhole, imploring for admission. "Louise, open the door! I beg; open the door—you will make yourself ill. What are you doing, Louise? For heaven's sake open the door."

"Go away. I am not making myself ill." No; she was drinking in a very elixir of life through that open window.

Her fancy was running riot along those days ahead of her. Spring days, and summer days, and all sorts of days that would be her own. She breathed a quick prayer that life might be long. It was only yesterday she had thought with a shudder that life might be long.

She arose at length and opened the door to her sister's importunities. There was a feverish triumph in her eyes, and she carried herself unwittingly like a goddess of Victory. She clasped her sister's waist, and together they descended the stairs. Richards stood waiting for them at the bottom.

Some one was opening the front door with a latchkey. It was Brently Mallard who entered, a little travel-stained, composedly carrying his grip-sack and umbrella. He had been far from the scene of accident, and did not even know there had been one. He stood amazed at Josephine's piercing cry; at Richards's quick motion to screen him from the view of his wife.

But Richards was too late.

When the doctors came they said she had died of heart disease—of joy that kills.

Mary E. Wilkins Freeman

Mary E. Wilkins Freeman

(1852–1930)

Mary E. Wilkins Freeman was born in New England, spent much of her life there, and wrote about the New England village life she knew. She was a popular and an astoundingly prolific writer—her work including some two hundred short stories, poetry, children's books, novels, and an autobiography. Freeman was one of the first women to be elected to the National Institute of Arts and Letters. Awarded the William Dean Howells Medal for Distinction in Fiction, she was cited by Hamlin Garland for having created "an unparalleled record of New England life." "Book after book flowed from her pen," he said, "each containing unfaltering portraits of lorn widowhood, crabbed age, wistful youth, cheerful drudgery, patient poverty, defiant spinsterhood." While Freeman understood the limitations of New England life, she also recognized its strengths. Her characters, many of whom lead solitary lives, often appear narrow and yet serene. Louisa Ellis, the heroine of "A New England Nun," one of Freeman's most popular stories, is typical not only of these solitary characters, but of another of Freeman's favorite character types—the strong-willed individualistic New England woman.

A NEW ENGLAND NUN

It was late in the afternoon, and the light was waning. There was a difference in the look of the tree shadows out in the yard. Somewhere in the distance cows were lowing and a little bell was tinkling; now and then a farm wagon tilted by, and the dust flew; some blue-shirted laborers with shovels over their shoulders plodded past; little swarms of flies were dancing up and down before the people's faces in the soft air. There seemed to be a gentle stir arising over everything for the mere sake of subsidence—a very premonition of rest and hush and night.

This soft diurnal commotion was over Louisa Ellis also. She had been peacefully sewing at her sitting-room window all the afternoon. Now she quilted her needle carefully into her work, which she folded precisely, and laid in a basket with her thimble and thread and scissors. Louisa Ellis could not remember that ever in her life she had mislaid one of these little feminine appurtenances, which had become, from long use and constant association, a very part of her personality.

Louisa tied a green apron round her waist, and got out a flat straw hat with a green ribbon. Then she went into the garden with a little blue crockery bowl, to pick some currants for her tea. After the currants were picked she sat on the back doorstep and stemmed them, collecting the stems carefully in her apron and afterward throwing them into the hencoop. She looked sharply at the grass beside the step to see if any had fallen there.

Louisa was slow and still in her movements; it took her a long time to prepare her tea; but when ready it was set forth with as much grace as if she had been a veritable guest to her own self. The little square table stood exactly in the center of the kitchen, and was covered with a starched linen cloth whose border pattern of flowers glistened. Louisa had a damask napkin on her tea tray, where were arranged a cut-glass tumbler full of teaspoons, a silver cream pitcher, a china sugar bowl, and one pink china cup and saucer. Louisa used china every day—something which none of her neighbors did. They whispered about it among themselves. Their daily tables were laid with common crockery, their sets of best china stayed in the parlor closet, and Louisa Ellis was no richer nor better bred than they. Still she would use the china. She had for her supper a glass dish full of sugared currants, a plate of little cakes, and one of light white biscuits. Also a leaf or two of lettuce, which she cut up daintily. Louisa was very fond of lettuce, which she raised to perfection in her little garden. She ate quite heartily, though in a delicate, pecking way; it seemed almost surprising that any considerable bulk of the food should vanish.

After tea she filled a plate with nicely baked thin corn cakes, and carried them out into the back yard.

"Caesar!" she called. "Caesar! Caesar!"

There was a little rush, and the clank of a chain, and a large yellow-and-white dog appeared at the door of his tiny hut, which was half hidden among the tall grasses and flowers. Louisa patted him and gave him the corn cakes. Then she returned to the house and washed the tea things, polishing the china carefully. The twilight had deepened; the chorus of the frogs floated in at the open window wonderfully loud and shrill, and once in a while a long sharp drone from a tree toad pierced it. Louisa took off her green gingham apron, disclosing a shorter one of pink-and-white print. She lighted her lamp, and sat down again with her sewing.

In about half an hour Joe Dagget came. She heard his heavy step on the walk, and rose and took off her pink-and-white apron. Under that was still another—white linen with a little cambric edging on the bottom; that was Louisa's company apron. She never wore it without her calico sewing apron over it unless she had a guest. She had barely folded the pink-and-white one with methodical haste and laid it in a table drawer when the door opened and Joe Dagget entered.

He seemed to fill up the whole room. A little yellow canary that had been asleep in his green cage at the south window woke up and fluttered wildly, beating his little yellow wings against the wires. He always did so when Joe Dagget came into the room.

"Good evening," said Louisa: She extended her hand with a kind of solemn cordiality.

"Good evening, Louisa," returned the man, in a loud voice.

She placed a chair for him, and they sat facing each other, with the table between them. He sat bolt upright, toeing out his heavy feet squarely, glancing with a good-humored uneasiness around the room. She sat gently erect, folding her slender hands in her white-linen lap.

"Been a pleasant day," remarked Dagget.

"Real pleasant," Louisa assented, softly. "Have you been haying?" she asked, after a little while.

"Yes, I've been haying all day, down in the ten-acre lot. Pretty hot work."

"It must be."

"Yes, it's pretty hot work in the sun."

"Is your mother well today?"

"Yes, mother's pretty well."

"I suppose Lily Dyer's with her now?"

Dagget colored. "Yes, she's with her," he answered, slowly.

He was not very young, but there was a boyish look about his large face. Louisa was not quite so old as he, her face was fairer and smoother, but she gave people the impression of being older.

"I suppose she's a good deal of help to your mother," she said, further.

"I guess she is; I don't know how mother'd get along without her," said Dagget, with a sort of embarrassed warmth.

"She looks like a real capable girl. She's pretty-looking too," remarked Louisa.

"Yes, she is pretty fair looking."

Presently Dagget began fingering the books on the table. There was a square red autograph album, and a Young Lady's Gift Book which had belonged to Louisa's mother. He took them up one after the other and opened them; then laid them down again, the album on the Gift Book.

Louisa kept eyeing them with mild uneasiness. Finally she rose and changed the position of the books, putting the album underneath. That was the way they had been arranged in the first place.

Dagget gave an awkward little laugh. "Now what difference did it make which book was on top?" said he.

Louisa looked at him with a deprecating smile. "I always keep them that way," murmured she.

"You do beat everything," said Dagget, trying to laugh again. His large face was flushed.

He remained about an hour longer, then rose to take leave. Going out, he stumbled over a rug, and trying to recover himself, hit Louisa's work basket on the table, and knocked it on the floor.

He looked at Louisa, then at the rolling spools; he ducked himself awkwardly toward them, but she stopped him. "Never mind," said she; "I'll pick them up after you're gone."

She spoke with a mild stiffness. Either she was a little disturbed, or his nervousness affected her and made her seem constrained in her effort to reassure him.

When Joe Dagget was outside he drew in the sweet evening air with a sigh, and felt much as an innocent and perfectly well-intentioned bear might after his exit from a china shop.

Louisa, on her part, felt much as the kind-hearted, long-suffering owner of the china shop might have done after the exit of the bear.

She tied on the pink, then the green apron, picked up all the scattered treasures and replaced them in her work basket, and straightened the rug. Then she set the lamp on the floor and began sharply examining the carpet. She even rubbed her fingers over it, and looked at them.

"He's tracked in a good deal of dust," she murmured. "I thought he must have."

Louisa got a dustpan and brush, and swept Joe Dagget's track carefully.

If he could have known it, it would have increased his perplexity and uneasiness, although it would not have disturbed his loyalty in the least. He came twice a week to see Louisa Ellis, and every time, sitting there in her delicately sweet room, he felt as if surrounded by a hedge of lace. He was afraid to stir lest he should put a clumsy foot or hand through the fairy web, and he had always the consciousness that Louisa was watching fearfully lest he should.

Still the lace and Louisa commanded perforce his perfect respect and patience and loyalty. They were to be married in a month, after a singular courtship which had lasted for a matter of fifteen years. For fourteen out of the fifteen years the two had not once seen each other, and they had seldom exchanged letters. Joe had been all those years in Australia, where he had gone to make his fortune, and where he had stayed until he made it. He would have stayed fifty years if it had taken so long, and come home feeble and tottering, or never come home at all, to marry Louisa.

But the fortune had been made in the fourteen years, and he had come home now to marry the woman who had been patiently and unquestioningly waiting for him all that time.

Shortly after they were engaged he had announced to Louisa his determination to strike out into new fields and secure a competency before they should be married. She had listened and assented with the sweet serenity which never failed her, not even when her lover set forth on that long and uncertain journey. Joe, buoyed up as he

by a Woman writt

was by his sturdy determination, broke down a little at the last, but Louisa kissed him with a mild blush, and said good-by.

"It won't be for long," poor Joe had said, huskily; but it was for fourteen years.

In that length of time much had happened. Louisa's mother and brother had died, and she was all alone in the world. But greatest happening of all—a subtle happening which both were too simple to understand—Louisa's feet had turned into a path, smooth maybe under a calm, serene sky, but so straight and unswerving that it could only meet a check at her grave, and so narrow that there was no room for anyone at her side.

Louisa's first emotion when Joe Dagget came home (he had not apprised her of his coming) was consternation, although she would not admit it to herself, and he never dreamed of it. Fifteen years ago she had been in love with him—at least she considered herself to be. Just at that time, gently acquiescing with and falling into the natural drift of girlhood, she had seen marriage ahead as a reasonable feature and a probable desirability of life. She had listened with calm docility to her mother's views upon the subject. Her mother was remarkable for her cool sense and sweet, even temperament. She talked wisely to her daughter when Joe Dagget presented himself, and Louisa accepted him with no hesitation. He was the first lover she had ever had.

She had been faithful to him all these years. She had never dreamed of the possibility of marrying anyone else. Her life, especially for the last seven years, had been full of a pleasant peace; she had never felt discontented nor impatient over her lover's absence; still, she had always looked forward to his return and their marriage as the inevitable conclusion of things. However, she had fallen into a way of placing it so far in the future that it was almost equal to placing it over the boundaries of another life.

When Joe came she had been expecting him, and expecting to be married for fourteen years, but she was as much surprised and taken aback as if she had never thought of it.

Joe's consternation came later. He eyed Louisa with an instant confirmation of his old admiration. She had changed but little. She still kept her pretty manner and soft grace, and was, he considered, every whit as attractive as ever. As for himself, his stent was done; he had turned his face away from fortune seeking, and the old winds of romance whistled as loud and sweet as ever through his ears. All the song which he had been wont to hear in them was Louisa; he had for a long time a loyal belief that he heard it still, but finally it seemed to him that although the winds sang always that one song, it had another name. But for Louisa the wind had never more than murmured; now it had gone down, and everything was still. She listened for a little while with half-wistful attention; then she turned quietly away and went to work on her wedding clothes.

Joe had made some extensive and quite magnificent alterations in his house. It was the old homestead; the newly-married couple would live there, for Joe could not desert his mother, who refused to leave her old home. So Louisa must leave hers. Every morning, rising and going about among her neat maidenly possessions, she felt as one looking her last upon the faces of dear friends. It was true that in a measure she could take them with her, but, robbed of their old environments, they would appear in such new guises that they would almost cease to be themselves.

Then there were some peculiar features of her happy solitary life which she would probably be obliged to relinquish altogether. Sterner tasks than these graceful but half-needless ones would probably devolve upon her. There would be a large house to care for; there would be company to entertain; there would be Joe's rigorous and feeble old mother to wait upon; and it would be contrary to all thrifty village traditions for her to keep more than one servant.

Louisa had a little still, and she used to occupy herself pleasantly in summer weather with distilling the sweet and aromatic essences from roses and peppermint and spearmint. By-and-by her still must be laid away. Her store of essences was already considerable, and there would be no time for her to distill for the mere pleasure of it. Then Joe's mother would think it foolishness; she had already hinted her opinion in the matter.

Louisa dearly loved to sew a linen seam, not always for use, but for the simple, mild pleasure which she took in it. She would have been loath to confess how more than once she had ripped a seam for the mere delight of sewing it together again. Sitting at her window during long sweet afternoons, drawing her needle gently through the dainty fabric, she was peace itself. But there was small chance of such foolish comfort in the future. Joe's mother, domineering, shrewd old matron that she was even in her old age, and very likely even Joe himself, with his honest masculine rudeness, would laugh and frown down all these pretty but senseless old maiden ways.

Louisa had almost the enthusiasm of an artist over the mere order and cleanliness of her solitary home. She had throbs of genuine triumph at the sight of the windowpanes which she had polished until they shone like jewels. She gloated gently over her orderly bureau drawers, with their exquisitely folded contents redolent with lavender and sweet clover and very purity. Could she be sure of the endurance of even this? She had visions, so startling that she half repudiated them as indelicate, of course masculine belongings strewn about in endless litter; of dust and disorder arising necessarily from a course masculine presence in the midst of all this delicate harmony.

Among her forebodings of disturbance, not the least was with regard to Caesar. Caesar was a veritable hermit of a dog. For the greater part of his life he had dwelt in his secluded hut, shut out from the society of his kind and all innocent canine joys. Never had Caesar since his early youth watched at a woodchuck's hole; never had he known the delights of a stray bone at a neighbor's kitchen door. And it was all on account of a sin committed when hardly out of his puppyhood. No one knew the possible depth of remorse of which this mild-visaged, altogether innocent-looking old dog might be capable; but whether or not he had encountered remorse, he had encountered a full measure of righteous retribution. Old Caesar seldom lifted up his voice in a growl or a bark; he was fat and sleepy; there were yellow rings which looked like spectacles around his dim old eyes; but there was a neighbor who bore on his hand the imprint of several of Caesar's sharp white youthful teeth, and for that he had lived at the end of a chain, all alone in a little hut, for fourteen years. The neighbor, who was choleric and smarting with the pain of his wound, had demanded either Caesar's death or complete ostracism. So Louisa's brother, to whom the dog had belonged, had built him his little kennel and tied him up. It was now fourteen years since, in a flood of youthful spirits, he had inflicted that memorable bite, and

Mary E. Wilkins Freeman

with the exception of short excursions, always at the end of the chain, under the strict guardianship of his master or Louisa, the old dog had remained a close prisoner. It is doubtful if, with his limited ambition, he took much pride in the fact, but it is certain that he was possessed of considerable cheap fame. He was regarded by all the children in the village and by many adults as a very monster of ferocity. St. George's dragon could hardly have surpassed in evil repute Louisa Ellis's old yellow dog. Mothers charged their children with solemn emphasis not to go too near to him, and the children listened and believed greedily, with a fascinated appetite for terror, and ran by Louisa's house stealthily, with many sidelong and backward glances at the terrible dog. If perchance he sounded a hoarse bark, there was a panic. Wayfarers chancing into Louisa's yard eyed him with respect, and inquired if the chain were stout. Caesar at large might have seemed a very ordinary dog and excited no comment whatever; chained, his reputation overshadowed him, so that he lost his own proper outlines and looked darkly vague and enormous. Joe Dagget, however, with his good-humored sense and shrewdness, saw him as he was. He strode valiantly up to him and patted him on the head, in spite of Louisa's soft clamor of warning, and even attempted to set him loose. Louisa grew so alarmed that he desisted, but kept announcing his opinion in the matter quite forcibly at intervals. "There ain't a better-natured dog in town," he would say, "and it's down-right cruel to keep him tied up there. Some day I'm going to take him out."

Louisa had very little hope that he would not, one of these days, when their interests and possessions should be more completely fused in one. She pictured to herself Caesar on the rampage through the quiet and unguarded village. She saw innocent children bleeding in his path. She was herself very fond of the old dog, because he had belonged to her dead brother, and he was always very gentle with her; still she had great faith in his ferocity. She always warned people not to go too near him. She fed him on ascetic fare of corn mush and cakes, and never fired his dangerous temper with heating and sanguinary diet of flesh and bones. Louisa looked at the old dog munching his simple fare, and thought of her approaching marriage and trembled. Still no anticipation of disorder and confusion in lieu of sweet peace and harmony, no forebodings of Caesar on the rampage, no wild fluttering of her little yellow canary, were sufficient to turn her a hair's-breadth. Joe Dagget had been fond of her and working for her all these years. It was not for her, whatever came to pass, to prove untrue and break his heart. She put the exquisite little stitches into her wedding garments, and the time went on until it was only a week before her wedding day. It was a Tuesday evening, and the wedding was to be a week from Wednesday.

There was a full moon that night. About nine o'clock Louisa strolled down the road a little way. There were harvest fields on either hand, bordered by low stone walls. Luxuriant clumps of bushes grew beside the wall, and trees—wild cherry and old apple trees—at intervals. Presently Louisa sat down on the wall and looked about her with mildly sorrowful reflectiveness. Tall shrubs of blueberry and meadow-sweet, all woven together and tangled with blackberry vines and horsebriers, shut her in on either side. She had a little clear space between them. Opposite her, on the other side of the road, was a spreading tree; the moon shone between its boughs, and the leaves twinkled like silver. The road was bespread with a beautiful shifting dapple of silver and shadow; the air was full of a mysterious sweetness. "I wonder if it's wild grapes?" murmured Louisa. She sat there some time. She was just thinking of rising, when she heard footsteps and low voices, and remained quiet. It was a lonely place, and she felt a little timid. She thought she would keep still in the shadow and let the persons, whoever they might be, pass her.

But just before they reached her the voices ceased, and the footsteps. She understood that their owners had also found seats upon the stone wall. She was wondering if she could not steal away unobserved, when the voice broke the stillness. It was Joe Dagget's. She sat still and listened.

The voice was announced by a loud sigh, which was as familiar as itself. "Well," said Dagget, "you've made up your mind, then, I suppose?"

"Yes," returned another voice; "I'm going day after tomorrow."

"That's Lily Dyer," thought Louisa to herself. The voice embodied itself in her mind. She saw a girl tall and full-figured, with a firm, fair face, looking fairer and firmer in the moonlight, her strong yellow hair braided in a close knot. A girl full of a calm rustic strength and bloom, with a masterful way which might have beseemed a princess. Lily Dyer was a favorite with the village folk; she had just the qualities to arouse the admiration. She was good and handsome and smart. Louisa had often heard her praises sounded.

"Well," said Joe Dagget, "I ain't got a word to say."

"I don't know what you could say," returned Lily Dyer.

"Not a word to say," repeated Joe, drawing out the words heavily. Then there was a silence. "I ain't sorry," he began at last, "that that happened yesterday—that we kind of let on how we felt to each other. I guess it's just as well we knew. Of course I can't do anything any different. I'm going right on an' get married next week. I ain't going back on a woman that's waited for me fourteen years, an' break her heart."

"If you should jilt her tomorrow, I wouldn't have you," spoke up the girl, with sudden vehemence.

"Well, I ain't going to give you the chance," said he; "but I don't believe you would, either."

"You'd see I wouldn't. Honor's honor, an' right's right. An' I'd never think anything of any man that went against 'em for me or any other girl; you'd find that out, Joe Dagget."

"Well, you'll find out fast enough that I ain't going against 'em for you or any other girl," returned he. Their voices sounded almost as if they were angry with each other. Louisa was listening eagerly.

"I'm sorry you feel as if you must go away," said Joe, "but I don't know but it's best."

"Of course it's best. I hope you and I have got common sense."

"Well, I suppose you're right." Suddenly Joe's voice got an undertone of tenderness. "Say, Lily," said he, "I'll get along well enough myself, but I can't bear to think—You don't suppose you're going to fret much over it?"

"I guess you'll find out I shan't fret much over a married man."

"Well, I hope you won't—I hope you won't, Lily. God knows I do. And—I hope—one of these days—you'll—come across somebody else—"

"I don't see any reason why I shouldn't." Suddenly her tone changed. She spoke in a sweet, clear voice, so loud that she could have been heard across the street. "No, Joe Dagget," said she, "I'll never marry any other man as long as I live. I've got good sense, an' I ain't going to break my heart nor make a fool of myself; but I'm never going to be married, you can be sure of that. I ain't that sort of a girl to feel this way twice."

Louisa heard an exclamation and a soft commotion behind the bushes; then Lily spoke again—the voice sounded as if she had risen. "This must be put a stop to," said she. "We've stayed here long enough. I'm going home."

Louisa sat there in a daze, listening to their retreating steps. After a while she got up and slunk softly home herself. The next day she did her housework methodically; that was as much a matter of course as breathing; but she did not sew on her wedding clothes. She sat at her window and meditated. In the evening Joe came. Louisa Ellis had never known that she had any diplomacy in her, but when she came to look for it that night she found it, although meek of its kind, among her little feminine weapons. Even now she could hardly believe that she had heard aright, and that she would not do Joe a terrible injury should she break her troth plight. She wanted to sound him without betraying too soon her own inclinations in the matter. She did it successfully, and they finally came to an understanding; but it was a difficult thing, for he was as afraid of betraying himself as she.

She never mentioned Lily Dyer. She simply said that while she had no cause of complaint against him, she had lived so long in one way that she shrank from making a change.

"Well, I never shrank, Louisa," said Dagget. "I'm going to be honest enough to say that I think maybe it's better this way; but if you'd wanted to keep on, I'd have stuck to you till my dying day. I hope you know that."

"Yes, I do," said she.

That night she and Joe parted more tenderly than they had done for a long time. Standing in the door, holding each other's hands, a last great wave of regretful memory swept over them.

"Well, this ain't the way we've thought it was all going to end, is it, Louisa?" said Joe.

She shook her head. There was a little quiver on her placid face.

"You let me know if there's ever anything I can do for you," said he. "I ain't ever going to forget you, Louisa." Then he kissed her, and went down the path.

Louisa, all alone by herself that night, wept a little, she hardly knew why; but the next morning, on waking, she felt like a queen who, after fearing lest her domain be wrested away from her, sees it firmly insured in her possession.

Now the tall weeds and grasses might cluster around Caesar's little hermit hut, the snow might fall on its roof year in and year out, but he never would go on a rampage through the unguarded village. Now the little canary might turn itself into a peaceful yellow ball night after night, and have no need to wake and flutter with wild terror against its bars. Louisa could sew linen seams, and distill roses, and dust and polish and fold away in lavender, as long as she listed. That afternoon she sat with her needlework at the window, and felt fairly steeped in peace. Lily Dyer, tall and erect and blooming went past; but she felt no qualm. If Louisa Ellis had sold her birthright she did not know it; the taste of the pottage was so delicious, and had been her sole satisfaction for so long. Serenity and placid narrowness had become to her as the birthright itself. She gazed ahead through a long reach of future days strung together like pearls in a rosary, every one like the others, and all smooth and flawless and innocent, and her heart went up in thankfulness. Outside was the fervid summer afternoon; the air was filled with the sounds of the busy harvest of men and birds and bees; there were halloos, metallic clatterings, sweet calls, and long hummings. Louisa sat, prayerfully numbering her days, like an uncloistered nun.

Dorothy Richardson

Dorothy Richardson

(1873–1957)

Pilgrimage, a thirteen-volume semiautobiographical account of a young woman's quest for self-discovery, took Dorothy Richardson over twenty years to complete. She began with the intention of creating "a feminine equivalent of the current masculine realism." But she gradually became preoccupied by "a stranger in the form of contemplated reality having for the first time in her experience its own say, and apparently justifying those who acclaim writing as the surest means of discovering the truth about one's own thoughts and beliefs." The first publisher to whom she sent her work returned it, claiming he could not understand what it was about. Hiding the returned manuscript in a trunk, Richardson continued to write. "I knew I must go on," she later explained. "You get a moment of feeling committed." It was to Richardson's work that the term "stream of consciousness" first was applied. Characterized by Ford Madox Ford as "the most abominably unknown contemporary writer," Richardson was one of the innovators of modern fiction. She was also one of the first writers to so fully explore the thoughts and beliefs of a modern woman.

Miriam Henderson, Richardson's central character, is a young Englishwoman, living at the beginning of the twentieth century, and keenly aware of feminism. The first selection from *Pilgrimage* describes Miriam's torment at discovering how, for a woman, "there was nothing to turn to. Books were poisoned. Art. All the achievements of men." The second selection describes Miriam's relationship with "Hypo"—a character based on H. G. Wells—a relationship that leads her to realize how women need and are denied homage.

FROM THE TUNNEL

PILGRIMAGE, VOLUME II, CHAPTER XXIV

"There; how d'ye like that, eh? A liberal education in twelve volumes, with an index. Read them when ye want to. See?" . . .

They looked less, set up like that in a row, than when they had lain about on the floor of the den . . . taking up Dante and Beethoven at tea time.

by a Woman writt

"Books posted? I wonder I'm not more rushed. I say—v'you greased all Hancock's and the pater's instruments?"

He knows I'm slacking . . . he'll tell the others when they come back. . . .

Mr. Leyton's door shut with a bang. He would be sitting reading the newspaper until the next patient came. The eternal sounds of laughter and dancing came up from the kitchen. The rest of the house was perfectly still. Her miserable hand reopened the last page of the index. There were five or six more entries under "Woman."

If one could only burn all the volumes; stop the publication of them. But it was all books, all the literature in the world, right back to Juvenal . . . whatever happened, if it could all be avenged by somebody in some way, there was all that . . . the classics, the finest literature—"unsurpassed." Education would always mean coming in contact with all that. Schoolboys got their first ideas. . . . *How* could Newnham and Girton women endure it? How could they go on living and laughing and talking?

And the modern men were the worst . . . "We can now, with all the facts in our hands, sit down and examine her at our leisure." There was no getting away from the scientific facts . . . *inferior*; mentally, morally, intellectually, and physically . . . her development arrested in the interest of her special functions . . . reverting later towards the male type . . . old women with deep voices and hair on their faces . . . leaving off where boys of eighteen began. If that is true everything is as clear as daylight. "Woman is not undeveloped man but diverse" falls to pieces. Woman is undeveloped man . . . if one could die of the loathsome visions . . . I *must* die. I can't go on living in it . . . the whole world full of *creatures*; half-human. And I am one of the half-human ones, or shall be, if I don't stop now.

Boys and girls were much the same . . . women stopped being people and went off into hideous processes. What for? What was it all for? Development. The wonders of science. The wonders of science for women are nothing but gynaecology—all those frightful operations in the *British Medical Journal* and those jokes—the

Dorothy Richardson

hundred golden rules. . . . Sacred functions . . . highest possibilities
. . . sacred for what? The hand that rocks the cradle rules the world?
The Future of the Race? What world? What race? Men. . . . Nothing
but men; for ever.

If, by one thought, all the men in the world could be stopped,
shaken, and slapped. There *must*, somewhere, be some power that
could avenge it all . . . but if these men were right, there was not.
Nothing but Nature and her decrees. Why was nature there? Who
started it? If nature "took good care" this and that . . . there must
be somebody. If there was a trick, there must be a trickster. If there
is a god who arranged how things should be between men and
women, and just let it go and go on I have no respect for him. I
should like to give him a piece of my mind. . . .

It will all go on as long as women are stupid enough to go on
bringing men into the world . . . even if civilized women stop the
colonials and primitive races would go on. It is a nightmare.

They invent a legend to put the blame for the existence of humanity
on woman and, if she wants to stop it, they talk about the wonders
of civilization and the sacred responsibilities of motherhood. They
can't have it both ways. They also say women are not logical.

They despise women and they want to go on living—to reproduce
—themselves. None of their achievements, no "civilization," no art,
no science can redeem that. There is no pardon possible for man.
The only answer to them is suicide; all women ought to agree to
commit suicide.

The torment grew as the August weeks passed. There were strange
interesting things unexpectedly everywhere. Streets of great shuttered
houses, their window boxes flowerless, all grey, cool and quiet and
untroubled, on a day of cool rain; the restaurants were no longer
crowded; torturing thought ranged there unsupported, goaded to
madness, just a mad feverish swirling in the head, ranging out, driven
back by the vacant eyes of little groups of people from the country.

by a Woman writt

Unfamiliar people appeared in the parks and streets, talking and staring eagerly about, women in felt boat-shaped hats trimmed with plaid ribbons—Americans. They looked clever—and ignorant of worrying thoughts. Men carried their parcels. But it was just the same. It was impossible to imagine these dried, yellow-faced women with babies. But if they liked all the fuss and noise and talk as much as they seemed to do. . . . If they did *not*, what were they doing? What was everybody *doing*? So busily.

Sleeplessness, and every day a worse feeling of illness. Every day the new torture. Every night the dreaming and tossing in the fierce, stifling, dusty heat, the awful waking, to know that presently the unbearable human sounds would begin again; the torment of walking through the streets, the solitary torment of leisure to read again in the stillness of the office; the moments of hope of finding a fresh meaning; hope of having misread.

There was nothing to turn to. Books were poisoned. Art. All the achievements of men were poisoned at the root. The beauty of nature was tricky femininity. The animal world was cruelty. Humanity was based on cruelty. Jests and amusements were tragic distractions from tragedy. Religion was the only hope. But even there there was no hope for women. No future life could heal the degradation of having been a woman. Religion in the world had nothing but insults for women. Christ was a man. If it was true that he was God taking on humanity—he took on *male* humanity . . . and the people who explained him, St. Paul and the priests, the Anglicans and the Nonconformists, it was the same story everywhere. Even if religion could answer science and prove it wrong there was no hope, for women. And no intelligent person can prove science wrong. Life is poisoned, for women, at the very source. Science is true and will find out more and more, and things will grow more and more horrible. Space is full of dead worlds. The world is cooling and dying. Then why not stop *now*?

"Nature's great Salic Law will never be repealed." "Women can never reach the highest places in civilization." Thomas Henry

Dorothy Richardson

Huxley. With side-whiskers. A bouncing complacent walk. Thomas Henry Huxley. (*Thomas Babington Macaulay.*) The same sort of walk. Eminent men. Revelling in their cleverness. "The Lord has delivered him into my hand." He did not believe in any future for anybody. But he built his life up complacently on home and family life while saying all those things about women, lived on them and their pain, ate their food, enjoyed the comforts they made ... and wrote conceited letters to his friends about his achievements and his stomach and his feelings.

What is it in me that stands back? Why can't it explain? My head will burst if it can't explain. If I die now in wild anger it only makes the thing more laughable on the whole. .... That old man lives quite alone in a little gas-lit lodging. When he comes out, he is quite alone. There is nothing touching him anywhere. He will go quietly on like that till he dies. But he is me. I saw myself in his eyes that day. But he must have money. He can live like that with nothing to do but read and think and roam about, because he has money. It isn't fair. Some woman cleans his room and does his laundry. His thoughts about women are awful. It's the best way ... but I've made all sorts of plans for the holidays. After that, I will save and never see anybody and never stir out of Bloomsbury. The woman in black works. It's only in the evenings she can roam about seeing nothing. But the people she works for know nothing about her. She knows. She is sweeter than he. She is sweet. I like her. But he is more me.

FROM DAWN'S LEFT HAND

PILGRIMAGE, VOLUME IV, FROM CHAPTER IX

Again the side-door of a small restaurant in a narrow street. Again a dingy waiter leading the way up an ill-lit staircase. Again the conflict between her desire to be a sympathetic presence and her resentment of his ignorance of her perfect awareness of the conflict in him, between his bourgeois scruples and his secret, new-comer's delight in what he had called his "slum." Again a distracting preoccupation with the world-wide vision of harpy disreputability offering facilities to the well-to-do. And again, more clearly than all, her whole being set against the plan that last week had perfectly foiled itself without instructing him . . .

Coercion. The unpardonable crime.

Unless he should realize that, and make a convincing recantation, he would wreck this occasion as he had wrecked all the others.

It was his worst fault?

The thought occurred to her, coming as if from outside her mind and gleaming for an instant in the murky darkness, that presently she might discreetly discuss this subject with him. He might listen in the way he sometimes had done when suddenly and irrelevantly she said something with all the force of her nature. And this particular certainty was perhaps her strongest social certainty.

Philosophizing: Well, it was what she most wanted, to remove a barrier of which he was aware without understanding its nature. It would be difficult, almost impossible, in a half-lit, shamefaced room. Perhaps the same room. Whose features, in memory, had already attained a kind of beauty.

But to-night the journey ended in a brightly lit sitting-room with table laid. And instantly the evening was endless. They were alone, in endless time.

Piling her outdoor things upon a sheeny shamefaced armchair in a dark corner near a window through the slats of whose dilapidated Venetian blinds came the bluish light of a street lamp, she felt the remains of the day's preoccupations fall away and strength return, flowing in from the promise of leisure, making her hope she was less tired than she felt. Far away from him and from her surroundings her spirit seemed to flee, demanding peace, and to-night, at no matter what cost in apparent idiocy or ill-humour, she *would* reach that central peace; go farther and farther into the heart of her being and be there, as if alone, tranquilly, until fully possessed by that something within her that was more than herself. If not, if she remained outside it, if he succeeded in making her pretend,

Dorothy Richardson

though he never knew she was pretending, to be an inhabitant of his world, then again they would squabble and part.

As they both came forward into the central light and he rounded off the tuneless humming that had accompanied his disrobing and had been meant to signal self-possession, with a cheerful cadenza on a tone increased in fullness like that of an opera orchestra while the hero enters, and still said no word, she felt time and space open out between them, infinitely available: the gift of last week's evening, of their first evening of being alone and inaccessible.

And paused in deep gratitude to life and to him, just short of the lit table, and turned away to the mirror with her hands to her hair as though arranging it. Immediately his humming broke forth anew; this time to answer her silent abstraction, to tell her they were *both* tranquilly at home and at leisure.

Gazing into the depths of the mirror's fly-blown damp-mottled reflection of a dark curtain screening a door in the opposite wall, she was aware of herself there in the picture, lit from behind, obstructing the light that presently again would lie across the mirror when she turned to join the party: him, and herself representing to him a set of memories amongst other sets of memories. A set covering about ten years of his life, covering the period that had seen him emerge from obscurity to celebrity in his world that was so alien to her own.

In and out of every year of his ascent her life had been woven. She had been a witness, and was now a kind of compendium for him of it all, one of his supports, one of those who through having known the beginnings, through representing them every time she appeared, brought to him a realization of his achievements.

He was two people. A man achieving, becoming, driving forward to unpredictable becomings, delighting in the process, devoting himself, compelling himself, whom so frankly he criticized and so genuinely deplored, to a ceaseless becoming, ceaseless assimilating of anything that promised to serve the interests of a ceaseless becoming for life as he saw it. And also a man seeming uncreated, without any existence worth the name.

If presently he should ask, really wishing, impersonally, to hear of movements, of any kind of accomplishment: "Well, what have you been up to since last week?" and she should answer, as a hundred times she had answered: "Living," he would emit the little chuckle, half amusement at what he considered an evasion and half disapproval of the spectacle of a life spent, as lately he had so often said, "in agreeable loafing that leads nowhere."

But then he would say also, in moods of reflective impersonal contemplation: "You 've taken your freedom, Miriam, won it in the teeth of difficulties in a way that compels my admiration. You 've lived, you still live, you know, only just above the poverty line, and it hasn't bashed you." And so many other descriptive commentaries, recognizable, impersonal classifications of all sorts. And yet she remained, felt, unknown to him. And whatever selves he might reveal to her, selves he hinted at, none of which she had any desire to become, she must remain unknown. For so dismally, in every one, he saw only what they were becoming or might become, and of the essential individual knew, and wanted to know, nothing at all.

The dreary young waiter came in with the soup and once more the room asserted its character and Hypo, sharply aware of him, began at once to edit his ideas of the occasion by his manner of supervising his arrangements with a half-friendly, half-patronizing approval, and succeeded only in making the mournful young man strain yet higher the eyebrows permanently a little lifted by the disappointing difference between the realities of his life in London and his dreams thereof in his far-away continental home.

He shuffled away and the room recovered: the fly-blown mirror, the faded artificial flowers, the obtrusive sofa, were redeemed by the table's circle of golden light, now populous and become one with all the circles of golden light within which she had sat down to feast.

Taking her place, she felt more than the usual familiar sense of everlastingness that came forward in her at the moment of sitting down to table with beloved people, and stayed until the breaking forth of conversation drove it into the background. Here it was, blissfully beating its wings in the disgraceful room and coming this time not only from the past but from past and future alike; for ever.

She held to it, savouring its strange new quality, its power of so intensifying the radiance in which they sat, that everything beyond it was a darkness obliterating the walls of the room, extending back and back, right along the receding years of their intermittent friendship.

Called by his unusual silence to glance across the separating inches, she saw that he was being grave, apparently quietly abstracted. Honestly, quite honestly and sincerely he was playing up to her, venturing unarmed into the desert shared life became for him whenever deliberate, incessant gaiety was in abeyance, whose destructive power he yet knew as well as he knew its joys.

Robbed of the subtle curves drawn about them by his watchful readiness for witty improvisation or facetious retort, robbed of the authoritative complacency they wore during his ceaseless social occupation of definition and commentary at every turn of every occasion, his features were homely, reverted to his very homely type, the raw material of his personal appearance. Only his brow, the side of it left free from limply forward-falling wisps of hair, asserted independence, above his momentarily invisible eyes; thought-moulded, moulded by the theories and thoughts that built up his mental life.

She was at once charmed and touched by this surely painful experiment, the result of his willingness to try to meet her on her own ground, or at any rate her own terms; for the ground she lived on he believed to be merely a mistaken self-importance.

Turning away her eyes from the strange spectacle of him abdicated and docile, she became aware of the thoughts behind his experiment. He was curious as to what use she would make of the offered leadership, and at the same time sceptical, willing to give her time, at any rate time enough to prove to herself as well as to him that her silence was what he believed all feminine silence to be: a vacuous waiting.

His patience, unless she could almost hypnotize him by the intensity of her concentration, would give out. Long before she could attain. Well, let it give out.

Scarcely breathing, she dropped, aware at once by the way the now familiar objects of the room fused to a unity, as if seen from a distance, that she would remember them for ever, down and down, sure now, if she could hold out, of attaining at last in his presence for the first time, save now and again by accident, to possession of that self within herself who was more than her momentary self, and again and again, intermittently and unreliably, had charmed them both.

Almost arrived, almost down in the innermost sphere of happy solitude, drawing the first deep breath of its fresher air that was like air coming across the sea at night, air breathed above the waters of a bubbling spring, she was halted by the watchfulness of a swift glance, a ray immediately withdrawn.

In answer to her awareness, having first made sure of it, made sure her eyes would turn his way, he raised his spoon and flourished it in a neat little spiral above his plate, with eyes downcast, lips pouched, and eyebrows pathetically up in would-be childish appeal: a small pantomime suggesting that they should get on with their soup.

He was confessing his vow of silence, making game of it, revealing above his half-mocking, half-interested, sceptical submissiveness, his ceaseless mind presiding, its wide shallow definitions and interpretations all neatly in place.

With a flash of insight that freed her for ever, she felt, of jealousy of his relationships past, present, and future, she saw how very slight, how restricted and perpetually baffled must always be the communication between him and anything that bore the name of woman. Saw the price each one had paid with whom he had been intimate either in love or friendship, in being obliged to shut off, in order to meet him in his world, his shaped world, rationalized according to whatever scheme of thought was appealing to him at the moment, three-fourths of their being.

What could any one of them be for him beyond the fact that they were providers of what he regarded as vitalizing physical contacts, but sounding-boards for his ideas; admirers, supporters? Either they were disciples, holding on to and living in the light of one or other of the mutually contradictory interpretations of life perpetually evolved by men, all of them right and all wrong, and were therefore not women at all, but the "intelligent emancipated creatures" for whom he expressed so much admiration while fighting shy of them in his leisure hours because of their awful consistency and conscientiousness or because, as Jan said, "a rush of brains to the head usually made them rather plain in the face," or they played up whenever they were with him, trotted briskly about on his maps and diagrams, and lived for the rest of their time in their own deep world.

All this she felt to-night with the strength of two. Amabel was with her, young Amabel, with her mature experience of men, who had confirmed what hitherto she had thought might be inexperience, or a personal peculiarity: her certainty that between men and women there can be no direct communication.

There was no place in his universe for women who did not either sincerely, blindly, follow, or play up and make him believe they were following. All the others were merely pleasant or unpleasant biological material. Those who opposed: misguided creatures who must not be allowed to obstruct. The majority played up: for the sake of his society, his charm, the charm of enjoying and watching him enjoy the pranks of his lightning-swift intelligence. The temptation was great.

She knew she had not always resisted it.

Poor little man. Isolated without knowing the cause of his isolation. Representing, as he sat there, all his isolated fellowmen.

No, there was no room for jealousy of the association of any woman with any man; only perhaps of their privileges and some of their experiences.

People can meet only in God? The shape—she took her spoon and began on her soup, swiftly, rhythmically, seeing upon the tablecloth in front of her the shape—a triangle. Woman and man at either end of the base, the apex: God.

"Grace," she said, feeling now quite free, as if in solitude, to entertain herself with her own thoughts. "That is why people say Grace. At least, one of the reasons."

"Grace . . ." he began, provisionally, in the rather high-pitched tone that meant he was focusing something for which he had no prepared formula; but very gently so that he might, if she wished, be considered not to have spoken.

"Grace," she breathed, as if speaking to herself: "Grace, even if followed by *Snooks* . . . any one bearing such a name, called by it every day, must be influenced."

With "Gracie" and "Grice" sounding hideously in her ears as she reflected that the name, as spoken in English, was a bad example of what she might have wanted to express if her new interest in words as a factor in environment had really been brought into play, she felt his eyes turned upon her and away again as he bent, believing her engrossed, to his filled spoon, without attempting to interpose, by means of some characteristic sally, his bugle-call to some recognizable form of mental activity.

This was marvellous. As now and again in the past, but then only in the midst of distracting conflict, she felt her spirit expand freely in the room and gather to itself, in the immensity of leisure provided by each succeeding second, all that belonged to the occasion.

So prominent in the backward vista that it seemed now to be offering itself as a substitute for the one now surrounding them, the scene of their early conflicts and of the beginning of the false-true relationship now established between them came clearly before her inward eye: the room shaped like a one-armed signpost, the long, cushioned seat in the window looking out to sea, every detail of the room's contents that had flouted her in moments of despair over the absence of words to frame the truths that balanced his and refused to fit into his patterns.

She felt again the delight of the moment of facing silently, alone with him, the sea's distant misty blue behind the nearer blue brilliance of delphiniums and saw again the window-framed loveliness deepen as quite gravely and simply he implored her to remain, for the whole morning dependably there, supporting. Again felt that morning immediately become endless. It did not matter that his consciousness had forgotten all this. Actually, it was the moment preceding this present one. Interruption had fallen upon it. Upon all the opportunities he had made, it had punctually fallen.

But now interruption was banished.

"This is very nice and domestic. You are having your first share of domesticity, Miretta."

She looked across the few inches of space that separated them as across a gulf on the hither side of which he sat awaiting response to his adroit attempt to steer her thoughts, and met his eyes and saw re-enthroned in them the comedic sprite that gave him ceaseless entertainment and would not let him live.

Dorothy Richardson

Having given her the chance of steering the conversation and waited, according to his own reckoning, for dark ages, in vain, he now resumed his usual role in any shared experience: conductor, perpetually defining.

It was true. This *was* perhaps her share of domestic life. Perhaps all she had felt on sitting down to table was the result of a plunge into that zone of experience, now irrevocable and to be bearing fruit for ever.

"Been flying, almost desperately, from domesticity, all m'life."

"Yes. . . . *Yes*. Lucky Miriam. Sailing free. You *are* lucky, you know. Not domesticity, then. Isolation; in space. But that unfortunate young man 'll be coming in again. Don't go too far into space before we 've done with him."

"Women carry all the domesticity they need about with them. That is why they can get along alone so much better than men."

That had launched him; and to the now quite strange sound of his voice, as new and strange as it had been the first time she heard it, she comfortably went on thinking; reminding herself of the many wives in whose eyes she had surprised private meditation going its way behind an appearance of close attention to a familiar voice.

Half turned towards his talk, eating her soup as though her listening supplied her present animation, she considered the strangeness, the perversity of his perpetual denial of the being far away within himself who believed all she wanted him to believe and knew all she wanted him to know. The one who had written the phrase of which his words had just reminded her.

No cunning, no kind of clever calculation could have worked the miracle of that letter. So complete that she had forgotten it, although without it she would not have been here to-night. But it was not until now that she saw it as proof of all he denied.

It was scientific evidence, surely more interesting and valuable, if less directly profitable, than the kind of evidence by which he set such store, and to this, the fact that it was *scientific* evidence she held eagerly, the whole of her mind seeming to be vocal at once above the sounds made by the waiter returned and who now was a friend, one of the strange human family, being and knowing, behind all the surface appearances and comings and goings. Ignoring them both, she prepared to communicate, with all these voices that were speaking at once within her, each presenting a different aspect of what she wanted to say and leaving her to choose the one that would best secure his attention.

But when they were once more alone she felt careless, defiant of any careful presentation. To whatever she might say, he would give an attention that for this evening at least was centred on herself. The beating within her of what seemed at once life and light, was making her breath come unsteadily and her voice shook a little as she said:

"It was in the middle of the morning," and then steadied, for its sound, so personal and yet so strange, the thin small thread of sound, however smooth and pleasant and musical, going out into space to represent—in a manner that left with every word so much denied and so little so partially stated—one person to another, was warning her that the evidence, if it were to convince, must be given in his language of "honest fact."

"There had been," she went on, looking straight ahead and filling out her tone to carry herself past any obstructive witticism of word or manner he might find necessary for the decoration of his retirement from discourse, "a letter from a friend by the first post. Various letters, of course, from various friends. But just that one letter standing out from the rest. It doesn't matter why it stood out. The reasons may be good, bad, indifferent, anything you like." His eyes moved from her face; his thoughts, while the point of her discourse remained uncertain, had touched the subject's possibilities and his set of generalizations about it—including the one, a little hampering her discourse, about the feminine habit of writing long, personal letters that so easily degenerated into a pleasant waste of time— and, with these ready to hand, had dropped away.

"The point is that there could not possibly be another of these very special letters, which in any case always came by the first post, until the next day. Came a rat-tat. I *do* dislike that form, don't you? *Came* this and that; even in poetry. Perhaps because "came" is such a poor sound. Won't bear the weight of suspense. . . . Now *kahm*—" Reverie advanced upon her, suggesting the interest to be found in considering the relative powers of English and German words. He cherished Saxon English for its sanguine force and rich earthiness, but did not know how continuously vivid was German, with its unaltered, ancient pictoriality, every other word describing an action or an object so as to bring it before the eyes; even the terminology of philosophy being directly descriptive.

"Proceed, Miriam."

"*Kahm*, then, the eleven o'clock rat-tat, which I hear every day unmoved and which, as I have explained, on this particular day could not be bringing me anything, brought me to my feet in a way that no other rat-tat has ever done in the whole of my life. With my heart beating, and telling me much more plainly than speech could do that there was, down there in the letter-box, only one letter, instead of the usual posse of business letters and circulars, and that it was for *me*."

"Yes. One has these curious premonitions, in certain moods. Certain states of heightened perception. One is exalted and luminous."

He knew, then, and accepted this kind of experience, had perhaps gone through it himself, and yet remained incurious. She could tell him no more. Even if he were different, believing in an unseen world and an unseen power in communication with every single soul, even if he could suddenly be turned into a believer and her own man and partner, she could not tell, in words, what had happened in the moment of reading. He was in the midst of truth, surrounded by it as she knew it to be, but not willing to attend to its intimations. So the sacred moment was apart in her own personal and private life, though it was he who had found the words to describe its cause.

"Art, sex, and religion; one and the same," she said briskly, "but that doesn't matter. What matters—"

"Tell me, was that letter from me? Nice Miriam; *your* letters are exactly like yourself. Was it?"

"That doesn't matter. The shock, coming from outside, inside, life-as-it-seems-to-be was in having, as it were, read the letter before it came and reacted to it when my rational mind *knew* it couldn't be there."

And the letter was *not*, in a sense, from him.

"There's no outside that is not—"

"Yes. There *is*. We can move, see, hear, feel some how beyond our immediate selves. We can. We do."

And now again the waiter came in, creating diversions with his presence and more food and again departed, leaving Hypo talking of discoveries that would supply scientific explanations for a set of phenomena not at present understood.

She smiled and stretched cool limbs full of strength that an hour ago were so fevered with weariness and, in the deep silence flowing in from the past over the sound of his words and all the words that ever would be used to convey thoughts about life, she demanded of herself whether she cared for him in the smallest degree or for any one or anything so much as the certainty of being in communion with something always there, something in which and through which people could meet and whose absence, felt with people who did not acknowledge it, made life at once impossible, made it a death worse than any dying.

"Religious people in general are in some way unsatisfactory. Not fully alive. Exclusive. Irreligious people are unsatisfactory in another way. Defiant."

A violin, squeaking and scraping in the street below, making his answer inaudible because it was taking all her attention. Its halting sounds, the uncertain notes scraped out into the air of the gloomy street, were addressing themselves to what was always waiting, just within reach, just beyond the always breaking, always disappearing fragments of every kind of life . . . *Eve's little aria.* Playing itself, appealingly, into her heart. Hearing it now, not in Eve's rendering, nor in that of the decrepit musician down there, but in its own perfection, which now she was realizing for the first time, she was smitten by its meditative beauty and by the power with which it called her to herself. It was his enemy. It asserted, quietly, confidently, and, in coming to her at this moment out of the far past and showing it remaining in herself more deeply than the raw new years that had succeeded it and were still formless and void, as if gently chiding her while it overwhelmed her with its tenderness, all that he denied.

"Gluck," she breathed, bending her head to listen.

"Glook, dear Miriam," he said swiftly, and raised his glass.

And she remembered how years ago, when first hovering between relief and admiration for the mental freedom of the Wilson atmosphere, and uncertainty as to the liberties Hypo had taken with the shape of social life, she had told Eve, in a letter written from the

Brooms' villa, from the midst of all the old beliefs, that she felt, in not renouncing the friendship of a divorced, remarried man, she was selling her soul to the devil. And how Eve had written imploring her to give him up.

And now she was surrounded by people all of whom Eve would see as "living in sin." And was about to join their ranks.

Raising her hand to keep him from further speech, she listened with all her strength and moved as she listened away and away, not back into the past, but forward, it seemed, into a future that belonged to it and drew her to itself, to where by nature she belonged.

Crashing across what now seemed to be Eve's own voice and brought a picture of her as she used to stand, gently waiting, without words, when her feelings had been hurt, came the sound of a heavy vehicle along the narrow street.

"You *are* a dear, Miriam," he said in his most delighted voice. "I wish I had your power of complete enthusiasm at a moment's notice. You *do* enjoy life, you know."

"That is one of the loveliest little shapes of music, of its kind, there can be."

There ought to be homage. There was a woman, not this thinking self who talked with men in their own language, but one whose words could be spoken only from the heart's knowledge, waiting to be born in her.

Now here, really, was a point for him: men want recognition of their work, to help them to believe in themselves. They want lime-light and approval, even if they are only hanging a picture, crookedly, in order to bring them confirmation of the worth of what they do. Unless in some form they get it, all but the very few—the stoic philosophical ones who are apt to have a crooked smile, and a pipe in one corner of it, and not much of an opinion of humanity, but a sort of blasphemous, unconsciously destructive, blind, kindly *tolerance*—are miserable. Women, then, want recognition of themselves, of what they are and represent, before they can come fully to birth. Homage for what they are and represent.

He was incapable of homage. Or had given all he had and grown sceptical and dead about it. Left it somewhere. But without a touch of it she could not come fully to birth for him. In that sense all women *are* Undine. Only through a man's recognition can they come to their full stature. But so are men, in their different way. It was his constricted, biological way of seeing sex that kept him blind. Beauty, even, was to him beauty by contrast with Neanderthal man . . .

"The trouble with Miretta is that one can't take liberties with a philosopher."

She smiled from far away, from where if only he knew and could have patience just to look at what she saw and fully submit himself to its truth, see and feel its truth, she could travel towards him. But at least this evening he was serene, not annoyed both with himself and with her as in last week's dimly lit room where yet in memory he seemed so much nearer to her than in this golden light. This evening he knew that the barrier was not of her own deliberate placing.

"Now with others than Miretta"—flattery—"one just takes them in one's arms and immediately there is no barrier."

"Not because I am different. Because there is a psychological barrier. We 've not talked enough."

"Talking comes afterwards, believe me."

He dropped a kiss on her shoulder.

"You *are* a pretty creature, Miriam. I wish you could see yourself."

With the eyes of Amabel, and with her own eyes opened by Amabel, she saw the long honey-coloured ropes of hair framing the face that Amabel found beautiful in its "Flemish Madonna" type, falling across her shoulders and along her body where the last foot of their length, red-gold, gleamed marvellously against the rose-tinted velvety gleaming of her flesh. Saw the lines and curves of her limbs, their balance and harmony. Impersonally beautiful and inspiring. To him each detail was "pretty," and the whole an object of desire.

With an impersonal sacredness they appeared before her, less imaginable as objects of desire than when swathed, as in public they had been all her life.

This mutual nakedness was appeasing rather than stimulating. And austere, as if it were a first step in some arduous discipline.

His body was not beautiful. She could find nothing to adore, no ground for response to his lightly spoken tribute. The manly structure, the smooth, satiny sheen in place of her own velvety glow was interesting as partner and foil, but not desirable. It had no power

Dorothy Richardson

to stir her as often she had been stirred by the sudden sight of him walking down a garden or entering a room. With the familiar clothes, something of his essential self seemed to have departed.

Leaving him pathetic.

The impulse seemed reckless. But when she had leaned forward and clasped him, the warm contact drove away the idea that she might be both humiliating and annoying him and brought a flood of solicitude and suggested a strange action. And as gently she rocked him to and fro the words that came to her lips were so unsuitable that even while she murmured "My little babe, just born," she blushed for them, and steeled herself for his comment.

Letting him go, she found his arms about her in their turn and herself, surprised and not able with sufficient swiftness to contract her expanded being that still seemed to encompass him, rocked unsatis-factorily to and fro while his voice, low and shy and with the inappropriate unwelcome charm in it of the ineffectual gestures of a child learning a game, echoed the unsuitable words.

She leaned back surveying him with downcast eyes, dismayed to feel in him the single, simple, lonely helplessness of the human soul from which his certainties, though they seemed blind, had made her imagine him exempt, and wanting now only to restore him as swiftly as possible to his own world, even at the price of pretending she believed in it. With this determination came a sudden easy certainty of being able to rescue his evening from any sense of failure and disappointment.

Looking up at him with a plan in her mind that in his present state of simplicity did not seem impossible, she met his voice:

"Lost lady. Your reputation 's in shreds, Miriam, virginal though you be."

"Yes. Come and have coffee at my Donizetti's. Open till midnight. One of those little Italian-Swiss places where everything is fried in the same fat."

She had risked the chances of the suggestion by apologizing for it. With an ingenious piece of flattery he would bring the occasion to an end and get away to his own world, with a formula for his evening that would satisfy every test he was likely to apply to it.

"We 'll have a hansom," he said, making for his piled clothes, with the little creak in his voice that was there only when he was on the way to something that promised entertainment. "A hansom," he repeated with comforting ineptitude, "evade the east wind."

Reflected in the mirror she saw as if it were elsewhere and invisible, save by an effort of imagination she did not wish to make, the spectacle of him in conflict with garments and drew her eyes back to her own image just in time to see before it was shadowed by the influence of the haste that was needed if she were to be ready in time to escape the embarrassment of his misguided observation, how radiant it was in the promise of side-by-side companionship.

"We always have an east wind. It 's a portent."

"We 'll elude it. I deplore your superstitions, Miriam, and adore your shamelessness in adhering to them. If I don't look out I shall end by adoring the superstitions."

As they took their places in a vacant corner, without losing any of the joy that had possessed her when the absurd plan suggested itself, she saw the miserable little interior through his eyes. But the sight of his face wearing the curves it had only when everything was going very well, made her carelessly happy and sent her mind on a private tour all round the well-known space, reviving the memories stored up in it. Her early solitude. Eleanor, blissful here in brief immeasurable intervals between difficulty and difficulty. Michael, in conflict and in truce. Selina, courteously enduring a unique experience, restraining her withering disapproval until the moment before they left. She lost without regret the meaning of the words coming from his side of the table and was prevented from turning to inquire by the sight of little Donizetti bringing his plump, short person as quickly as possible down the narrow gangway, turning sideways where projecting chairs impeded his advance, with china-blue eyes coldly inspecting Hypo from a distance and remaining keen and stern when he arrived and turned them upon herself and only sending forth the kindly ray of the smile that smoothed away the lines drawn by disapproval on his well-padded brow when she gave her order, in a voice expressing for him and for herself so much more than her delight in this single occasion that when she turned back to Hypo she knew that already he must have come into possession of some of the wealth accumulated here.

But though for the moment he was incredibly sitting at ease and

Dorothy Richardson

happy here in her world and her life, he would presently need distractions. Forcing herself to ignore the fact that she had on her hands a man accustomed to be "animated" and to meet "animation," she at once recovered the depth of her surroundings, from which she found herself glancing at the picture that was the result of trying on Amabel the effect of her own belief in the impossibility of association between men and women: Amabel at breakfast with Basil in his shooting-box, sitting there in morning light, lovely in her blue kimono, fresh and amusing and delightful and apparently amused and delighted, and Basil, opposite, believing that the behaviour and the talk with which she was filling the gap, to him the enchanting behaviour and the delightful talk and laughter of an amazingly intelligent child-woman, was spontaneous and as pleasing to herself as to him; having no idea of the difficulty, the sheer hard work of holding herself in his world and keeping him at his ease even for an hour.

She stole yet another flash of time to contemplate the alternatives that would confront her in looking across at him as if about to speak: "pally" conversational remarks, the small talk, in their own coinage, for men only, of the woman who has abdicated, fancies she has become a friend and not only is, but looks, a satellite; the sprightly, amusing, half-cynical, social-revelation kind of talk, adapted to male blindness in social life and vastly entertaining them in their unoccupied moments, and giving women the reputation for scandal-mongering from which most men are free only by reason of their social blindness and incapacity; the man-to-man, generalized talk that must go forward in a language each of whose terms leaps a gap and goes confidently forward and finally leaves both them, and the women who contrive without reservations to adopt their mentality and their methods, in a desert of agnosticism.

In conning over his experience of these varieties of interchange, she grew self-conscious, aware of having slipped too far away, and sadly anticipated that in the second about to follow the one that was flashing by, he would, assuming the blankness of her mind, be amiably embarking upon one of his entertaining, life-darkening improvisations.

Marlis Schwieger

Anaïs Nin

Anaïs Nin

(1903–   )

At eleven, Anaïs Nin sailed from Spain to the United States with her mother and brothers. Her father, a celebrated composer and pianist, had separated from the family, and during the journey, Nin began a diary "to persuade my absent father to return." Now well over 150 manuscript volumes long, her *Diary* is one of the richest and most illuminating accounts of a woman artist ever written. In the twenties, Nin went to France, where she continued to write, underwent psychoanalysis, and became part of a literary group which included Henry Miller and Lawrence Durrell. After the outbreak of World War II, she returned to the United States. At first, unable to find a publisher for her works, she bought a printing press and published them herself. For years, Nin's writings were known mainly to a small literary circle, and she herself better known for her friendships with other artists than for her own writing.

Nin has written novels, short stories, and critical works as well as the *Diary.* As in the *Diary,* in her novels and stories, she has often attempted to evoke the psychic life of women—their dreams, their fears, their fantasies. Nin has attempted to speak not only for herself, but "for many women." Often misunderstood, often called "childish" and "curious," she has persisted in writing as she sees fit. The woman artist, Nin has written, "has to create something different from man. . . . She has to sever herself from the myth man creates, from being created by him, she has to struggle with her own cycles, storms, terrors which man does not understand."

FROM THE DIARY OF ANAÏS NIN, VOLUME II, 1934–1939

From [*February, 1937*]

I must continue the diary because it is a feminine activity, it is a personal and personified creation, the opposite of the masculine alchemy. I want to remain on the untransmuted, untransformed, untransposed plane. This alchemy called creation, or fiction, has become for me as dangerous as the machine. Feelings and emotions are diverted at the source, used as the fuel to other purpose. What comes out of the factory: painting, sculpture, poetry, rugs, architecture, novels, I now regard with fear. It is too far from the truth of the moment. Perceived by feeling, during the life, not after.

It resembles the moment when I felt that with Rank I saw too much, unveiled too much, the psychological terminus. Too much awareness, without accompanying experience, is a skeleton without the flesh of life.

Analysis has made three errors:

1. Idealism. In struggling against the negative, destructive element in relationships, it also sets up a falsely idealistic one, a perfect balance, an absolute, which is humanly impossible.

2. It considers all escape as bad, as evasion. Some of these escapes are mobilities into creative areas, towards light or sun, new growth, new departures or renewals.

3. The desire to get back into the womb can become, in a creative way, a making of a womb out of the whole world, including everything in the womb (the city, the enlarged universe of *Black Spring*, of *The Black Book*), the all-englobing, all-encompassing womb, holding everything. Not being able to re-enter the womb, the artist becomes the womb. Analysis does not take into account the creative products of neurotic desires.

From [*March, 1937*]

I cannot remember what I saw in the mirror as a child. Perhaps a child never looks at a mirror. Perhaps a child, like a cat, is so much inside of himself that he does not see himself in the mirror. He sees a child. The child does not remember what he looks like. Later I remembered what I looked like. But when I look at photographs of myself one, two, three, four, five years old, I do not recognize myself. The child is *one*. At one with himself. Never outside of himself. I can remember what I did but not the reflection of what I did. No reflections. Six years old. Seven years old. Eight years old. Nine. Ten. Eleven. No images. No reflections. Feelings. I can feel what I felt about my father's white mice, the horror they inspired in me, the revolting odor, the taste of a burnt omelette my father made for us while my mother was sick and expecting Joaquin in Berlin. The feel of the beach in Barcelona, the feel of the balcony there, the fear of death and the writing of a testament, the feelings in church, in the street. Sounds in the Spanish courtyard, singing, a memory of a gaiety which was to haunt me all my life, totally absent from America. The face of the maid Ramona, the music in the streets, children dancing on the sidewalks. Voices. The appearance of others, the long black mustache of Granados, the embrace of the nuns, drowning me in veils as they leaned over. No picture in the mind's eye of what I wore. The long black stockings of Spanish children I saw in a photograph. I do remember my passion for penny "surprise" packages, the passion for surprise. Yet at the age of six the perfection of the blue bow on my hair, shaped like a butterfly, preoccupied me, since I insisted that my godmother tie it because she tied it better than anyone else. I must have seen this bow in the mirror then. I do not remember whether I saw this bow, the little girl in the very short white-lace-edged dress, or again a photograph taken in Havana where all my cousins and I stood in a row according to our heights, all wearing enormous ribbons and short white dresses. In the mirror there never was a child. The first mirror had a frame of white wood. In it there is no Anaïs Nin, but Marie Antoinette with a white lace cap, a long black dress, standing on a pile of chairs, the chariot, riding to her beheading. No Anaïs Nin. An actress playing all the parts of characters in French history. I am Charlotte Corday plunging a knife into the tyrant Marat. I am, of course, Joan of Arc. At fourteen, the portrayal of a Joan burning at the stake was my brother's favorite horror story.

The first mirror in which the self appears is very large, it is inlaid inside of a brown wood wall in the room of a brownstone house. Next to it the window pours down so strong a light that the rest of the room is not reflected in the mirror. The image of the girl who approaches it is brought into luminous relief. Against a foggy darkness, the girl of fifteen stands with frightened eyes. She is looking at her dress, a dress of shiny worn blue serge, which was fixed up for her out of an old one belonging to a cousin. It does not fit her. It is meager. It looks poor. The girl is looking at the worn shiny dark-blue serge dress with shame. It is the day she has been told in school that she is gifted for writing. They had come purposely into the class to tell her. In spite of being a foreigner, in spite of having to use the dictionary, she had written the best essay in the class. She who was always quiet and who did not wish to be noticed, was told to come up the aisle and speak to the English teacher before everyone, to hear the compliment. And the joy, the dazzling joy which had first struck her was instantly killed by the awareness of the dress. I did not want to get up, to be noticed. I was ashamed of this meager dress with a shine on it, its worn air, its orphan air, its hand-me-down air.

There is another mirror framed in brown wood. The girl is looking at the new dress which transfigures her. What an extraordinary change. She leans over very close to look at the humid eyes, the humid mouth, the moisture and luminousness brought about by the change of dress. She walks up very slowly to the mirror, very slowly, as if she did not want to frighten reflections away. Several times, at fifteen, she walks very slowly towards the mirror. Every girl of fifteen has put the same question to a mirror: "Am I beautiful?" The face is masklike. It does not smile. It does not want to charm the mirror, or deceive the mirror, or flirt with it and gain a false answer. The girl is in a trance. She does not want to frighten the reflection away herself. Someone has said she is very pale. She approaches the mirror and stands very still like a statue. Immobile. Waxy. She never makes a gesture. Surprised. Somnambulistic? She only moves to become someone else, impersonating Sarah Bernhardt, Mélisande, *La Dame aux Camélias*, Madame Bovary, Thaïs. She is never Anaïs Nin who goes to school, and grows vegetables and flowers in her backyard. She is immobile, haunting, like a figure moving in a dream. She is decomposed before the mirror into a hundred personages, recomposed into paleness and immobility. Silence. She is watching for an expression which will betray the spirit. You can never catch the face alive, laughing, or loving. At sixteen she is looking at the mirror with her hair up for the first time. There is always the question. The mirror is not going to answer it. She will have to look for the answer in the eyes and faces of the boys who dance with her, men later, and above all the painters.

Writing as a woman. I am becoming more and more aware of this. All that happens in the real womb, not in the womb fabricated by man as a substitute. Strange that I should explore this womb of real flesh when, of all women, I seem the most idealized, the most legendary, a myth, a dream. And it is this descending into the real womb, luring men into it, struggling to keep men there, and struggling to free him of woman to help him create another womb, which fascinates me. The diary ended in Fez, in a city, in a street, in a labyrinth for me, because that was the city which looked most deeply like the womb, with its Arabian Nights gentleness, tranquility and mystery. My self, woman, womb, with grilled windows, veiled eyes. Tortuous streets, secret cells, labyrinths and more labyrinths.

From [*August, 1937*]

Beautiful flow between Durrell, Henry, Nancy and me. It is while we talk together that I discover how we mutually nourish each other, stimulate each other. I discover my own strength as an artist, for Henry and Durrell often ally themselves against me. Henry's respect is also reawakened by Durrell's admiration for me. My feeling for woman's inarticulateness is reawakened by Nancy's stutterings and stumblings, and her loyalty to me as the one who does not betray woman but seeks to speak for her. A marvelous talk, in which Henry unmasked Durrell and me, and when Durrell said: "And now we must unmask Henry," I answered: "We can't, because he has done it himself." Henry is the strongest because he is not afraid of being alone. Larry is afraid. I am afraid. And we confessed it.

They suddenly attacked my personal relation to all things, by personification of ideas. I defended myself by saying that relating was an act of life. To make history or psychology alive I personify it. Also everything depends on the nature of the personal relationship. My self is like the self of Proust. It is an instrument to connect life and the myth. I quoted Spengler, who said that all historical patterns are reproduced in individual man, entire historical evolutions are reproduced in one man in one lifetime. A man could experience, in a personal way, a Gothic, a Roman, or a Western period. Man is cheating when he sits for a whole evening talking about Lao-tze, Goethe, Rousseau, Spengler. It would be closer to the truth if he said, instead of Lao-tze, Henry—instead of Goethe, some poet we know now—

by a Woman writt

instead of Rousseau, his contemporary equivalent. It would be more honest if Larry said that it is Larry who feels irritation because symbolical wine does not taste as good as plain wine.

When they discussed the problem of my diary, all the art theories were involved. They talked about the geological changes undergone with time, and that it was the product of this change we called art. I asserted that such a process could take place instantaneously.

Henry said: "But that would upset all the art theories."

I said: "I can give you an example. I can feel the potentialities of our talk tonight while it is happening as well as six months later. Look at the birth story. It varies very little in its polished form from the way I told it in the diary immediately after it happened. The new version was written three years later. Objectivity may bring a more rounded picture, but the absence of it, empathy, feeling with it, immersion in it, may bring some other kind of connection with it."

Henry asked: "But then, why did you feel the need of rewriting it?"

"For a greater technical perfection. Not to re-create it."

Larry, who before had praised me for writing as a woman, for not breaking the umbilical connection, said: "You must rewrite *Hamlet*."

"Why should I, if that is not the kind of writing I wish to do?"

Larry said: "You must make the leap outside of the womb, destroy your connections."

"I know," I said, "that this is an important talk, and that it will be at this moment that we each go different ways. Perhaps Henry and Larry will go the same way, but I will have to go another, the woman's way."

At the end of the conversation they both said: "We have a real woman artist before us, the first one, and we ought not to put her down."

I know Henry is the artist because he does exactly what I do not do. He waits. He gets outside of himself. Until it becomes fiction. It is all fiction.

I am not interested in fiction. I want faithfulness.

All I know is that I am right, right for me. If today I can talk both woman's and man's language, if I can translate woman to man and man to woman, it is because I do not believe in man's objectivity. In all his ideas, systems, philosophies, arts come from a personal source he does not wish to admit. Henry and Larry are pretending to be impersonal. Larry has the English complex. But it is a disguise.

Poor woman, how difficult it is to make her instinctive knowledge clear!

"Shut up," says Larry to Nancy. She looks at me strangely, as if expecting me to defend her, explain her. Nancy. I won't shut up. I have a great deal to say, for June, for you, for other women.

As to all that nonsense Henry and Larry talked about, the necessity of "I am God" in order to create (I suppose they mean "I am God, I am not a woman"). Woman never had direct communication with God anyway, but only through man, the priest. She never created directly except through man, was never able to create as a woman. But what neither Larry nor Henry understands is that woman's creation far from being like man's must be exactly like her creation of children, that is it must come out of her own blood, englobed by her womb, nourished with her own milk. It must be a human creation, of flesh, it must be different from man's abstractions. As to this "I am God," which makes creation an act of solitude and pride, this image of God alone making sky, earth, sea, it is this image which has confused woman. (Man too, because he thinks God did it all alone, and he thinks he did it all alone. And behind every achievement of man lies a woman, and I am sure God was helped too but never acknowledged it.)

Woman does not forget she needs the fecundator, she does not forget that everything that is born of her is planted in her. If she forgets this she is lost. What will be marvelous to contemplate will not be her solitude but this image of woman being visited at night by man and the marvelous things she will give birth to in the morning. God alone, creating, may be a beautiful spectacle. I don't know. Man's objectivity may be an imitation of this God so detached from us and human emotion. But a woman alone creating is not a beautiful spectacle. The woman was born mother, mistress, wife, sister, she was born to represent union, communion, communication, she was born to give birth to life, and not to insanity. It is man's separateness, his so-called objectivity, which has made him lose contact, and then his reason. Woman was born to *be* the connecting link between man and his human self. Between abstract ideas and the personal pattern which creates them. Man, to create, must become man.

Woman has this life-role, but the woman•artist has to fuse creation and life in her own way, or in her own womb if you prefer. She has to create something different from man. Man created a world cut off from nature. Woman has to create within the mystery, storms, terrors, the infernos of sex, the battle against abstractions and art. She has to sever herself from the myth man creates, from being created by him, she has to struggle with her own cycles, storms, terrors which man does not understand. Woman wants to destroy aloneness, recover the original paradise. The art of woman must be born in the womb-cells of the mind. She must be the link between the synthetic products of man's mind and the elements.

I do not delude myself as man does, that I create in proud isolation. I say we are bound, interdependent. Woman is not deluded. She must create without these proud delusions of man, without megalomania, without schizophrenia, without madness. She must create that unity which man first destroyed by his proud consciousness.

Henry and Larry tried to lure me out of the womb. They call it objectivity. No woman died the kind of death Rimbaud died. I have never seen in a woman a skeleton like Fraenkel, killed by the dissections of analysis, the leprosy of egotism, the black pest of the brain cells.

Man today is like a tree that is withering at the roots. And most women painted and wrote nothing but imitations of phalluses. The world was filled with phalluses, like totem poles, and no womb anywhere. I must go the opposite way from Proust who found eternal moments in creation. I must find them in life. My work must be the closest to the life flow. I must install myself inside of the seed, growth, mysteries. I must prove the possibility of instantaneous, immediate, spontaneous art. My art must be like a miracle. Before it goes through the conduits of the brain and becomes an abstraction, a fiction, a lie. It must be for woman, more like a personified ancient ritual, where every spiritual thought was made visible, enacted, represented.

A sense of the infinite in the present, as the child has.

Woman's role in creation should be parallel to her role in life. I don't mean the good earth. I mean the bad earth too, the demon, the instincts, the storms of nature. Tragedies, conflicts, mysteries are personal. Woman must not fabricate. She must descend into the real womb and expose its secrets and its labyrinths. She must describe it as the city of Fez, with its Arabian Nights gentleness, tranquility and mystery. She must describe the voracious moods, the desires, the worlds contained in each cell of it. For the womb has dreams. It is not as simple as the good earth. I believe at times that man created art out of fear of exploring woman. I believe woman stuttered about herself out of fear of what she had to say. She covered herself with taboos and veils. Man invented a woman to suit his needs. He disposed of her by identifying her with nature and then paraded his contemptuous domination of nature. But woman is not nature only.

She is the mermaid with her fish-tail dipped in the unconscious. Her creation will be to make articulate this obscure world which dominates man, which he denies being dominated by, but which asserts its domination in destructive proofs of its presence, madness.

Note by Durrell: "Anaïs is *unanswerable*. Completely unanswerable. I fold up and give in. What she says is biologically true from the very navel strings."

From [*October, 1937*]

I glanced over what Henry was writing in *Tropic of Capricorn*, and there it was, the great anonymous, depersonalized world of sex. Instead of investing each woman with a different face, he takes pleasure in reducing all women to a biological aperture. That is not very interesting. His depersonalization is turning into an obsession with sex itself. It is not enough to take a woman to bed, man was given many other forms of expression and relationship. The only personal, individual experience he had was June, because she tor-

by a Woman writt

mented him, and was thus finally able to distinguish herself from the ocean of women. The way he focuses on sex is an obsession. He is in danger of becoming an Ego in a crowd. (The ego can only perceive a crowd, it cannot perceive an equal.) The crowd is a malleable thing, it can be dominated, dazzled, it's a public, it is faceless. This is the opposite of relationship.

If I could only awaken him to the consciousness of the *other.* One's life as a man is not in relation to the crowd, it is to the friend, the lover, the child.

He says: "I can have a good time with people who don't mean much to me." But this is not what nourishes our deepest life.

The entire mystery of pleasure in a woman's body lies in the intensity of the pulsation just before the orgasm. Sometimes it is slow, one-two-three, three palpitations which then project a fiery and icy liqueur through the body. If the palpitation is feeble, muted, the pleasure is like a gentler wave. The pocket seed of ecstasy bursts with more or less energy, when it is richest it touches every portion of the body, vibrating through every nerve and cell. If the palpitation is intense, the rhythm and beat of it is slower and the pleasure more lasting. Electric flesh-arrows, a second wave of pleasure falls over the first, a third which touches every nerve end, and now the third like an electric current traversing the body. A rainbow of color strikes the eyelids. A foam of music falls over the ears. It is the gong of the orgasm. There are times when a woman feels her body but lightly played on. Others when it reaches such a climax it seems it can never surpass. So many climaxes. Some caused by tenderness, some by desire, some by a word or an image seen during the day. There are times when the day itself demands a climax, days of cumulative sensations and unexploded feelings. There are days which do not end in a climax, when the body is asleep or dreaming other dreams. There are days when the climax is not pleasure but pain, jealousy, terror, anxiety. And there are days when the climax takes place in creation, a white climax. Revolution is another climax. Sainthood another.

FROM THE DIARY OF ANAÏS NIN, VOLUME III, 1939-1944

From [*January, 1943*]

Jaeger,[1] by being a woman, by her particular intuition as a woman, has caught a truth not known to any male analyst: the guilt for creating which is strong in woman. Creation linked with femininity and a threat to it. A threat to relation with man.

In a woman who loves man as much as I do, it becomes paralyzing. The feminine and the maternal having developed protection and nourishment, not war, destruction, or revolution for the sake of new worlds. I had guilt for writing about those I loved, exposing the character of the father. Henry never weighed the consequences of his portraits. I feel them as a danger to love.

Secrets. Need to disguise. The novel was born of this. If I used myself as a character it was because it was an experiment with the suitable object, as in chemistry. It is easy to work in one's own mine, to dig for oil or gold on one's own property. I never met any character but Henry capable of living out so much. The desire to know intimately drives one back into the only honest "I" who tested and lived out what it describes.

I considered Henry's work far more important than my own.

I tried to efface my creation with a sponge, to drown my creation because my concept of devotion and the roles I had to play clashed with my creative self.

I opposed creation, its sincerity and revelation, to the disguised self. Creation and revelation threaten my loves; threatened the roles my love forced me to play. In love I played a role to give each man whatever he needed or wanted at the cost of my life.

[1] Martha Jaeger, Anaïs Nin's psychoanalyst.

In creation I would reveal what I am, or all the truth.

I have a fear of public recognition.

Those who live for the world, as Henry does, always lose their personal, intimate life.

I told Jaeger the lamentable story of my publications.

D. H. Lawrence, published by Edward Titus a few months before his divorce, which caused him to go bankrupt. The book was but partially distributed, half lost, not sent to reviewers, and no royalties, and not even copies for myself.

Michael Fraenkel loaned me the money to print *House of Incest*, but lost interest in it when it was out and did not distribute it as he had promised. No reviews.

Lawrence Durrell backed the publication of *Winter of Artifice*. Obelisk issued it a week before the war. No distribution. No reviews.

Can Jaeger say to all this that the veil which concealed me was of my own making? Had guilt suffocated my work—does it envelop me in a fog, guide my destiny? What is fatality? *Fatalité intérieur?* Other women who produced far lesser works have gained reputations.

I thought my obscure destiny was that of greater mysteries and subtler influences.

But Jaeger smiles. Guilt. Guilt everywhere.

I did not want to rival man. Man was my brothers, younger than I, Joaquin and Thorvald. I must protect them, not outshine them. I did not want to be a man. Djuna Barnes was masculine. George Sand.

I did not want to steal man's creation, his thunder.

Creation and femininity seemed incompatible. The *aggressive* act of creation.

"Not aggressive," said Jaeger, "*active.*"

I have a horror of the masculine "career" woman.

To create seemed to me such an assertion of the strongest part of me that I would no longer be able to give all those I love the feeling of their being stronger, and they would love me less.

An act of independence would be punished by desertion. I would be abandoned by all those I loved.

Men fear woman's strength. I have been deeply aware of men's weakness, the need to guard them from my strength.

I have made myself less powerful, have concealed my powers.

At the press, I make Gonzalo believe he has discovered this, he has suggested that improvement, that he is cleverer, stronger. I have concealed my abilities like an evil force that would overwhelm, hurt, or weaken others.

I have crippled myself.

Dreams of Chinese woman with bound feet.

I have bound myself spiritually.

I have associated creation with ruthlessness, absence of scruples, indifference to consequences as I see it in Henry. (His story about his father and mother, a cruel caricature.)

I see strongly creative women crush their men. I fear this. I have feared all aggressiveness, all attacks, all destruction. Above all, self-assertion.

Jaeger said: "All you are trying to do is to throw off this mother role imposed on you. You want a give-and-take relationship."

Jaeger, by being true to the woman, creating the woman in me, by her particular intuition as a woman, has penetrated truths not observed by either Allendy or Rank. The creator's guilt in me has to do with my femininity, my subjection to man.

Also with my maternal self in conflict with my creative self. A negative form of creation.

Also the content of my work is related to the demon in me, the adventure-loving, and I do feel this adventurousness a danger to my loves.

Guilt about exposing the father.

Secrets.

Need of disguises.

Fear of consequences.

Great conflict here. Division.

If only I could invent, invent other characters. Objective work which would not involve guilt. Rank said woman could not invent. Will begin to describe others minutely. I was more at ease with myself as a character because it is easier to excavate on one's own property. I could be used for all experiences, was protean, unlimited.

When I started out with an invented character, based always on someone I knew, and then sought to expand, I found myself inside restricted forms, limited outlines, characters who could not go far enough into experience. I felt in a tight mold, and returned to my experience which I tried to transpose into other women.

But this was a misconception. You do not get rid of the self by giving it away, by annihilation. When a child is uprooted it seeks to make a center from which it cannot be uprooted. That was a safety island, but now I must relinquish this too.

Friday morning I went to Jaeger with all my notes on creation. My material is novel, and in a sense adds to an unsolved problem. Jaeger is concerned with this. It was more than analysis, I feel we are beginning to create together. She is my guide, but I can see that I am a good subject. I feel elated and strong because something is being created, and I feel something is being discovered which baffled men analysts. Rank always admitted that man-made psychology might not apply to woman. He honestly threw up his hands at Jaeger's problems.

What I consider my weaknesses are feminine traits: incapacity to destroy, ineffectualness in battle.

"I am the same," said Jaeger.

It is strange and wonderful that the analysis was conducted this time by way of the emotions. It was her feminine compassion, her feminine intuition which discovered the maternal complex, and the conflict before creation.

I represent, for other women too, the one who wanted to create with, by, and through her femininity.

I am a good subject because I have lived out everything, and because contrary to most creative women of our time I have not imitated man, or become man.

It is the creative self which will rescue me. Constitutionally I am more or less doomed to suffer, and I have had little relief from anxiety and doubts, but the displacement is taking place harmoniously and I am entering a larger realm.

Jaeger quoted the legend of the woman who was ordered to cross the river and would not, because she did not want to leave love

Anaïs Nin

behind. But when she finally crossed she found love on the other side. I brought up the fear of disconnection and solitude.

The evolution of woman. I am living it and suffering it for all women. I have loved as woman loves.

BIRTH

"The child," said the doctor, "is dead."

I lay stretched on a table. I had no place on which to rest my legs. I had to keep them raised. Two nurses leaned over me. In front of me stood the doctor with the face of a woman and eyes protuding with anger and fear. For two hours I had been making violent efforts. The child inside of me was six months old and yet it was too big for me. I was exhausted, the veins in me were swelling with the strain. I had pushed with my entire being. I had pushed as if I wanted this child out of my body and hurled into another world.

"Push, push with all your strength!"

Was I pushing with all my strength? All my strength?

No. A part of me did not want to push out the child. The doctor knew it. That is why he was angry, mysteriously angry. He knew. A part of me lay passive, did not want to push out anyone, not even this dead fragment of myself, out in the cold, outside of me. All in me which chose to keep, to lull, to embrace, to love, all in me which carried, preserved, and protected, all in me which imprisoned the whole world in its passionate tenderness, this part of me would not thrust out the child, even though it had died in me. Even though it threatened my life, I could not break, tear out, separate, surrender, open and dilate and yield up a fragment of a life like a fragment of the past, this part of me rebelled against pushing out the child, or anyone, out in the cold, to be picked up by strange hands, to be buried in strange places, to be lost, lost, lost. . . . He knew, the doctor. A few hours before he adored me, served me. Now he was angry. And I was angry with a black anger at this part of me which refused to push, to separate, to lose.

"Push! Push! Push with all your strength!"

I pushed with anger, with despair, with frenzy, with the feeling that I would die pushing, as one exhales the last breath, that I would push out everything inside of me, and my soul with all the blood around it, and the sinews with my heart inside of them, choked, and that my body itself would open and smoke would rise, and I would feel the ultimate incision of death.

The nurses leaned over me and they talked to each other while I rested. Then I pushed until I heard my bones cracking, until my veins swelled. I closed my eyes so hard I saw lightning and waves of red and purple. There was a stir in my ears, a beating is if the tympanum would burst. I closed my lips so tightly the blood was trickling. My legs felt enormously heavy, like marble columns, like immense marble columns crushing my body. I was pleading for someone to hold them. The nurse laid her knee on my stomach and shouted: "Push! Push! Push!" Her perspiration fell on me.

The doctor paced up and down angrily, impatiently. "We will be here all night. Three hours now. . . ."

The head was showing, but I had fainted. Everything was blue, then black. The instruments were gleaming before my eyes. Knives sharpened in my ears. Ice and silence. Then I heard voices, first talking too fast for me to understand. A curtain was parted, the voices still tripped over each other, falling fast like a waterfall, with sparks, and cutting into my ears. The table was rolling gently, rolling. The women were lying in the air. Heads. Heads hung where the enormous white bulbs of the lamps were hung. The doctor was still walking, the lamps moved, the heads came near, very near, and the words came more slowly.

They were laughing. One nurse was saying: "When I had my first child I was all ripped to pieces. I had to be sewn up again, and then I had another, and had to be sewn up, and then I had another. . . ."

The other nurse said: "Mine passed like an envelope through a letter box. But afterwards the bag would not come out. The bag would not come out. Out. Out. . . ." Why did they keep repeating themselves. And the lamps turning. And the steps of the doctor very fast, very fast.

"She can't labor any more, at six months nature does not help. She should have another injection."

Anaïs Nin

I felt the needle thrust. The lamps were still. The ice and the blue that was all around came into my veins. My heart beat wildly. The nurses talked: "Now that baby of Mrs. L. last week, who would have thought she was too small, a big woman like that, a big woman like that, a big woman like that. . . ." The words kept turning, as on a disk. They talked, they talked, they talked. . . ."

Please hold my legs! Please hold my legs! Please hold my legs! *PLEASE HOLD MY LEGS!* I am ready again. By throwing my head back I can see the clock. I have been struggling four hours. It would be better to die. Why am I alive and struggling so desperately? I could not remember why I should want to live. I could not remember anything. Everything was blood and pain. I have to push. I have to push. That is a black fixed point in eternity. At the end of a long dark tunnel. I have to push. A voice saying: "Push! Push! Push!" A knee on my stomach and the marble of my legs crushing me and the head so large and I have to push.

Am I pushing or dying? The light up there, the immense round blazing white light is drinking me. It drinks me slowly, inspires me into space. If I do not close my eyes it will drink all of me. I seep upward, in long icy threads, too light, and yet inside there is a fire too, the nerves are twisted, there is no rest from this long tunnel dragging me, or am I pushing myself out of the tunnel, or is the child being pushed out of me, or is the light drinking me. Am I dying? The ice in the veins, the cracking of the bones, this pushing in darkness, with a small shaft of light in the eyes like the edge of a knife, the feeling of a knife cutting the flesh, the flesh somewhere is tearing as if it were burned through by a flame, somewhere my flesh is tearing and the blood is spilling out. I am pushing in the darkness, in utter darkness. I am pushing until my eyes open and I see the doctor holding a long instrument which he swiftly thrusts into me and the pain makes me cry out. A long animal howl. That will make her push, he says to the nurse. But it does not. It paralyzes me with pain. He wants to do it again. I sit up with fury and I shout at him: "Don't you dare do that again, don't you dare!"

The heat of my anger warms me, all the ice and pain are melted in the fury. I have an instinct that what he has done is unnecessary, that he has done it because he is in a rage, because the hands on the clock keep turning, the dawn is coming and the child does not come out, and I am losing strength and the injection does not produce the spasm.

I look at the doctor pacing up and down, or bending to look at the head which is barely showing. He looks baffled, as before a savage mystery, baffled by this struggle. He wants to interfere with his instruments, while I struggle with nature, with myself, with my child and with the meaning I put into it all, with my desire to give and to hold, to keep and to lose, to live and to die. No instrument can help me. His eyes are furious. He would like to take a knife. He has to watch and wait.

I want to remember all the time why I should want to live. I am all pain and no memory. The lamp has ceased drinking me. I am too weary to move even towards the light, or to turn my head and look at the clock. Inside of my body there are fires, there are bruises, the flesh is in pain. The child is not a child, it is a demon strangling me. The demon lies inert at the door of the womb, blocking life, and I cannot rid myself of it.

The nurses begin to talk again. I say: let me alone. I put my two hands on my stomach and very softly, with the tips of my fingers I drum drum drum drum drum drum on my stomach in circles. Around, around, softly, with eyes open in great serenity. The doctor comes near with amazement on his face. The nurses are silent. Drum drum drum drum drum drum in soft circles, soft quiet circles. Like a savage. The mystery. Eyes open, nerves begin to shiver . . . a mysterious agitation. I hear the ticking of the clock . . . inexorably, separately. The little nerves awake, stir. But my hands are so weary, so weary, they will fall off. The womb is stirring and dilating. Drum drum drum drum drum. I am ready! The nurse presses her knee on my stomach. There is blood in my eyes. A tunnel. I push into this tunnel, I bite my lips and push. There is a fire and flesh ripping and no air. Out of the tunnel! All my blood is spilling out. Push! Push! Push! It is coming! It is coming! It is coming! I feel the slipperiness, the sudden deliverance, the weight is gone. Darkness. I hear voices. I open my eyes. I hear them saying: "It was a little girl. Better not show it to her." All my strength returns. I sit up. The doctor shouts: "Don't sit up!"

"Show me the child!"

"Don't show it," says the nurse, "it will be bad for her." The nurses try to make me lie down. My heart is beating so loud I can hardly hear myself repeating: "Show it to me." The doctor holds it up. It looks dark and small, like a diminutive man. But it is a little girl. It has long eyelashes on its closed eyes, it is perfectly made, and all glistening with the waters of the womb.

FROM WINTER OF ARTIFICE

Twenty years after her father deserted her, the narrator of *Winter of Artifice* is reunited with him. At first, she tries to revive her love for him, but gradually she comes to see his weaknesses and her own need to break away from him.

Realizing more and more that she did not love him she felt a strange joy, as if she were witnessing a just punishment for his coldness as a father when she was a child. And this suffering, which in reality she made no effort to inflict since she kept her secret, gave her joy. It made her feel that she was balancing in herself all the injustice of life, that she was restoring in her own soul a kind of symmetry to the events of life.

It was the fulfillment of a spiritual symmetry. A sorrow here, a sorrow there. Abandon yesterday, abandon today. Betrayal today, betrayal tomorrow. Two equally poised columns. A deception here, a deception there, like twin colonnades: a love for today, a love for tomorrow; a punishment to him, a punishment to the other . . . and one for herself. . . . Mystical geometry. The arithmetic of the unconscious which impelled this balancing of events.

She felt like laughing whenever her father repeated that he was lucid, simple, logical. She knew that this order and precision were only apparent. He had chosen to live on the surface, and she to descend deeper and deeper. His fundamental desire was to escape pain, hers to face all of life. Instead of coming out of his shell to face the disintegration of their relationship he eluded the truth. He had not discovered as she had that by meeting the person she feared to meet, by reading the letter she feared to read, by giving life a chance to strike at her she had discovered that it struck less cruelly than her imagination. To imagine was far more terrible than reality, because it took place in a void, it was untestable. There were no hands with which to strike or defend oneself in that inner chamber of ghostly tortures. But in living the realization summoned energies, forces, courage, arms and legs to fight with so that war almost became a joy. To fight a real sorrow, a real loss, a real insult, a real disillusion, a real treachery was infinitely less difficult than to spend a night without sleep struggling with ghosts. The imagination is far better at inventing tortures than life because the imagination is a demon within us and it knows where to strike, where it hurts. It knows the vulnerable spot, and life does not, our friends and lovers do not, because seldom do they have the imagination equal to the task.

He told her that he had stayed awake all night wondering how he would bring himself to tell a singer that she had no voice at all.

"There was almost a drama here yesterday with Laura about that singer. I tried to dissuade her from falling in love with me by assuring her she was simply the victim of a mirage which surrounds every artist, that if she came close to me she would be disillusioned. So yesterday after the singing we talked for three quarters of an hour and when I told her I would not have an affair with her (at another period of my life I might have done it, for the game of it, but now I have other things to live for) she began to sob violently and the rimmel came off. When she had used up her handkerchief I was forced to lend her mine. Then she dropped her lipstick and I picked it up and wiped it with another of my handkerchiefs. After the first fits of tears she began to calmly make up her face, wiping off the rouge that had been messed up by the tears. When she left I threw the handkerchiefs into the laundry. The *femme de chambre* picked them up and left all the laundry just outside the door of my room while she was cleaning it. Laura passed by, saw them and immediately thought I had deceived her. I had to explain everything to her; I told her I had not told her about this woman because I did not want to seem to be boasting all the time about women pursuing me."

She did not mind his philandering, but she was eager for the truth. She knew that he was telling a lie, because when a woman weeps the rimmel comes off, but not the lipstick, and besides, all elegant women have acquired a technique of weeping which has no such fatal effect on the make-up. You wept just enough to fill the eyes with tears and no more. No overflow. The tears stay inside the cups of the eyes, the rimmel is preserved, and yet the sadness is sufficiently expressive. After a moment one can repeat the process with the same dexterity which enables the garçon to fill a liqueur glass exactly to the brim. One tear too much could bring about a catastrophe, but these only came uncontrolled in the case of a deep love.

She was smiling to herself at his naive lies. The truth probably was that he had wiped his own mouth after kissing the singer.

He was playing around now as before, but he hated to admit it to himself, and to her, because of the ideal image he carried in himself, the image of a man who could be so deeply disturbed and altered by the love of a long-lost daughter that his career as a Don Juan had come to an abrupt end.

This romantic gesture which he was unable to make attracted him so much that he had to pretend he was making it, just as she had often pretended to be taking a voyage by writing letters on the stationery of some famous ocean liner.

"I said to Laura: do you really think that if I wanted to deceive you I would do it in such an obvious and stupid way, right here in our own home where you might come in any moment?"

What her father was attempting was to create an ideal world for her in which Don Juan, for the sake of his daughter, renounced all women. But she could not be deceived by his inventions. She was too clairvoyant. That was the pity of it. She could not believe in that which she wanted others to believe in—in a world made as one wanted it, an ideal world. She no longer believed in an ideal world.

And her father, what did he want and need? The illusion, which she was fostering, of a daughter who had never loved any one but him? Or did he find it hard to believe her too? When she left him in the south, did he not doubt her reason for leaving him?

When she went about dreaming of satisfying the world's hunger for illusion did she know it was the most painful, the most insatiable hunger? Did she not know too that she suffered from doubt, and that although she was able to work miracles for others she had no faith that the fairy tale would ever work out for herself? Even the gifts she received were difficult for her to love, because she knew that they would soon be taken away from her, just as her father had been taken away from her when she loved him so passionately, just as every home she had as a child had been disrupted, sold, lost, just as every country she became attached to was soon changed for another country, just as all her childhood had been loss, change, instability.

When she entered his house which was all in brown, brown wood on the walls, brown rugs, brown furniture, she thought of Spengler writing about brown as the color of philosophy. His windows were not open on the street, he had no use for the street, and so he had made the windows of stained glass. He lived within the heart of his own home as Orientals live within their citadel. Out of reach of passers-by. The house might have been anywhere—in England, Holland, Germany, America. There was no stamp of nationality upon it, no air from the outside. It was the house of the self, the house of his thoughts. The wall of the self-created without connection with the crowd, or country or race.

He was still taking his siesta. She sat near the long range of files, the long, beautiful, neat rows of files, with names which set her dreaming: China, Science, Photography, Ancient Instruments, Egypt, Morocco, Cancer, Radio, Inventions, The Guitar, Spain. It required hours of work every day: newspapers and magazines had to be read and clippings cut out, dated, glued. He wove a veritable spider web about himself. No man was ever more completely installed in the realm of possessions.

He spent hours inventing new ways of filling his cigarette holder with an anti-nicotine filter. He bought drugs in wholesale quantities. His closets were filled with photographs, with supplies of writing paper and medicines sufficient to last for years. It was as if he feared to find himself suddenly empty handed. His house was a storehouse of supplies which revealed his way of living too far ahead of himself, a fight against the improvised, the unexpected. He had prepared a fortress against need, war and change.

In proportion to her father's capacity for becoming invisible, untouchable, unattainable, in proportion to his capacity for metamorphosis, he had made the most solid house, the strongest walls, the heaviest furniture, the most heavily loaded bookcases, the most completely filled and catalogued universe. Everything to testify to his presence, his duration, his signature to a contract to remain on earth, visible at moments through his possessions.

In her mind she saw him asleep upstairs, with his elbow under his chin, in the most uncomfortable position which he had trained himself to hold so as not to sleep with his mouth open because that was ugly. She saw him asleep without a pillow, because a pillow under the head caused wrinkles. She pictured the bottle of alcohol which her mother had laughingly said that he bottled himself in at night in order to keep young forever. . . .

He washed his hands continuously. He had a mania for washing and disinfecting himself. The fear of microbes played a very important part in his life. The fruit had to be washed with filtered water. His mouth must be disinfected. The silverware must be passed over an alcohol lamp like the doctor's instruments. He never ate the part of the bread which his fingers had touched.

Her father had never imagined that he may have been trying to cleanse and disinfect his soul of his lies, his callousness, his deceptions. For him the only danger came from the microbes which attacked the body. He had not studied the microbe of conscience which eats into the soul.

When she saw him washing his hands, while watching the soap foaming she could see him again arriving behind stage at a concert, with his fur-lined coat and white silk scarf, and being immediately surrounded by women. She was seven years old, dressed in a starched dress and white gloves, and sitting in the front row with her mother and brothers. She was trembling because her father had said severely: "And above all, don't make a cheap family show of your enthusiasm. Clap discreetly. Don't have people notice that the pianist's children are clapping away like noisy peasants." This enthusiasm which must be held in check was a great burden for a child's soul. She had never been able to curb a joy or sorrow: to restrain meant to kill, to bury. This cemetery of strangled emotions—was it this her father was trying to wash away? And the day she told him she was pregnant and he said: "Now you're worth less on the market as a woman" . . . was this being washed away? No insight into the

feelings of others. Passing from hardness to sentimentality. No inter-
mediate human feeling, but extreme poles of indifference and weakness which never made the human equation. Too hot or too cold,
blood cold and heart weak, blood hot and heart cold.

While he was washing his hands with that expression she had seen
on the faces of people in India thrust into the Ganges, of Egyptians
plunged into the Nile, of Negroes dipped into the Mississippi, she
saw the fruit being washed and mineral water poured into his glass.
Sterilized water to wash away the microbes, but his soul unwashed,
unwashable, yearning to be free of the microbe of conscience. . . .
All the water running from the modern tap, running from this modern
bathroom, all the rivers of Egypt, of India, of America . . . and he
unwashed . . . washing his modern body, washing . . . washing . . .
washing. . . . A drop of holy water with which to exorcise the guilt.
Hands washed over and over again in the hope of a miracle, and no
miracle comes from the taps of modern washstands, no holy water
flows through leaden pipes, no holy water flows under the bridges
of Paris because the man standing at the tap has no faith and no
awareness of his soul: he believes he is merely washing the stain of
microbes from his hands. . . .

She told her father she must leave on a trip. He said: "You are
deserting me!"

He talked rapidly, breathlessly, and left very hurriedly. She
wanted to stop him and ask him to give her back her soul. She hated
him for the way he descended the stairs as if he had been cast out,
wounded by jealousy.

She hated him because she could not remain detached, nor
remain standing at the top of the stairs watching him depart. She
felt herself going down with him, within him, because his pain and
flight were so familiar to her. She descended with him, and lost
herself, passed into him, became one with him like his shadow. She
felt herself empty, and dissolving into his pain. She knew that when
he reached the street he would hail a taxi, and feel relief at escaping
from the person who had inflicted the wound. There was always the
power of escape, and rebellion.

The organ grinder would play and the pain would gnaw deeper, bitterer. He would curse the lead-colored day which intensified the sorrow because they both were born inextricably woven into the moods of nature.

He would curse his pain which distorted faces and events into one long, continuous nightmare.

She wanted to beg her father to say that he had not felt all this, and assure her that she had stayed at the top of the stairs, with separate, distinct feelings. But she was not there. She was walking with him, and sharing his feelings. She was trying to reach out to him and reassure him. But everything about him was fluttering like a bird that had flown into a room by mistake, flying recklessly and blindly in utter terror. The pain he had eluded all his life had caught him between four walls. And he was bruising himself against walls and furniture while she stood there mute and compassionate. His terror so great that he did not sense her pity, and when she moved to open the window to allow him to escape he interpreted the gesture as a menace. To run away from his own terror he flew wildly against the window and crushed his feathers.

Don't flutter so blindly, my father!

She grew suddenly tired of seeing her father always in profile, of seeing him always walking on the edge of circles, always elusive. The fluidity, the evasiveness, the deviations made his life a shadow picture. He never met life full-face. His eyes never rested on anything, they were always in flight. His face was in flight. His hands were in flight. She never saw them lying still, but always curving like autumn leaves over a fire, curling and uncurling. Thinking of him she could picture him only in motion, either about to leave, or about to arrive; she could see better than anything else, as he was leaving, his back and the way his hair came to a point on his neck.

She wanted to bring her father out in the open. She was tired of his ballet dancing. She would struggle to build up a new relationship.

But he refused to admit he had been lying. He was pale with anger. No one ever doubted him before—so he said. To be doubted blinded him with anger. He was not concerned with the truth or falsity of the situation. He was concerned with the injury and insult she was guilty of, by doubting him.

"You're demolishing everything," he said.

"What I'm demolishing was not solid," she answered. "Let's make a new beginning. We created nothing together except a sand pile into which both of us sink now and then with doubts. I am not a child. I cannot believe your stories."

He grew still more pale and angry. What shone out of his angry eyes was pride in his stories, pride in his ideal self, pride in his delusions. And he was offended. He did not stop to ask himself if she were right. She could not be right. She could see that, for a moment at any rate, he believed implicitly in the stories he had told her. If he had not believed in them so firmly he would have been humiliated to see himself as a poor comedian, a man who could not deceive even his own daughter.

"You shouldn't be offended," she said. "Not to be able to deceive your own daughter is no disgrace. It's precisely because I have told you so many lies myself that I can't be lied to."

"Now," he said, "you are accusing me of being a Don Juan."

"I accuse you of nothing. I am only asking for the truth."

"What truth?" he said, "I am a moral being, far more moral than you."

"That's too bad. I thought we were above questions of good and evil. I am not saying you are bad. That does not concern me. I am saying only that you are *false* with me. I have too much intuition."

"You have no intuition at all concerning me."

"That might have affected me when I was a child. Today I don't mind what you think of me."

"Go on," he said. "Now tell me, tell me I have no talent, tell me I don't know how to love, tell me *all that your mother used to tell me.*"

"I have never thought any of these things."

But suddenly she stopped. She knew her father was not seeing her any more, but always that judge, that past which made him so uneasy. She felt as if she were not herself any more, but her mother, her mother with a body tired with giving and serving, rebelling at his selfishness and irresponsibility. She felt her mother's anger and despair. For the first time her own image fell to the floor. She saw her mother's image. She saw the child in him who demanded all love and did not know how to love. She saw the child incapable of an act of protection, strength, or self-denial. She saw the child hiding behind her courage, the same child hiding now under Laura's protection. She was her mother telling him again that as a human being he was a failure. And perhaps she had told him too that as a musician he had not given enough to justify his limitations as a human being. All his life he had been playing with people, with love, playing *at* love, playing *at* being a pianist, playing *at* composing. Playing because to no one or nothing could he give his whole soul.

There were two regions, two tracts of land, with a bridge in between, a slight, fragile bridge like the Japanese bridges in the miniature Japanese gardens. Whoever ventured to cross the bridge fell into the abyss. So it was with her mother. She had fallen through and been drowned. Her mother thought he had a soul. She had fallen there in that space where his emotions reached their limit, where the land opened in two, where circles fell open and rings were unsoldered.

Was it her mother talking now? She was saying: "I am only asking you to be honest with yourself. I admit when I lie, but you never admit it. I am not asking for anything except that you be real."

"Now say I am superficial."

"At this moment you are. I wanted you to face me and be truthful."

He paced up and down, pale with anger.

It seemed to her that her father was not quarreling with her but with his own past, that what was coming to light now was his underlying feeling of guilt towards her mother. If he saw in her now an avenger it was only because of his fear that his daughter might accuse him too. Against her judgment he had erected a huge defense: the approbation of the rest of the world. But in himself he had never quite resolved the right and the wrong. He, too, was driven now by a compulsion to say things he never intended to say, to make her the symbol of the one who had come to punish, to expose his deceptions, to prove his worthlessness.

And this was not the meaning of her struggle with him. She had not come to judge him but to dissolve the falsities. He feared so much that she had come to say: "the four persons you abandoned in order to live your own life, to save yourself, were crippled," that he did not hear her real words. The scene was taking place between two ghosts.

Her father's ghost was saying: "I cannot bear the slightest criticism. Immediately I feel judged, condemned."

Her own ghost was saying: "I cannot bear lies and deceptions. I need truth and sincerity."

They could not understand each other. They were gesticulating in space. Gestures of despair and anger. Her father pacing up and down, angry because of her doubts of him, forgetting that these doubts were well founded, forgetting to ask himself if she was right or not. And she in despair because her father would not understand, because the fragile little Japanese bridge between the two portions of his soul would not hold her even for a moment, she walking with such light feet, trying to bring messages from one side to another, trying to make connections between the real and the unreal.

She could not see her father clearly any more. She could see only the hard profile cutting the air like a swift stone ship, a stone ship moving in a sea unknown to human beings, into regions made of granite rock. No more water, or warmth, or flow between them. All communication paralyzed by the falsity. Lost in the fog. Lost in a cold, white fog of falsity. Images distorted as if they were looking through a glass bowl. His mouth long and mocking, his eyes enormous but empty in their transparency. Not human. All human contours lost.

And she thinking: I stopped loving my father a long time ago. What remained was the slavery to a pattern. When I saw him I thought I would be happy and exalted. I pretended. I worked myself up into ecstasies. When one is pretending the entire body revolts. There come great eruptions and revolts, great dark ravages, and above all, a joylessness. A great, bleak joylessness. Everything that is natural brings joy. He was pretending too—he had to win me as a trophy, as a victory. He had to win me away from my mother, had to win my approbation. Had to win me because he feared me. He feared the judgment of his children. And when he could not win me he suffered in his vanity. He fought in me his own faults, just as I hated in him my own faults.

Anaïs Nin

Certain gestures made in childhood seem to have eternal repercussions. Such was the gesture she had made to keep her father from leaving, grasping his coat and holding on to it so fiercely that she had to be torn away. This gesture of despair seemed to prolong itself all through her life. She repeated it blindly, fearing always that everything she loved would be lost.

It was so hard for her to believe that this father she was still trying to hold on to was no longer real or important, that the coat she was touching was not warm, that the body of him was not human, that her breathless, tragic desire had come to an end, and that her love had died.

Great forces had impelled her towards symmetry and balance, had impelled her to desert her father in order to close the fatal circle of desertion. She had forced the hour-glass of pain to turn. They had pursued each other. They had tried to possess each other. They had been slaves of a pattern, and not of love. Their love had long ago been replaced by the other loves which gave them life. All those parts of the self which had been tied up in a tangle of misery and frustration had been loosened imperceptibly by life, by creation. But the feelings they had begun with twenty years back, he of guilt and she of love, had been like railroad tracks on which they had been launched at full speed by their obsessions.

Today she held the coat of a dead love.

This had been the nightmare—to pursue this search and poison all joys with the necessity of its fulfillment. To discover that such fulfillment was not necessary to life, but to the myth. It was the myth which had forbidden them to deny their first ideal love or to recognize its illusory substance. What they called their destiny—the railroad track of their obsessions.

At last she was entering the Chinese theater of her drama and could see the trappings of the play as well as the play itself, see that the settings were made of the cardboard of illusion. She was passing behind the stage and could stop weeping. The suffering was no longer real. She could see the strings which ruled the scenes, the false storms and the false lightning.

She was coming out of the ether of the past.

by a Woman writt

The world was a cripple. Her father was a cripple. In striking out for his own liberty, to save his life, he had struck at her, but he had poisoned himself with remorse.

No need to hate. No need to punish.

The last time she had come out of the ether it was to look at her dead child, a little girl with long eyelashes and slender hands. She was dead.

The little girl in her was dead too. The woman was saved. And with the little girl died the need of a father.

Dilys Laing

Dilys Laing

(1906–1960)

Dilys Laing died at fifty-three, little known to the general public but much admired by other poets. In her lifetime, she published four books of poetry and a novel; at the time of her death, she had been at work on another novel. Laing began publishing at twelve. At fourteen, she was editor of the children's page of the *Vancouver Daily Sun*. A few years later, she was on the editorial staff of the *Victoria Daily Colonist*. As she grew older, Laing devoted herself more to poetry. She wrote, gave readings, married, and bore a son. Personal, compassionate, and candid, her work ranges from light humorous verse to poems of anguish at the injustice and cruelty in the world. Some of Laing's most interesting poems are about herself as a woman—about her sensuality, about girlhood, about motherhood, about her identification and dissatisfaction with women's traditional roles.

VILLANELLE

Proud inclination of the flesh,
most upright tendency, salute
in honor of the secret wish.

Slant attitude. When anglers fish
they hold their rods in this acute
proud inclination of the flesh

as purely in the waters thrash
the living fish like silver fruit
in honor of the secret wish.

For who's so risky or so rash
he would forbid this absolute
proud inclination of the flesh?

No woman, truly. Let her blush
and hide her thoughts. Herself she'll suit
in honor of the secret wish.

by a Woman writt

Let scholars all their reasons thresh—
this argument they'll not refute:
proud inclination of the flesh
in honor of the secret wish.

VENUS PETRIFIED

All the windows are shining. A great waltz flows
out of the house into the breathing dark.
Dancers come through a casement door that throws
a rhomb of honey onto indigo grass.
By twos they move among the elms and pines,
secret as deer evasive in a park.

The house, that seems a vessel blown in glass,
a phantom dwelling held erect by vines,
brims with a light the color of Moselle,
and high beyond the roof the meteors pour
like bright leaves scattering from a shaken bough
through black October.

                    Shallow tides of Strauss
swell to orgasmic oceans in my brain
and memory is a storm I can't repel.

Swept by the fury to go through that door
I try to move, but stand from foot to brow
rigid. My blood has run and left no stain.

I am that statue at the garden's end
which, crazed, and scarred with lichen, keeps the form
of Venus startled, hands poised to defend
what nothing threatens. I struggle to unbend
arms that the noonday sun can never warm.

The spilling windows blur and the whole house
flares, like a single star, with straws of light
and blinds me.

Dilys Laing

When the dark has healed my sight
the blood beats through my stone, and I discern
the old foundations bandaged thick with fern.

THE DOUBLE GOER

The woman took a train
away away from herself.
She thought: I need a change
and wheels make revolutions.
I'm half a century old
and must be getting somewhere.
And so she futured on
away from her own presence.

The landscape boiled around her
like a pan of beans.
A man without a face
made her ticket holy.
Adventure thrilled her nerves
restless rapture shook her.
Love is in the next seat,
she mused, and strength and glory
are over the hill, and I
grow younger as I leave
my me behind.

The telephone wires were staves
of a quintet score.
The hills were modulations
through the circle of keys.
Freedom is music, she thought,
smiling at the conductor.
This is your station, lady,
he snapped, and on the downbeat
she stepped to the vita nuova.

by a Woman writt

A crowd had come to meet her
and they were fond in greeting:
husband, child, and father,
mother, and all the neighbors.

They travel as fast as I do,
she thought, and turned to climb
back to freedom's flying.
The door was shut. The train
streamed off like spilled water.

She faced the crowd and cried:
I love you all but one:
the one who wears my face.
She is the one I fled from.

They said: You took her with you
and brought her back again.
You look sick. Welcome home.

THE LITTLE GIRLS

The eyes of the little girls are lit with projects
like windows honey-gold at edge of night.
The little girls are houses, swept and dusted,
busy and sane and proud with purposes.

I was a child who clutched the amulet
of childhood in a terror of time. I saw
archangels, worshipped trees, expected God.

The heavens of these children are within their reach.
Sweeping their elders' floors, they dream of love.

When Bertha tells me with a crystal smile
that Girl Scouts meet on Friday; when Kathleen
boasts that she's learning how to bake at school;
when Betty, making beds, fattens the pillows
with confident hands, I marvel and look back
at scented cedar pagodas ringed around

Dilys Laing

the solitary spirit of a child
who like a spindly deer ran from the trap
of house and hurried up the nearest slope
to push the horizon out and keep time still.

I love these girls as we can only love
what is mysteriously different from us.
I was the flare that cools into a poet.
They are the earth that every turning spring
breaks through the snow and branches into a world.

LET THEM ASK THEIR HUSBANDS

> *And if they will learn anything let*
> *them ask their husbands at home:*
> *for it is a shame for women to speak*
> *in the church*—I Corinthians 14:35.

In human need
of the familiar
I see God
woman-shaped

for God created
woman in Her own image
and I have
my Pauline pride.

LOT'S DAUGHTER

You, being grown and little pleased by growth,
look back to childhood with an envious eye
that sees no snare in the remembered heath,
no shadow in the clockless golden day.

You see your yesterday self: why-saying child
armed with enchanted formulae direct
from servants' tongues or books whose words were spelled
trustingly into thought, then into act.

by a Woman writt

Time is illumined with inverted light:
the past all whole, the present weird with fault.
Look back no more. The child's eyes burn with hate
watching the woman harden into salt.

EGO

Vague, submarine, my giant twin
swims under me, a girl of shade
who mimics me. She's caught within
a chickenwire of light that's laid
by netted waves on floor of sand.
I dare not look. I squeeze my lids
against that apparition and
her nightmare of surrounding squids,
her company of nounless fright.
She is the unknown thing I am
and do not wish to see. In flight
I swim the way my comrades swam
and hide among them. Let me keep
their safety's circle for a charm
against that sister in the deep
who, huge and mocking, plans me harm.

VETERANS

Women receive
the insults of men
with tolerance,
having been bitten
in the nipple
by their toothless gums.

PRIVATE ENTRY IN THE DIARY
OF A FEMALE PARENT

He is my own fault. Let me see it straight.
I got him willfully, with joy, and hatched him

Dilys Laing

a long time intimately, and in him warmed
the flaws and fineness of two ancestries,
before I had my bellyful of him
at last and threw him neck and crop
into the doctor's expert rubber hands.
Since then I've suckled, kissed and smacked him
while he has sucked and wet and beaten me
or all but beaten me, although I rise
out of the ashes at short intervals.
The end will be, perhaps, the end of me,
which will, I humbly guess, be his beginning.

SONNET TO A SISTER IN ERROR

"Whilst the dull manage of a servile house
Is held by some our utmost art and use."
—ANNE, COUNTESS OF WINCHILSEA (1661–1720)

Sweet Anne of Winchilsea, you were no hellion
intent on setting the broad world to rocking.
The long court dress concealed the long blue stocking,
the easy manner masked the hard rebellion.
With light foot stirruped on the Muses' stallion
you ambled privately, afraid of shocking
the Maids of Honor who excelled at mocking
the matchless rose with stitches small and million.

Staunch Anne! I know your trouble. The same tether
galls us. To be a woman and a writer
is double mischief, for the world will slight her
who slights "the servile house," and who would rather
make odes than beds. Lost lady! Gentle fighter!
Separate in time, we mutiny together.

PRAYER OF AN OVULATING FEMALE

I bring no throat-slit kid
no heart-scooped victim
no captive decapitated
and no self-scourged flesh.

by a Woman writt

I bring you, Domina,
Mother of women,
a calendula in a pot
a candle and a peach
an egg and a
split condom.

Ave Mater
Mulierum!
may no blood flow
nec in caelo
nec in terra
except according
to the calendar.

Margaret Walker

Margaret Walker

(1915–   )

By the time she was eight, Margaret Walker knew she "wanted to learn to write books." At ten, she was fascinated by the story of her great-grandmother, a slave, a story Walker was later to tell in her novel, *Jubilee*. As a young woman, Walker worked with the WPA Writers' Project in Chicago, training herself to write poetry. "Every spare moment of my early years," she has written, "was devoted to learning and developing this skill." In 1942, she won the Yale Series of Younger Poets Award for a volume of her poetry, *For My People*. In it, she wrote of her pride in her heritage, of her hatred of racism, of the need for her people to struggle for freedom. Walker went on to become a college teacher and the mother of four children, and to write articles, short stories, and poetry. "I believe my role in the struggle," she has written, "is the role of a writer. Everything I have ever written or hoped to write is dedicated to that struggle, to our hope of peace and dignity and freedom in the world, not just as black people, or as Negroes, but as free human beings in a world community."

FOR MY PEOPLE

For my people everywhere singing their slave songs repeat-
          edly: their dirges and their ditties and their blues and
          jubilees, praying their prayers nightly to an unknown
          god, bending their knees humbly to an unseen power;

For my people lending their strength to the years, to the gone
          years and the now years and the maybe years, washing
          ironing cooking scrubbing sewing mending hoeing
          plowing digging planting pruning patching dragging
          along never gaining never reaping never knowing and
          never understanding;

For my playmates in the clay and dust and sand of Alabama
          backyards playing baptizing and preaching and doc-
          tor and jail and soldier and school and mama and

cooking and playhouse and concert and store and hair
and Miss Choomby and company;

For the cramped bewildered years we went to school to learn
to know the reasons why and the answers to and the
people who and the places where and the days when,
in memory of the bitter hours when we discovered we
were black and poor and small and different and
nobody cared and nobody wondered and nobody
understood;

For the boys and girls who grew in spite of these things to be
man and woman, to laugh and dance and sing and
play and drink their wine and religion and success, to
marry their playmates and bear children and then die
of consumption and anemia and lynching;

For my people thronging 47th Street in Chicago and Lenox
Avenue in New York and Rampart Street in New
Orleans, lost disinherited dispossessed and happy
people filling the cabarets and taverns and other
people's pockets needing bread and shoes and milk
and land and money and something—something all
our own;

For my people walking blindly spreading joy, losing time
being lazy, sleeping when hungry, shouting when
burdened, drinking when hopeless, tied and shackled
and tangled among ourselves by the unseen creatures
who tower over us omnisciently and laugh;

For my people blundering and groping and floundering in
the dark of churches and schools and clubs and
societies, associations and councils and committees
and conventions, distressed and disturbed and deceived and devoured by money-hungry glory-craving
leeches, preyed on by facile force of state and fad and
novelty, by false prophet and holy believer;

Margaret Walker

For my people standing staring trying to fashion a better
way from confusion, from hypocrisy and misunder-
standing, trying to fashion a world that will hold all
the people, all the faces, all the adams and eves and
their countless generations;

Let a new earth rise. Let another world be born. Let a bloody
peace be written in the sky. Let a second generation
full of courage issue forth; let a people loving freedom come to growth. Let a beauty full of healing
and a strength of final clenching be the pulsing in
our spirits and our blood. Let the martial songs be
written, let the dirges disappear. Let a race of men
now rise and take control.

DARK BLOOD

There were bizarre beginnings in old lands for the making
of me. There were sugar sands and islands of fern
and pearl, palm jungles and stretches of a never-
ending sea.

There were the wooing nights of tropical lands and the cool
discretion of flowering plains between two stalwart
hills. They nurtured my coming with wanderlust. I
sucked fevers of adventure through my veins with
my mother's milk.

Someday I shall go to the tropical lands of my birth, to the
coasts of continents and the tiny wharves of island
shores. I shall roam the Balkans and the hot lanes of
Africa and Asia. I shall stand on mountain tops and
gaze on fertile homes below.

And when I return to Mobile I shall go by the way of
Panama and Bocas del Toro to the littered streets
and the one-room shacks of my old poverty, and

by a Woman writt

blazing suns of other lands may struggle then to
reconcile the pride and pain in me.

LINEAGE

My grandmothers were strong.
They followed plows and bent to toil.
They moved through fields sowing seed.
They touched earth and grain grew.
They were full of sturdiness and singing.
My grandmothers were strong.

My grandmothers are full of memories
Smelling of soap and onions and wet clay
With veins rolling roughly over quick hands
They have many clean words to say.
My grandmothers were strong.
Why am I not as they?

KISSIE LEE

Toughest gal I ever did see
Was a gal by the name of Kissie Lee;
The toughest gal God ever made
And she drew a dirty, wicked blade.

Now this here gal warn't always tough
Nobody dreamed she'd turn out rough
But her Grammaw Mamie had the name
Of being the town's sin and shame.

When Kissie Lee was young and good
Didn't nobody treat her like they should
Allus gettin' beat by a no-good shine
An' allus quick to cry and whine.

Till her Grammaw said, "Now listen to me,
I'm tiahed of yoah whinin', Kissie Lee.
People don't never treat you right,
An' you allus scrappin' or in a fight.

Margaret Walker

"Whin I was a gal wasn't no soul
Could do me wrong an' still stay whole.
Ah got me a razor to talk for me
An' aftah that they let me be."

Well Kissie Lee took her advice
And after that she didn't speak twice
'Cause when she learned to stab and run
She got herself a little gun.

And from that time that gal was mean,
Meanest mama you ever seen.
She could hold her likker and hold her man
And she went thoo life jus' raisin' san'.

One night she walked in Jim's saloon
And seen a guy what spoke too soon;
He done her dirt long time ago
When she was good and feeling low.

Kissie bought her drink and she paid her dime
Watchin' this guy what beat her time
And he was making for the outside door
When Kissie shot him to the floor.

Not a word she spoke but she switched her blade
And flashing that lil ole baby paid:
Evvy livin' guy got out of her way
Because Kissie Lee was drawin' her pay.

She could shoot glass doors offa the hinges,
She could take herself on the wildest binges.
And she died with her boots on switching blades
On Talladega Mountain in the likker raids.

LONG JOHN NELSON
AND SWEETIE PIE

Long John Nelson and Sweetie Pie
Lived together on Center Street.

by a Woman writt

Long John was a mellow fellow
And Sweetie Pie was fat and sweet.

Long John Nelson had been her man
Long before this story began;
Sweetie cooked on the Avenue.
Long John's loving was all he'd do.

When Sweetie Pie came home at night
She brought his grub and fed him well
Then she would fuss and pick a fight
Till he beat her and gave her hell.

She would cuss and scream, call him black
Triflin' man git outa my sight;
Then she would love him half the night
And when he'd leave she'd beg him back.

Till a yellow gal came to town
With coal black hair and bright blue gown
And she took Long John clean away
From Sweetie Pie one awful day.

Sweetie begged him to please come back
But Long John said, "I'm gone to stay."
Then Sweetie Pie would moan and cry
And sing the blues both night and day:

"Long John, Baby, if you'll come back
I won't never call you black;
I'll love you long and love you true
And I don't care what else you do."

But Long John said, "I'm really through."
They're still apart this very day.
When Long John got a job to do
Sweetie got sick and wasted away.

Then after she had tried and tried
One day Sweetie just up and died.

Then Long John went and quit his job
And up and left his yellow bride.

CHILDHOOD

When I was a child I knew red miners
dressed raggedly and wearing carbide lamps.
I saw them come down red hills to their camps
dyed with red dust from old Ishkooda mines.
Night after night I met them on the roads,
or on the streets in town I caught their glance;
the swing of dinner buckets in their hands,
and grumbling undermining all their words.

I also lived in low cotton country
where moonlight hovered over ripe haystacks,
or stumps of trees, and croppers' rotting shacks
with famine, terror, flood, and plague near by;
where sentiment and hatred still held sway
and only bitter land was washed away.

WHORES

When I grew up I went away to work
where painted whores were fascinating sights.
They came on like whole armies through the nights—
their sullen eyes on mine, their mouths a smirk,
and from their hands keys hung suggestively.
Old women working by an age-old plan
to make their bread in ways as best they can
would hobble past and beckon tirelessly.

Perhaps one day they'll all die in the streets
or be surprised by bombs in each wide bed;
learning too late in accustomed dread
that easy ways, like whores on special beats,
no longer have the gift to harbor pride
or bring men peace, or leave them satisfied.

by a Woman writt

STREET DEMONSTRATION

*"Hurry up Lucille or we won't get
arrested with our group."
(An eight year old demonstrator, 1963)*

We're hoping to be arrested
And hoping to go to jail
We'll sing and shout and pray
For Freedom and for Justice
And for Human Dignity
The fighting may be long
And some of us will die
But Liberty is costly
And ROME they say to me
Was not built in one day.

*Hurry up, Lucille, Hurry up
We're Going to Miss Our Chance to go to Jail.*

GIRL HELD
WITHOUT BAIL

*"In an unjust state the only place
for a just man is in jail."*

I like it here just fine
And I don't want no bail
My sister's here
My mother's here
And all my girl friends too.
I want my rights
I'm fighting for my rights
I want to be treated
Just like *anybody* else
I want to be treated
Just like *everybody* else

*I like it fine in Jail
And I don't want no Bail.*

Margaret Walker

NOW

Time to wipe away the slime
from inner rooms of thinking,
and covert skin of suffering;
indignities and dirt
and helpless degradation;
from furtive relegation
to the back doors and dark alleys
and the balconies of waiting
in the cleaning rooms and closets
with the washrooms and the filthy
privies marked "For Colored Only"
and the drinking-soda-fountains
tasting dismal and disgusting
with a dry and dusty flavor
of the deep humiliation;
hearing vulgars shout to mothers
"Hey you, nigger girl, and girlie!
Auntie, Ant, and Granny;
My old mammy was a wonder
and I love those dear old darkies
who were good and servile nigras
with their kerchiefed heads and faces
in their sweet and menial places."
Feeling hate and blood commingled
in a savage supplication
full of rites and ceremonies
for the separate unequal—
re-enforced by mobs who mass
with a priest of cult and klan
robed and masked in purest White
marking Kleagle with a Klux
and a fiery burning cross.
Time to wipe away the slime.
Time to end this bloody crime.

Sylvia Ashton-Warner

Sylvia Ashton-Warner

In a preface to her journal, *Myself*, Sylvia Ashton-Warner wrote, "love was my big trouble when I was young—still is, to be frank. . . . My need of and dependence on it." A teacher in her native New Zealand, Ashton-Warner wrote a highly acclaimed account of the methods she devised for her Maori pupils. Later, she published *Myself*, in which she revealed a more personal side of her early years as a teacher—her love affair, the violence in her own nature, the conflicts between her love for her husband and children and her desire not "to go down under marriage and babies as glamorous girls do, never to be heard of again." *Three*, Ashton-Warner's recent work, is about a middle-aged widow, who goes to live with her severely ill son, his wife, and a boarder called "Hamlet." In *Three*, as in her other works, Ashton-Warner speaks personally, frankly, of her need for independence and of her care for those she loves.

FROM MYSELF

From *February, 1941*

This is evening with the children in bed and K back at school. I must get back to study soon. I've forgotten all I learned at training college about how to teach. All I can remember about teaching is how I myself was taught when young. That strict traditional way: spare the rod and spoil the child and that. And how we'd line up for reading and sums and get the strap if we got any wrong. The sing-song tables in the morning and the strap for every spelling word wrong. All good at the time, I think, because we thought it was all right—and no one allowed to speak. But we didn't learn that at college. I've got to relearn what I was supposed to have learned. This very evening I mean to write a letter to the Country Library Service to get some books to study.

And not only for that reason. I don't mean to go down under marriage and babies as glamorous girls do, never to be heard of again. Down at heel, straggly hair and nothing important to say. I can't see why I need to. I can't see why marriage should wipe out my personality, why I should let it, I mean. Somehow . . . I don't know how what with home, school and family . . . I mean to recover and keep the things I did when single; I mean some time to be what I had meant to be—in the first place a worthwhile person, not just for myself but for those who love me. I mean to so organize my loaded time that I'll retain some for myself to paint, do music, read and even learn to write. I'm not one of these people who were born for nothing.

I'm dreadfully tired. Now I'll go to bed and hope for a good night's sleep without Dannie waking, without a nightmare about the Coast, without anxiety about the war which might take K, without remembering in shame my anger at Olga—yes, anger, not mere irritation—without worrying about forgetting how to teach, if I ever knew, without bleakly counting my bead-dreams that I dreamed when I was single about how I would live my life: a glamorous mysterious vivid life in the capitals of the world with those of my own kind—artists, musicians and writers. And lovers demanding a look from me, and friends thinking me wonderful. Paris, Rome, New York . . . roaming, roaming, fascinated. Getting on and off ships and trains and planes, the last word in fashion. Without remembering those dreams and seeing them against what I am now: a forgotten girl on the top of a hill drearily teaching Maoris. A forgotten girl.

"Jacob, have you finished your work?"

"Please no."

"Tiny has. Look, all that." I held up Tiny's exercise.

"Please she copied it off . . . off—" glancing about him experimentally—"off Whitu."

"Please I didn't," from Tiny. "Please I copied it out of myself."

"Jacob, bring me your exercise book. Let me see it."

"Please I . . . please it's not here."

"Where is it?"

"Please at home."

"I told you not to take your book home. You'll have to go home and get it. Up you get . . . off! Go home and get your book."

Sylvia Ashton-Warner

"Please I can't."

"You've got legs!"

"Please yes. But the canoe it's not there."

"What's the canoe got to do with it?"

"My grandfather took it."

"Where?"

"Please he took our canoe downriver to the other pa because there's a tangi there because a man got drowned last night. He was eeling."

"What have *eels* got to do with your exercise book?"

Tiny beside me, who is truly tiny like a little black beetle, said, "Please Jacob he live on the other side of the river. He comes to school in the canoe."

"Am I to believe that a boy of Jacob's size goes to and fro across that wide deep river in a canoe every day?"

"Please, my big sisters bring me. They in Mr. Hen'son's room."

I paused. I'd lost the thread. With elbow on table I covered my eyes with a hand while I tried to find it again but all I could see in my mind were canoes, drowned men, eels and a grandfather. "What was I talking about, Tiny?"

She brushed the black hair from her eyes. "Please about Jacob he hasn't did his writing."

Mercifully the bell rang for morning play.

"Jacob," I said, "here's some paper. You stay in and do your writing."

"Please I can't write outside of inside myself like Tiny."

Baffled. "Look. Don't any of you children know my name yet?"

"Please yes."

"Please stop calling me Please!"

They looked puzzled.

"What is my name?" I said.

"Please M's Hen'son."

"Just answer 'Mrs. Henderson.' "

Chorus, "Jus' answer M's Hen'son."

"Mrs. Henderson."

"M's Hen'son."

"Now do you know it?"

"Please yes."

If you can call that teaching.

"Really," to K over morning tea, "my teaching. I haven't *started* to teach. There's no communication. We're supposed to be using the same language but we just don't understand each other. I dunno..."

"I'll give you an outline of a lesson. Now for a writing lesson you ..."

"But you see they're not thinking about what they're writing about or about what I'm teaching. I'm teaching about 'bed' and 'can' but they were thinking about canoes and grandfathers and drowned men and eels. It seems to me ... I seem to be *rude* to *intrude*."

"That's just it. Well, dear, that's what we're paid to do, just that: intrude."

Intrude. For once I won't intrude. It's really time for reading about the bed, the can, and I can jump. I can skip and I can run. But I can't bring myself to do it. I'll follow them into their own minds and fraternize there; their minds are full of grandfathers, canoes and eels and the river and so, indeed, is mine. I call them to my feet for a story, swiftly improvising.

March 6 · My two little boys, Three and Two, backfired into school today, both crying and bleeding from a fall down the steps, and although I was teaching something important, number, I dismissed my classes and took the babies home and dressed their little wounds. I put them in the big chair and gave them tea. Never would this have happened had I not been teaching. To me, never will teaching be other than a necessary source of income, a profession drifted into on account of the hours, the holidays and the fact that others did it. *Never!*

Sunday, March 9 · Among the things about K that astound me is the way he takes his teaching seriously as though it were something other than a source of income. Up close it looks as if his work is also his *hobby*. At college we called it sheer betrayal. I don't know how he can be so *open* about it! At school he's a headmaster and not my husband. For all that, however, I did drift into a drawing lesson with his seniors while he took my little ones for wonderful games on the lawn outside, so that when he came in afterwards and saw for himself that his big ones were busy and happy he was as amazed as they were and as I was too, at what was happening beneath their fingers. Big daisies, yellow-centered, petals red-tipped, serrated with the sun and the shadow on them. In a low voice looking about, "This is what I love to see . . . activity. Do you like it?"

"Yes I do," surprised.

Approval from my headmaster. "Do you think it is good?" begged the wife.

"Of course I do," finish.

Oh, why can't he kiss me? Will I ever accustom myself to no applause . . . well, not enough, I mean? And will I ever get used to my lover-husband turning into a cold headmaster?

From *August*

But although spring is benevolent, rages remain. With dreams crashing in on reality and reality crashing in on dreaming during the hours before school, I'm in an exclusive rage when I get there to find Rosina and Rosie Tahore late, Tiny's nails dirty and somebody's teeth unbrushed. How I went for them! I flung my tongue round like a cat-o'-nine-tails so that my pleasant peaceful infant room became little less than a German concentration camp as I took out on the children what life should have got. Moreover, Frannie was sick today, lying on a bed of cushions by the big school fire where he slept and wept alternately until I dismissed my classes early, carried my lamb home and nursed him like a mother. If only I were not teaching . . .

Yet they've receded lately, the nightmares, when hidden in sleep I beat the children, not with my tongue at all but with a stick till it breaks into the smallest pieces, too small to use. No, not from the tenderness of spring in the flowered, forested valley and not only from my concentrated study but from something strangely new: tentatively, reluctantly, I'm becoming interested in no less than my

by a Woman writt

infant room. From the reading I do in the early hours before the household wakes, how could I not become interested? Freud, Adler, Lipmann, Scheiner, Jung and Bertrand Russell explaining life and children, and all the poetry at night. I am my own University, I my own Professor.

Is it possible that teaching small children could be more than a source of income, more than a way of paying your bills? Today, remembering the people I read, no longer able to bear my shame at growling at little children, I turned my ever-seeking mind toward evolving some system of marks: ticks for good behavior, crosses for bad, with the result that all day my tongue has not got away. Yet never have I had a better-mannered class, or better work either. Spring after the atrocious winter it could be, more careful planning, but mainly the study I do. At last I'm beginning to extricate myself from the only conception of teaching I remembered since I resumed on the Coast—the manner in which I was taught myself—and am recollecting what I learned in college. It was latent there all the time.

From *March 22*

On Sunday evening with the children in bed and Pauline writing letters I talked to K about the design. "The intellect is the tool to find the truth. It's a matter of sharpening it. Since I've been studying I'm much keener-witted. That's one reason I'm learning to milk the cow. I'm going to take over your afternoon's work sometimes and you can have the time for more study. I can chop wood and feed the fowls. We'll share the time."

"I can't possibly allow you to do rough work, chop wood and do the fowls. Not when you have the desire and the ability and the opportunity to do what you do."

I was surprised to hear this.

He continued, "What I thought two months ago and what I think now are two different things. I've tried to be broader about your going away. People who can do the work you do should be allowed to do it and those who can't should hew the wood and draw the water, feed the fowls, chop the wood and milk Susie."

This distressed me.

Sylvia Ashton-Warner

He went on, "There's no need for you to take on my afternoon work."

"But my work loses its value unless you are happy. Everything loses its value. Your contentment comes before my work."

"I'm happy."

"No you're not."

He looked at me with interest. I went on, "You're not getting as much time for study as I am. You're the real mother of this family; I'm just one of the children. We must share the time."

He pushed the kettle over the flames. "But your study means more to you than mine does to me."

"I question it. But in any case that's not my point. Your work means more to me than my own does to me because your work involves your contentment and that comes before my work with me."

He was interested but looked doubtful.

"It's the truth," I added. "Unless you are happy in your work mine is valueless to me."

K examined my face as though he was seeing it for the first time.

"It may not be apparent," I said, "but I love you and you come first in the world with me, before everything, before anybody. You and the children. My family and home are more to me than my work. If it came to the choice it would be my work that went overboard. No doubt I've appeared to be a failure in the home but that is not indicative. Do you feel I've failed you in the home?" I called on all my courage to ask this question which could draw a devastating answer.

He put out two cups and saucers. "Well, it has crossed my mind that you shouldn't have married."

Catastrophe! "But I've been a good mother! Look at me all through my babies. How I stuck to them on the Coast."

"Yes. But, what I mean is that a person, any person, with your inclinations should not marry. You should have gone on with your work. Marriage has sidetracked you."

Desperately on the defensive, "I wash and dress the little boys in the morning, and Jonquil. I feed them."

"I know. What I mean is that people like you with talents and ideas should be undisturbed by marriage."

"Ah . . . but you see! I wouldn't have had these desires at all if

I hadn't married. When I didn't teach and had no babies I hardly lifted a brush. Hardly did a thing. The *need* to study, to do, to make, to think, *arises* from being married. I need to be married to work."

He poured the boiling water on the tea. "I still think that you should be allowed your work in preference to my being allowed mine. Your desire is stronger than mine."

"That's quite possible. But I'm still going to hurry up and learn to milk Susie and take over your jobs sometimes."

We had tea, ran off the dishes and went to bed. Neither of us lowered the flag, neither won, and we haven't talked about that since, but the part about his coming before my work must have registered and held for there's been a tenderness in his manner toward me like the reappearance of the sun, and that close feeling has returned.

March 24 • As it happened, when K had to dash off without notice to his ailing father I did take on his jobs and loved it. Wore his sou'wester in the rain and his enormous gum boots, fed his fowls and chopped all the wood, cared for the sitting hen and fed the cat. Pauline and Ruth (the Maori housekeeper) did the inside work. I stripped the pear tree from a ladder and with a saw, bottled eight large bottles of pears and stored the rest . . . although I've got to admit that Mando milked Susie. . . .

From *November 12*

Hurrying up the road in the rain I reflected on my position in my small vital circle and my influence on them. It tells only too vividly on my family and Saul. When I'm unhappy my sorrow and violence cast all about me and everybody pays, right down to the baby, whereas now with my impulses back in their normal channel, now that I am happy, the school alone is different and our home—at least my home—is incredibly joyful. Though I can't say that of Saul's.

I am aware of how much I mean to each one: K, Jonquil, Frannie and Dannie, and Saul too. For some reason that is obscure to me they all turn to me and seek my love and I pour on them *thousands* of kisses. Except when at Selah, my body is not my own. My mouth, my face, my waist, my breasts, my hands . . . sheer common property. I'm the only one to see K's garden, the only one to walk round Saul's; I'm the one without whose goodnight kiss no one will go to bed. At this time I'm first with them all. Why does each need my love so much? You'd think my elusiveness in continual slipping away would lessen their call on me.

What a time of life this is—thirty-one years old. How long will this last? I wonder. It was not always like this in the past . . . so shy in my adolescence, so apart in my childhood . . . and cannot always be. Some day I may be looking back on these days when arms were endlessly round my neck, my body seldom my own; some day I may find myself sitting at a table with all the silence I want, possibly more than I want. There may be large echoing rooms and corridors, and stairs and stunning views, none of which would put its arms round my neck and want to make love to me, call to me in the night, unless I'm like Mando's mother smothered under with the kisses of grandchildren—what grandchildren are for, I suppose. A woman's arms need never be empty.

Now that I feel better, temporarily, I must honor all this love by trying to be gentler and kinder, by forgiving more readily and teaching more sensitively. Love has the quality of informing almost everything—even one's work.

FROM THREE

Back at my table I write some letters and go out again to post them, then walk out across the hot green Common crying for Jonquil and my love in his grave. On the sweet grass open to the sky I sit middle-aged and I ponder on what has angered them. Intrusion on a love affair of course, accumulating over the weeks to the level of that universally feared term: "in-law interference." A girl trying to win her husband back and a father for her son in the face of the strongest relationship known to man: mother-and-son. I lived through this when I was young. I must go away and at once.

But Julian's life is at stake. How can I go as long as he needs me; who would bring him his early tea he craves after the night, the man with a new view of water; bring him a full-scale breakfast in bed while his wife and his friend continue to sleep the beautiful mornings away, sleeping and sleeping the beautiful mornings of their youth away; who'd make his bed, fold his pajamas and buy him three new pillows; iron his shirts and hang them up for the first time since he married; bake him scones for morning tea and a gooseberry pie for lunch, and make him blackberry jam; who but his mother would clean the kitchen to hold back creeping squalor . . . and the dozens of extras for convalescence known only to a senior woman? Sleepers till eleven don't do these things.

Moreover if I abruptly left the scene would a man already shocked survive this further crisis? He'd end up in hospital or back at home . . . yet I must go, I must go. On the sweet grass, the uncomplicated grass with a welcome for all, or at least without resistance, as the swift cars beat by, as the black people, the brown people, the copper-tinted people in their native clothing interweave the white, in view of the grandeur of the trees enclosing where we live . . . I know that I must go.

Back in my non-living room however I cannot discipline the thought that my family is only the length of this hall away yet do not wish to see me. I try to scan the *Advertiser* I've brought home to find another flat but again I'm dying of thirst. Moreover since I mean to leave him I claim the right to just look at him. For the third time I tread step by creaking step the length of his home, past the Halfway House of his room and open this door.

Still reading, and I smile on them but as I put the kettle on the gas neither speaks to me nor I to them. I turn to the perfection of the trees in the park below reminding me of how lovely life can be in the balance of their shapes and their shadows. The TV is still on with no sound. At least I have *seen* Julian. Before I go perhaps I could hear his voice and draw a glance upon me. "Would you like a cup of tea, Jule?"

A plate and knife for my fruit take me back much later and here is Angelique seated at the table in a creative fervor preparing the

Sylvia Ashton-Warner

supper. Seeing her at work with rows of spices, neatly divided heaps of vegetables, the meat laid out and all these exotic twentieth-century utensils I've never seen before, who could believe any lack of method or the creative intent? It flares its own proof. Passing I say, "You have many gifts."

Cheeks flushed, she smiles.

It hours along, the evening, until I do hear the longed-for creaking of a slow step in the hall, my door opens and here is the tall form with the hollowed eyes looking at me speechless.

"Come in, Jule."

He does.

"Sit down."

He sits in the low green chair first then changes to the bed.

"Don't you find that chair comfortable? Too small, a woman's chair?"

"It's my back."

"Your back!"

"It's tender round this area. The chairs press on it." His voice has not yet recovered its deep virile pitch.

I question him in concern.

"But I've got an appointment at the hospital for a follow-up check." He is standing again but in the doorway he smiles at me briefly as though he recognized me. What a gift! In mind I lay a hand on his arm but only in mind. That would be revealing a feeling, an offense against London.

Ryvita and fruit. Who am I anyway to be fed well? Only an intruder on the young. Yet astonishingly he appears at my door again and asks if I've had enough.

"Yes, plenty."

"What did you have?"

I tell him.

"I'll ask Angelique to bring up some supper when it is cooked."

"Oh no, no, don't do that. I've already refused it."

He stands at my table as though he had things to say with no energy with which to say them, and soon he goes with this same effort at a smile from the door. Knowing the time is near when I'll not see him again, I'll remember these efforts of his.

About another hour and I hear this slow shuffling of feet grown too thin to fill his slippers and here he is with a tray. "Here's your supper."

I don't at once look up from my work.

"Do you want it?"

"Oh yes I want it."

"Angelique told me to bring it up."

"You're both very kind, very patient with me."

No speech left.

"They used to bring me my dinner at home."

"Did they?"

God what a labor talking to me.

Yet he remains standing heavy with much or nothing to say, with no resources to say it, with no room for trivialities since his encounter with death, then slowly walks out and closes the door exactly as he has found it. That's our Julian walking out, mine and his father's, to whom his father spoke his last word, "Wonderful." Nor must I forget that Julian too is afflicted with memory although he never mentions it. I store the sounds of each last step creaking in the hall, last words, last looks and last smiles to remember later.

Wonderfully he comes to get my tray.

"That was stunning." Then foolishly, fatuously, "Do stay for a little talk. I love it when you come in. You don't disturb me."

"Don't I?"

"Sit down, Dear."

Not on the chair but the bed again.

"Of course, yes. The back."

Loaded with nothing to say, the pause. Should have been in bed hours ago, and his supper brought to him.

"This could be home in the evening. You'd never know it was the heart of London."

"No."

The traffic has slackened outside in the street. He takes my tray.

Sylvia Ashton-Warner

At the door, "I'm sorry. I've never got anything to say these days. Nothing."

"I understand." And this is the last for the night I'm sure, but he brings up our two coffees. "I'll send you in a taxi tomorrow to the hospital for your appointment."

"Yes."

"I mean to go and see your college next week. How do you get there, tube?"

"Train."

"But you take a tube to get to the train?"

"Yes."

Mother prattling. As he turns to go, "Leave the door open, Jule. I only keep it shut in case the typing gets on your nerves."

"We don't hear it."

We. "Don't you? Good. I'd far rather have it open. But I keep it shut in the morning though Angelique says nothing wakes her, ever."

"*Never!*" He picks up our cups and goes.

Yet again he returns when I'm in bed to bring the evening paper. "Well, you ought to sleep better after that supper."

"I'm sure to."

"Don't take any notice of my moods. I get them. Angelique knows them. She says, 'Is it anything I do?' But no."

"You've got that dreamy bewildered look you had in Bombay when we saw you off on the plane, when you were sickening and we didn't know it."

He smiles from the doorway. "I'm going through the moral and spiritual crisis you're supposed to get at thirty."

"Are you thirty?"

"Thirty-two. Two years late with my crisis."

"I follow."

"Well, goodnight."

"Goodnight, Dear, goodnight."

Moods. Like the cycle of the London weather. Flirting with his wife in the morning, rejecting his mother in the afternoon, tending me in the evening. Well, we knew didn't we that we'd have a shocked convalescent? I cannot leave him yet.

The large London trees outside my windows in the early city light and the green of the Common through them. As the blackness of the night recedes so does the nadir of yesterday. The child I am forgets so quickly.

Before I go roaming this afternoon I've got to gulp the Gap again to give Jule his taxi fare and find him also emerged from his darkness. He stands here dressed, feet astride as his father would, one hand pocketed, the other on a hip, and he is smiling wonderfully, looking as happy as I've seen him so far. Astounding how happy he can be without his mother about, alone with Angelique. She is ironing the table napkins, an unlikely sight, which gives her a new air of authority as the responsible wife. With Julian nearby it makes a relaxing genuinely domestic scene. "Here's your taxi fare, dear man."

"I don't know about that," he smiles. Folding the notes, "I think I'll go by tube and return by taxi."

"It may be all right. What do you think about that, Ange?"

"If he feels able," firmly.

So like his father. In mind my arms encircle him and my head rests on his breast. He laughs, "Going both ways by taxi makes me feel an invalid."

I don't think Angelique gets this word "invalid." What do you say?" she checks.

I return up the Gap not taking my leave, hearing behind me, "*What* do you say?"

"God!" he shouts, "the lack of communication in this house! No one understands what I mean." Like a bona fide husband roaring at his wife. "I said I would feel like an *invalid*."

Normal domesticity. I slip out as silently as the door will allow. Who cares whether I come or go?

I make wrong changes in the Underground surfacing all over London and am late turning homeward, caught in the six-to-seven rush in

Sylvia Ashton-Warner

the end. Even so I make another wrong change and have to retrace my route with all these too-heavy parcels. It is now nearing seven. Will they be wondering where I am? Never. Did they ask me where I was going? No. But does this matter? No more. Julian will be back from hospital talking to Angelique in the living room and Hamlet will be home with the TV on watching the Wimbledon finals, none with a thought of me in their heads, unless relief that I am gone. I'm glad I'm late. I'll slip into my room and they won't hear me. I'll have my fruit meal and a little Ryvita and, much later when the three of them are dining together cosily with the door-shut-eating intimacy, I'll put the new dress I've bought on her bed. Let them get on with their youth without me.

Though I'm seriously tired I'm happy. Julian's moods are no more than mine. I'm happy, not because I'm coming home to welcome and warmth but because I'm not. I have no home and am better without one. As from now, right here in the bursting train, strap-hanging in front of strong young men sitting white with their scowls, I start my new life. Never will anyone have occasion to use the term "intrusion" on me, or its worst form, "interference." I am only myself. Exhilaratingly.

Like a thief I climb the flights of stairs well after seven, unlock the door as carefully as . . .

"Hello?"

"Hello."

A step or two in the lounge. Both relaxing at ease with the tea things. Two, not three of them. Soft secluded intimacy, private, complete. The intimacy which I find only in mind. Homely and happy with me away. Calling me in is charity only. I smile with my parcels but don't sit down.

"Where have you been?" he asks.

"Oxford Street."

"Sit down," from Angelique.

I sit in the yellow Louis Quinze chair holding all my bags. "How did you get on at the hospital, Jule?"

"Quite good."

"Did you come home in a taxi?"

"I went both ways in the tube," returning the notes I gave him.

"A new doctor who had to hear the whole story over again. Said I could have picked up the amoeba anywhere, not necessarily in the tropics. India was only the incubation place, favorable climate." Until the subject is bare.

"I've got a present for you, Angelique."

Sparkles and dimples, "*Have* you?"

"My word I'm thirsty. I haven't had a drink since one o'clock."

Down goes the needle taking up the hem. "I'll make you some tea, Dear."

"They told me," from Julian, "I'm looking very well."

"You are. Marvelous. Just a bit more covering on that neck. What about lying on the divan, Dear," and I bring cushions for his head. "I'm thinking, Jule," back in my chair, "of taking off for a week or two, to see how you get on without me. I'll come back if you need me."

"But this is illogic! You're not going away. You're staying here. Why can't you relax and just *be*?"

"Yes it is illogic."

"Then why say it?"

"Unreasonableness."

Hands through hair. "Women are so illogic. They don't think. They find their baking going wrong and blame the baking powder but they haven't read the directions. They can't see a thing objectively. They react subjectively. They don't act, they react. You're staying *here*. That's settled."

I think.

"You're so appallingly sensitive. Just the slightest word, a touch, a breath and . . ."

"You're very welcome, Dear," from Angelique. "We want you to stay."

"I was only suggesting a trial to see how you get on."

"You don't have to do that. I'm all right."

"Angelique might need me."

Sylvia Ashton-Warner

"As soon as Angelique starts getting up in the morning . . ." a wary smile in her direction

"I don't want her to get up in the morning."

She glances at him from her sewing, her dark hair pouring.

Julian, "You don't have to be worried about me at all."

How can you expect such a thing from your mother?

"We want you to stay," he affirms.

"I'll do anything at all you wish me to. I'll go home tomorrow if you say it."

"But I haven't said this!" The hair again. "God, the illogic! The impossibility of communication in this house. The sheer operation alone of getting something through to somebody. I've just said you are staying *here*."

I flare for the first time in this household. "Angelique understands me better than you ever will. There's too much of your father in you!" I swing to her. "There's two of me. That's why I say one thing and then another, whichever one is uppermost. Only part of me wants to run away and hide and be free but the other part . . ."

"Yes, yes," from her, "the other part wants security."

"I want," I hurtle on, "to vanish . . ."

"*Here*," from Angelique.

"Do your vanishing act *here*," from him. "Shut the door, live apart and . . ."

"And," from her, "when you need company it is here."

"*Yes*," I sip the inspiring tea. "I mean to buy my own kettle and . . ."

From him, "That's what I've been saying all along. A kettle in your room." His eyes are wide as they are whenever seeing the future, having a future now to see, and he's including me in his future. "You don't like coming to the living room, do you?"

"I mean to equip my room. I was planning it in the tube. A kettle, a small cooker and that, maybe a tiny fridge. And I tell you this: once I'm equipped and independent you'll never see me. Never see me. And you won't be having me on your hands when I'm old either. I'll buy that flat at the corner and hire a nurse," at which he smiles for some reason.

He returns to clear up a point. "Where would you go, anyway? You've got nowhere to go."

"Oh, that's easy. I have friends who would snatch me up at a moment's notice right from under your noses and whisk me off forever. 'Just name the time and place' sort of thing."

"Angeleeque-eeque!" from the hall and here is Hamlet, romance in person, looking what he is, a man of the theatre. "Don't tell me I've come on again, he said, at the very moment when big things, lofty things are being . . . have I made a wrong entrance?"

"Your entrances are faultlessly timed." I smile.

"I do my best, he said, my best is sufficient. If I have offended it is because I never formulate the ideal action . . ."

You could be right, Hamlet.

"Look what I've got," from Angelique holding up her dress. "From my *mother-in-law*!" Then hastily amends, "Well I have to say that. What else do I use? I do not go to use her Christian name."

I get the message. Imagine the mother-in-law talk between them during the midnight hours; but I defend her against herself this time as I've defended her against Julian. "The term 'mother-in-law' is not to be so regretted. Why should you not use it? All the mothers-in-law I've ever known got on fine with their sons' wives as did Naomi and Ruth. These sour jokes about us are all off target. The most misused, mis-rated, misunderstood term in the language."

"Ye-e-es . . ." from Hamlet reflecting, but I don't think he believes himself.

I warm up, "Quite nice women suddenly have to wear this title with the stigma on it and a crown of thorns. We're so frightened of it that we change our nature to avoid it and in so doing we end up the classical mother-in-law we feared in the first place; so gravely have we twisted ourselves."

"They do their best," supplies Hamlet, "but their best is not sufficient. If they have offended it is because they never formulate the ideal action, he said, trying to make an impression."

Your use, the manner of your use of the term "mother-in-law," Angelique, I do not tongue, amounts to a statement of the burden I've been to you. Never mind, it will soon be over. From the time I equip my room, and I've begun today, there will be no mother-in-law. I'm free to run away and vanish right here; wonderful though heavy richness. What can be heavier in wealth than freedom? But it's time for me to withdraw, upon which brisk conversation penetrates the folding doors.

I put down my bags at last and walk to the windows framing the married trees, their branches intertwining like loving arms. Moods, I am thinking, moods. Not only Julian's but mine. Yesterday's hell, today's heaven. Poor Angelique, she's got *two* of us.

I am sure that Julian cares about me in spite of the knife-sharp edge of his truth, "There can never be independence for anyone at all under the same roof." I've not lost him to death so why lose a son? "All that lives must die, Passing through nature to eternity." A universal truth, but to me, particular. Why should I in peevish opposition take it to heart?

Muriel Rukeyser

Muriel Rukeyser

(1913–   )

Poet, biographer, translator, author of children's books and of a book on poetry, Muriel Rukeyser writes of contemporary life. She writes of politics, of war, and of the fragmentation of the modern psyche. While poetry is for her a way of understanding contemporary life, it is also a way of giving form and meaning to that life, of affirming it. This affirmation is exemplified in her work, "Nine Poems for the Unborn Child," where, pregnant and risking her own life, the narrator chooses life for her child. This affirmation also is exemplified in the poems on Ann Burlak, a labor leader, and Käthe Kollwitz, an artist, in both of which Rukeyser recognizes and celebrates the complexities of their lives. "However confused the scene of our life appears," Rukeyser writes in her book on poetry, "however torn we may be who now do face that scene, it can be faced, and we can go on to be whole."

In "The Poem as Mask," Rukeyser tells of the disguised way in which she wrote about herself. An appropriate conclusion for *by a Woman writt,* the poem suggests that women should turn to an art based not on "masks" nor on "mythologies," but on the real experiences of their lives.

WHO IN ONE LIFETIME

Who in one lifetime sees all causes lost,
Herself dismayed and helpless, cities down,
Love made monotonous fear and the sad-faced
Inexorable armies and the falling plane,
Has sickness, sickness. Introspective and whole,
She knows how several madnesses are born,
Seeing the integrated never fighting well,
The flesh too vulnerable, the eyes tear-torn.

She finds a pre-surrender on all sides:
Treaty before the war, ritual impatience turn
The camps of ambush to chambers of imagery.
She holds belief in the world, she stays and hides
Life in her own defeat, stands, though her whole world
    burn,
A childless goddess of fertility.

ANN BURLAK

Let her be seen, a voice on a platform, heard
as a city is heard in its prophetic sleep when
one shadow hangs over one side of a total wall
of houses, factories, stacks, and on the faces
around her tallies, shadow from one form.

An open square shields the voice, reflecting it
to faces who receive its reflections of light as
change on their features. She stands alone, sending
her voice out to the edges, seeing approach people
to make the ring ragged, to fill in blacker
answers.
           This is an open square of the lit world
whose dark sky over hills rimmed white with evening
squares lofts where sunset lies in dirty patterns
and rivers of mill-towns beating their broken bridges
as under another country full of air.
Dark offices evening reaches where letters take the light
even from palest faces over script.
Many abandon machines, shut off the looms,
hurry on glooming cobbles to the square. And many
are absent, as in the sky about her face, the birds
retreat from charcoal rivers and fly far.

The words cluster about the superstition mountains.
The sky breaks back over the torn and timid
her early city whose stacks along the river
flourished darkness over all, whose mottled sky
shielded the faces of those asleep in doorways
spread dark on narrow fields through which the father
comes home without meat, the forest in the ground
whose trees are coal, the lurching roads of autumn
where the flesh of the eager hangs, heavier by
its thirty bullets, barbed on wire. Truckdrivers
swing ungrazed trailers past, the woman in the fog
can never speak her poems of unemployment,

Muriel Rukeyser

the brakeman slows the last freight round the curve.
And riveters in their hardshell fling short fiery
steel, and the servant groans in his narrow room,
and the girl limps away from the door of the shady doctor.
Or the child new-born into a company town
whose life can be seen at birth as child, woman, widow.
The neighbor called in to nurse the baby of a spy,
the schoolboy washing off the painted word
"scab" on the front stoop, his mother watering flowers
pouring the milk-bottle of water from the ledge,
who stops in horror, seeing. The grandmother going
down to her cellar with a full clothes-basket,
turns at the shot, sees men running past brick,
smoke-spurt and fallen face.
                    She speaks of these:
the chase down through the canal, the filling-station,
stones through the windshield. The woman in the bank
who topples, the premature birth brought on by tear-gas,
the charge leaving its gun slow-motion, finding those
who sit at windows knowing what they see;
who look up at the door, the brutalized face appraising
strangers with holsters;   little blackened boys
with their animal grins, quick hands salvaging coal
among the slag of patriotic hills.

She knows the field of faces at her feet,
remembrances of childhood, likenesses of parents,
a system of looms in constellation whirled,
disasters dancing.
                    And behind her head
the world of the unpossessed, steel mills in snow flaming,
nine o'clock towns whose deputies' overnight power
hurls waste into killed eyes, whose guns predict
mirages of order, an empty coat before the blind.
Doorways within which nobody is at home.
The spies who wait for the spy at the deserted crossing,
a little dead since they are going to kill.

by a Woman writt

Those women who stitch their lives to their machines
and daughters at the symmetry of looms.

She speaks to the ten greatest American women:
The anonymous farmer's wife, the anonymous clubbed picket,
the anonymous Negro woman who held off the guns,
the anonymous prisoner, anonymous cotton-picker
trailing her robe of sack in a proud train,
anonymous writer of these and mill-hand, anonymous city-walker,
anonymous organizer, anonymous binder of the illegally wounded,
anonymous feeder and speaker to anonymous squares.

She knows their faces, their impatient songs
of passionate grief risen, the desperate music
poverty makes, she knows women cut down
by poverty, by stupid obscure days,
their moments over the dishes, speaks them now,
wrecks with the whole necessity of the past
behind the debris, behind the ordinary
smell of coffee, the ravelling clean wash,
the turning to bed, undone among savage night
planning and unplanning seasons of happiness
broken in dreams or in the jaundiced morning
over a tub or over a loom or over
the tired face of death.
                    She knows
the songs : *Hope to die, Mo I try, I comes out,
Owin boss mo, I comes out, Lawd, Owin boss mo*
food, money and life.
                    Praise breakers,
praise the unpraised who cannot speak their name.
Their asking what they need as unbelieved
as a statue talking to a skeleton.
They are the animals who devour their mother
from need, and they know in their bodies other places,
their minds are cities whose avenues are named
each after a foreign city. They fall when cities fall.
They have the cruelty and sympathy of those

Muriel Rukeyser

whose texture is the stress of existence woven
into revenge, the crime we all must claim.
They hold the old world in their new world's arms.
And they are the victims, all the splinters of war
run through their eyes, their black escaping face
and runaway eyes are the Negro in the subway
whose shadowy detective brings his stick
down on the naked head as the express pulls in,
swinging in locomotive roars on skull.
They are the question to the ambassador
long-jawed and grim, they stand on marble, waiting
to ask how the terms of the strike have affected him.
Answer : "I've never seen snow before. It's marvellous."
They stand with Ann Burlak in the rotunda, knowing
her insistent promise of life, remembering
the letter of the tear-gas salesman : "I hope
"this strike develops and a damn bad one too.
"We need the money."
                              This is the boundary
behind a speaker : Main Street and railroad tracks,
post office, furniture store. The soft moment before storm.
Since there are many years.
And the first years were the years of need,
the bleeding, the dragged foot, the wilderness,
and the second years were the years of bread
fat cow, square house, favorite work,
and the third years are the years of death.
The glittering eye all golden. Full of tears.
Years when the enemy is in our street,
and liberty, safe in the people's hands,
is never safe and peace is never safe.

Insults of attack arrive, insults
of mutilation. She knows the prophetic past,
many have marched behind her, and she knows
Rosa whose face drifts in the black canal,
the superstitions of a tragic winter

when children, their heads together, put on tears.
The tears fall at their throats, their chains are made
of tears, and as bullets melted and as bombs let down
upon the ominous cities where she stands
fluid and conscious. Suddenly perceives
the world will never daily prove her words,
but her words live, they issue from this life.
She scatters clews. She speaks from all these faces
and from the center of a system of lives
who speak the desire of worlds moving unmade
saying, "Who owns the world?" and waiting for the cry.

NINE POEMS
FOR THE UNBORN CHILD

I.

The childless years alone without a home
Flashed daily with the world's glimpse, happiness.
Always behind was the dark screen of loss
Hardly moving, like heavy hardly-moving cloud.
"Give me myself," or "Take me," I said aloud;
There was little to give, and always less to take.
Except the promise, except the promise darkness
Makes, night and daylight, miracle to come.

Flying over, I suddenly saw the traces
Of man : where man is, you may read the wind
In shadow and smoke, know how the wind is gone
And know the way of man;   in the fall of the plane
Into its levels, encounter the ancient spaces:
The fall to life, the cliff and strait of bone.

II.

They came to me and said, "There is a child."
Fountains of images broke through my land.
My swords, my fountains spouted past my eyes
And in my flesh at last I saw.   Returned

Muriel Rukeyser

To when we drove in the high forest, and earth
Turned to glass in the sunset where the wild
Trees struck their roots as deep and visible
As their high branches, the double planted world.
"There is no father," they came and said to me.
—I have known fatherless children, the searching, walk
The world, look at all faces for their father's life.
Their choice is death or the world.   And they do choose.
Earn their brave set of bone, the seeking marvelous look
Of those who lose and use and know their lives.

III.

There is a place.   There is a miracle.
I know the nightmare, the black and bone piano,
The statues in the kitchen, a house dissolving in air.
I know the lilac-turreted cathedral
Taking its roots from willows that changed before my eyes
When all became real, real as the sound of bells.
We earthly are aware of transformation;
Miraculously, life, from the old despair.

The wave of smooth water approaches on the sea-
Surface, a live wave individual
Linking, massing its color.   Moving, is struck by wind,
Ribbed, steepened, until the slope and ridge begin;
comes nearer, brightens.   Now curls, its vanishing
Hollows darken and disappear;   now high above
Me, the scroll, froth, foam of the overfall.

IV.

Now the ideas all change to animals
Loping and gay, now all the images
Transform to leaves, now all these screens of leaves
Are flowing into rivers, I am in love
With rivers, these changing waters carry voices,
Carry all children;   carry all delight.

by a Woman writt

The water-soothed winds move warm above these waves.
The child changes and moves among these waves.

The waves are changing, they tremble from waves of waters
To other essentials—they become waves of light
And wander through my sleep and through my waking,
And through my hands and over my lips and over
Me;   brilliant and transformed and clear,
The pure light.   Now I am light and nothing more.

v.

Eating sleep, eating sunlight, eating meat,
Lying in the sun to stare
At deliverance, the rapid cloud,
Gull-wing opposing sun-bright wind,
I see the born who dare
Walk on green, walk against blue,
Move in the nightlong flare
Of love on darkness, traveling
Among the rings of light to simple light,
From nowhere to nowhere.
And in my body feel the seasons grown.
Who is it in the dim room?   Who is there?

vi.

Death's threat!   Today I have known laughter
As if for the first time;   have seen into your eyes,
Death, past the still gaze, and found two I love.
One chose you gladly with a laugh advancing,
His hand full of guns, on the enemy in Spain.
The other living with the choice of life
Turning each day of living to the living day.
The strength, the grossness, spirit and gall of choice.

They came to me and said, "If you must choose,
Is it yourself or the child?"   Laughter I learned
In that moment, laughter and choice of life.

Muriel Rukeyser

I saw an immense ship trembling on the water
Lift by a gesture of hands.   I saw a child.   I saw
A red room, the eyes, the hands, the hands and eyes.

VII.

You will enter the world where death by fear and explosion
Is waited;   longed for by many;   by all dreamed.
You will enter the world where various poverty
Makes thin the imagination and the bone.
You will enter the world where birth is walled about,
Where years are walled journeys, death a walled-in act.
You will enter the world which eats itself
Naming faith, reason, naming love, truth, fact.

You in your dark lake moving darkly now
Will leave a house that time makes, times to come
Enter the present, where all the deaths and all
The old betrayals have come home again.
World where again Judas, the little child,
May grow and choose.   You will enter the world.

VIII.

Child who within me gives me dreams and sleep,
Your sleep, your dreams;   you hold me in your flesh
Including me where nothing has included
Until I said : I will include, will wish
And in my belly be a birth, will keep
All delicacy, all delight unclouded.

Dreams of an unborn child move through my dreams,
The sun is not alone in making fire and wave
Find meeting-place, for flesh and future meet,
The seal in the green wave like you in me,
Child.   My blood at night full of your dreams,
Sleep coming by day as strong as sun on me,
Coming with sun-dreams where leaves and rivers meet,
And I at last alive sunlight and wave.

IX.

Rider of dream, the body as an image
Alone in crisis.   I have seen the wind
Its tall cloud standing on a pillar of air,
The toe of the whirlwind turning on the ground.
Have known in myself hollow bodiless shade,
The shadow falling from the tree to the ground,
Have lost and lost and now at last am found
For a moment of sleep and waking, striking root.

Praise that the homeless may in their bodies be
A house that time makes, where the future moves
In his dark lake.   Praise that the cities of men,
The fields of men, may at all moments choose.
Lose, use, and live.   And at this daylight, praise
To the grace of the world and time that I may hope
To live, to write, to see my human child.

NIGHT FEEDING

Deeper than sleep but not so deep as death
I lay there dreaming and my magic head
remembered and forgot.   On first cry I
remembered and forgot and did believe.
I knew love and I knew evil:
woke to the burning song and the tree burning blind,
despair of our days and the calm milk-giver who
knows sleep, knows growth, the sex of fire and grass,
renewal of all waters and the time of the stars
and the black snake with gold bones.

Black sleeps, gold burns;   on second cry I woke
fully and gave to feed and fed on feeding.
Gold seed, green pain, my wizards in the earth
walked through the house, black in the morning dark.
Shadows grew in my veins, my bright belief,
my head of dreams deeper than night and sleep.

Muriel Rukeyser

Voices of all black animals crying to drink,
cries of all birth arise, simple as we,
found in the leaves, in clouds and dark, in dream,
deep as this hour, ready again to sleep.

WOMAN AS MARKET

—Forgetting and Remembering—

What was it? What was it?
Flashing beside me, lightning in daylight at the orange
    stand?
Along the ranks of eggs, beside the loaves of dark and
    light?
In a moment of morning, providing:
the moment of the eggplant?
            the lemons? the fresh eggs?
with their bright curves and curves of shadow?
the reds, the yellows, all the calling boxes.
What did those forms say? What words have I forgotten?
what spoke to me from the day?
God in the cloud? my life in my forgetting?
I have forgotten what it was
that I have been trying to remember

KÄTHE KOLLWITZ

I

Held between wars
my lifetime
            among wars, the big hands of the world of death
my lifetime
listens to yours.

The faces of the sufferers
ir the street, in dailiness,
their lives showing
through their bodies

by a Woman writt

a look as of music
the revolutionary look
that says   I am in the world
to change the world
my lifetime
is to love to endure to suffer the music
to set its portrait
up as a sheet of the world
the most moving the most alive
Easter and bone
and Faust walking among the flowers of the world
and the child alive within the living woman, music of man,
and death holding my lifetime between great hands
the hands of enduring life
that suffers the gifts and madness of full life, on earth, in
        our time,
and through my life, through my eyes, through my arms
        and hands
may give the face of this music in portrait waiting for
the unknown person
held in the two hands, you.

II

Woman as gates, saying :
"The process is after all like music,
like the development of a piece of music.
The fugues come back and

                            again and again
interweave.
A theme may seem to have been put aside,
but it keeps returning—
the same thing modulated,
somewhat changed in form.
Usually richer.
And it is very good that this is so."

A woman pouring her opposites.

Muriel Rukeyser

"After all there are happy things in life too.
Why do you show only the dark side?"
"I could not answer this. But I know—
in the beginning my impulse to know
the working life
                        had little to do with
pity or sympathy.
                    I simply felt
that the life of the workers was beautiful."

She said, "I am groping in the dark."

She said, "When the door opens, of sensuality,
then you will understand it too. The struggle begins.
Never again to be free of it,
often you will feel it to be your enemy.
Sometimes
you will almost suffocate,
such joy it brings."

Saying of her husband : "My wish
is to die after Karl.
I know no person who can love as he can,
with his whole soul.
Often this love has oppressed me;
I wanted to be free.
But often too it has made me
so terribly happy."

She said : "We rowed over to Carrara at dawn,
climbed up to the marble quarries
and rowed back at night. The drops of water
fell like glittering stars
from our oars."

She said : "As a matter of fact,
I believe
             that bisexuality
is almost   a necessary factor

in artistic production; at any rate,
the tinge of masculinity within me
helped me
         in my work."

She said : "The only technique I can still manage.
It's hardly a technique at all, lithography.
In it
        only the essentials count."

A tight-lipped man in a restaurant last night
        saying to me:
"Kollwitz?   She's too black-and-white."

III

Held among wars, watching
  all of them
  all these people
  weavers,
  Carmagnole

Looking at
  all of them
  death, the children
  patients in waiting-rooms
  famine
  the street
  the corpse with the baby
  floating, on the dark river

A woman seeing
  the violent, inexorable
  movement of nakedness
  and the confession of No
  the confession of great weakness, war,
  all streaming to one son killed, Peter;
  even the son left living; repeated,
  the father, the mother; the grandson
  another Peter killed in another war; firestorm·

Muriel Rukeyser

  dark, light, as two hands,
    this pole and that pole as the gates.

What would happen if one woman told the truth about
    her life?
    The world would split open

IV   SONG : THE CALLING-UP

Rumor, stir of ripeness
rising within this girl
sensual blossoming
of meaning, its light and form.
The birth-cry summoning
out of the male, the father
from the warm woman
a mother in response.

The word of death
calls up the fight with stone
wrestle with grief with time
from the material make
an art harder than bronze.

V   SELF-PORTRAIT

Mouth looking directly at you
eyes in their inwardness looking
directly at you
half light   half darkness
woman, strong, German, young artist
flows into
wide sensual mouth meditating
looking right at you
eyes shadowed with brave hand
looking deep at you
flows into
wounded brave mouth
grieving and hooded eyes
alive, German, in her first War

flows into
strength of the worn face
a skein of lines
broods, flows into
mothers among the war graves
bent over death
facing the father
stubborn upon the field
flows into
the marks of her knowing—
Nie Wieder Krieg
repeated in the eyes
flows into
"Seedcorn must not be ground"
and the grooved cheek
lips drawn fine
the down-drawn grief
face of our age
flows into
Pieta, mother and
between her knees
life as her son in death
pouring from the sky of
one more war
flows into
face almost obliterated
hand over the mouth forever
hand over one eye now
the other great eye
closed

Muriel Rukeyser

THE POEM AS MASK

Orpheus

When I wrote of the women in their dances and wildness,
    it was a mask,
on their mountain, god-hunting, singing, in orgy,
it was a mask; when I wrote of the god,
fragmented, exiled from himself, his life, the love gone
    down with song,
it was myself, split open, unable to speak, in exile from
    myself.

There is no mountain, there is no god, there is memory
of my torn life, myself split open in sleep, the rescued child
beside me among the doctors, and a word
of rescue from the great eyes.

No more masks! No more mythologies!

Now, for the first time, the god lifts his hand,
the fragments join in me with their own music.

Some other books published by Penguin
are described on the following pages.

Eleanor Flexner

MARY WOLLSTONECRAFT

This biography of Mary Wollstonecraft makes that pioneering eighteenth-century feminist as captivating now as she was in her own day. Eleanor Flexner draws on previously unused materials to show how an intelligent, high-strung woman lived as an individualist in spite of stifling convention, demanded equality at a time when females were little more than chattel, became the first great advocate of liberation for her sex, and wrote *A Vindication of the Rights of Woman,* a monumental achievement still relevant for the women of today. Nominated for a National Book Award, *Mary Wollstonecraft* was called by *Publishers Weekly* "a thoroughly researched and stylishly written biography . . . destined to be an important contribution to the literature of women's rights."

Edited by Jean Baker Miller, M.D.

PSYCHOANALYSIS AND WOMEN

The articles in this volume revise the traditional psychoanalytical approach to women. Feeling that women have been too long "kept in their place" by Freudian myths about penis envy, biological determinism, dependency, and masochism, the editor aims for a more realistic view. Included are articles by such eminent figures as Karen Horney, Alfred Adler, Clara Thompson, Gregory Zilboorg, Mary Jane Sherfey, Frieda Fromm-Reichmann, and Robert Seidenberg. Together, these writings dispel the old stereotypical attitudes with their phallocentric bias and go on to show that psychoanalysis can have a new relevance for women today. Jean Baker Miller is a practicing psychoanalyst.

Elizabeth Gould Davis

THE FIRST SEX

By looking at the superiority of woman to man, this unique book aims to give woman her rightful place in history. Drawing on science, mythology, and archaeology, Elizabeth Gould Davis comes up with some eye-opening facts to show that woman was first in the discovery of the arts and sciences, first in the march toward civilization, and first in physical efficiency. (For example: Biologically, man is a mutant of woman, since the Y chromosome is a stunted X. . . . Ancient civilizations such as the Sumerian were matriarchal societies where women ruled and men were servants.) Combining the expert documentation of *The Second Sex* with the lively controversy of *Sexual Politics, The First Sex* could well become the handbook of the women's movement.

Ruth Sidel

WOMEN AND CHILD CARE IN CHINA
A Firsthand Report

This report on the changing status of women and children in today's China has important implications for our own society. The emphasis is on the amazingly rapid liberation of Chinese women from their "bitter past." Now, Mrs. Sidel reports, the Chinese woman takes an active part in the life of the nation, and vast programs provide birth-control information, prenatal assistance, maternity leaves, and child-care facilities. Most especially, *Women and Child Care in China* looks at nurseries, nursery schools, and kindergartens and at the revolutionary methods they employ. Mrs. Sidel goes on to ask what aspects of the Chinese experience might be of value in the United States. With photographs by Victor W. Sidel.

Corinne J. Hutt

MALES AND FEMALES

In this review of the biological, psychological, and
sociological aspects of sexual differences in human
beings, the evidence presented argues strongly for
a sexual dimorphism in man—a dimorphism in
accord with the reproductive roles that men and
women, no less than other males and females, fulfill. Corinne J. Hutt is in the Department of Experi-
mental Psychology at Oxford University, England.